Performance and Reward Management

Performance and Reward Management

Tapomoy Deb

Ane Books Pvt. Ltd.
New Delhi ♦ Chennai

Performance and Reward Management
Tapomoy Deb

Price: Rs. 1495/-
Pages : xiv+262=276 (HB)
Size: 6.25 x 9.5 inch
Paper Quality (GSM):80

Published by
Ane Books Pvt. Ltd.
4821, Parwana Bhawan, 1st Floor, 24 Ansari Road, Darya Ganj,
New Delhi - 110 002, Tel.: +91(011) 23276843-44, Fax: +91(011) 23276863
e-mail: kapoor@anebooks.com, Website: www.anebooks.com

Branch Office:

- Avantika Niwas, 1st Floor, 19 Doraiswamy Road, T. Nagar,
  Chennai - 600 017, Tel.: +91(044) 28141554, 28141209
  e-mail: anebookschennai@gmail.com, rathinam@anebooks.com

ISBN: 978-81-90840-62-0

Printed at : Replika Press Pvt Ltd

To My Wife

Mrs. Swagata Deb

For Constantly Inspiring Me with
Her Values and Virtues

Acknowledgements

While authoring this book, I would like to express my sincere thanks particularly to Shri Anil Kaushik, Chief Editor and Publisher of Business Manager for encouraging and inspiring me to continue with my endeavour to provide contemporary concepts, pedagogy driven and lucid learning materials to my esteemed readers especially MBA students and their teaching staff. While his inspirational support cannot be measured; what has touched me is his humane approach.

I would also like to express my heart-felt gratitude to my parents, my mother Mrs. Maya Deb and my father, Mr. B.B. Deb. My mother has been my friend, philosopher and guide since my childhood. She has inculcated in me the values and virtues necessary to succeed in my personal and professional life with versatility, sincerity and modesty. Her vision, conviction, and strong determination have inspired me to relentless pursuit of excellence. I own her a great deal. This book is devoted to not just my but all mothers who guide the vision of their sons with their unconditional love, affection and morale support.

I shall be failing in my duties if I do not thank my publisher M/s Ane Books Pvt. Ltd., New Delhi especially Mr. Sunil Saxena and Mr. Jai Raj Kapoor for their generous support from project commissioning stage to its final printing. I also owe thanks to the reviewers who read the manuscript and offered valuable suggestions.

Preface

Performance and reward management has been part of human civilization since ancient times. Even in the ancient Indian and Chinese empires, there were royal performance raters. Performance is so ingrained in our life that nothing moves without it, be it personal lives, social life, academics, professions, or business. It would be appropriate to say that performance is the foundation of our society and reward is the pillar on which the whole body of individual and corporate success is built upon.

With the onset of globalization, the competitive scenario has changed forever. Organizations now have to be more agile, responsive, innovative and customer centric to stay afloat. In other words, organizations have to perform better and improve it each moment, each day, and each year. This is a Darwinian world, where only the fittest of the fit will thrive. This makes management and rewarding of performance at individual and group/organizational level critical. Managing people is essentially about improving individual performance for attaining organizational goals and objectives effectively in such a way that employees gets rewarded for their better performance and organization acquires increased competitiveness and leadership in the business world. This has facilitated the inclusion of Performance and Reward Management as an elective course in the human resource management specialization in MBA programmes.

Against this backdrop, this book "Performance and Reward Management" has been designed to provide a sequential and logical approach for unfolding the concepts and perspectives of performance and reward management. Care has been taken to make the theoretical discussions interesting, engaging and insightful for facilitating learning of the readers. Practice-based tools has been appended at the end of this book for enabling the students to understand real world HR practices on performance and reward programmes and to aid their internship programmes.

A good learning methodology for the students is to read the corresponding chapter prior to the lecture, and use the lecture to clarify concepts for developing deeper understanding of the subject. The material in the textbook is sufficiently self–explanatory and self–contained to facilitate easy grasping of the concepts and key terms by the students.

Although all care has been taken, but should you have a suggestion on any aspect connected with this book, you are most welcome to write to the publisher. I strongly believe that the path to excellence goes through hard work and an urge to improve that is beyond egotism.

Tapomoy Deb

Contents

Learning Objectives

At the conclusion of this chapter, you should be able to:

- Discuss performance and reward management linkages
- Understand the concept and perspectives of performance management
- Design a performance management model and strategy
- Explain the approaches and process of performance management
- Understand the influence of motivation, leadership, national and organizational culture on performance management
- Assess the implication of performance management on learning
- Focus concepts, features, significance, process and limitations of performance appraisal
- Explain performance coaching and its significance
- Describe the traditional and modern methods of performance appraisal
- Elucidate the concept of competency based performance management

1

Performance Management

1.1 Performance and Reward Management

With globalization of world economy, competition has become fierce and cut throat. Competition is no more limited to economies of scale but has assumed multi-dimension which embraces innovation, quality, cost, agility, responsiveness and self-renewal capabilities on the part of the organizations. With greater acceptance that employees create competitive advantage for their organizations through their skills, competencies and commitments, management of employee performance for gaining and sustaining organizational effectiveness has assumed paramount importance. Performance management is now a HR strategy to help align individual goals with organization's competitive priority, set performance expectations, facilitates and ensures achievement of performance expectations and link reward programmes for effective organizational outcomes as depicted in Fig. 1.1.

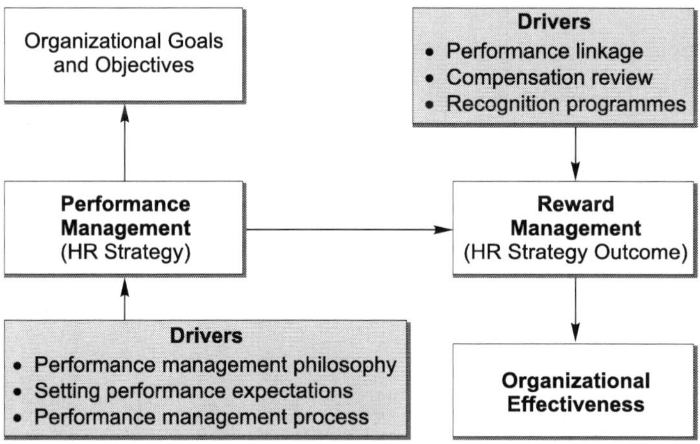

Fig. 1.1 Performance and Reward Management.

Performance management is an organization wide mechanism to align organizational and individual priorities, integrate efforts and ensure effective realization of results in such a way that organization sustains its competitiveness in the marketplace and the employee's gains intrinsic reward (job satisfaction, job involvement, succession planning, etc.) and extrinsic rewards (compensation, promotions, career progression). Thus, performance management ensures that individuals performing at or above par are rewarded adequately to maintain their performance level as an inducement. For employees performing below par are motivated to perform better in order to receive differentiating rewards given by the organization as a result of good performance. Hence, performance management and reward management are integrated system which seeks to compliment each other in order to achieve organizational success through enhanced employee performance. We shall discuss the essential constructs of performance and reward management in the following sections of the text.

Competence Development

At Bosch Ltd., competence and skill development programmes include scheduled training based on a systematic review and identification of existing and future gaps in the talent base. An online personnel assessment system linked to a training management module, support individual employee development.

At Indian Oil Corporation, the competencies and key result areas of pivotal roles in the organization are being reviewed and reframed in the current business context. With focus on building capabilities and core competencies, the Corporation's apex learning centre, Indian Oil Institute of Petroleum Management, such as 'Cutting Edge', 'Threshold' as well as specialized functional programmes focusing on enhancing business perspective, leadership and strategizing skills.

With firm belief in business strategies and robust HRD systems as the foundation for sustained growth, Indian Oil shall continue its endeavour to align individual aspirations of its employees with the corporate goals and objectives.

Source: Annual Report, 2007, Bosch Ltd., pp. 18 and Annual Report 2008, Indian Oil Corporation Ltd., pp.26.

1.2 Basic Concept of Performance

Performance may be viewed as behaviours or actions that are relevant to the goals of the organization and it is multidimensional. It follows that performance may be viewed as behaviour that leads to results. Behaviour refers to action of an individual in relation to his environment. Behaviour denotes the character and action of the individual. This implies that behaviour of different individuals is different due to varying environment or background or circumstances. Since behaviour also signifies response to environment therefore behaviour of the same individual varies from situation to situation. Furthermore, behaviour emanates from the character which leads to some action or reaction to a particular event, circumstance or situation. In other words, behaviour is a function of individual character and environmental demands which leads to some action. The final consequence of this action or sequence of actions expressed qualitatively or quantitatively is refereed to as result. This implies that behaviour is fundamental to result. But at the same time without result, behaviour is incomplete or meaningless. Therefore, in the organizational context, performance is a culmination of behaviour and result. Appropriate behaviour of employees is necessary to produce desired results. If the behaviour is inappropriate or negative the result is also likely to be inappropriate or negative. Hence, there is a need to systematically manage employees for eliciting desirable work behaviours which leads to desired results. When employees exhibit appropriate behaviour and action, the goals and objectives of the organization are achieved effectively. This is because the individual job or work goals of the employee's are linked with work unit or departmental goals and these departmental goals are further connected to organizational goals and objectives. Therefore, attainment of organizational goals and objectives is a sequence of interlinkages starting from the individual employee level and ending up at organizational level. Thus, managing performance is essentially about managing, developing and reinforcing appropriate individual behaviour for excellent results.

1.3 Definitions of Performance

A few noteworthy definitions of performance are as follows:

1. *"Performance is a function of both the behaviour and accomplishment of a person or group of people. Performance includes the action of a person or people and the result of the action or action".*

   — Stolovitch and Keeps

2. *"Performance means both behaviours and results. Behaviours emanate from the performer and transform performance from abstraction to action. Not just the instruments for results, behaviours are also outcomes in their own right the product of mental and physical effort applied to tasks and can be judged apart from results".*

   — Brumbrach

3. *"Performance has two components: a behaviour or activity and whatever that behaviour or activity accomplishes".*

   — Gilbert

Thus, performance includes activities and outcomes–behaviours and accomplishments.

The relationship between External Environment and Employee Performance required is as depicted in Fig. 1.2.

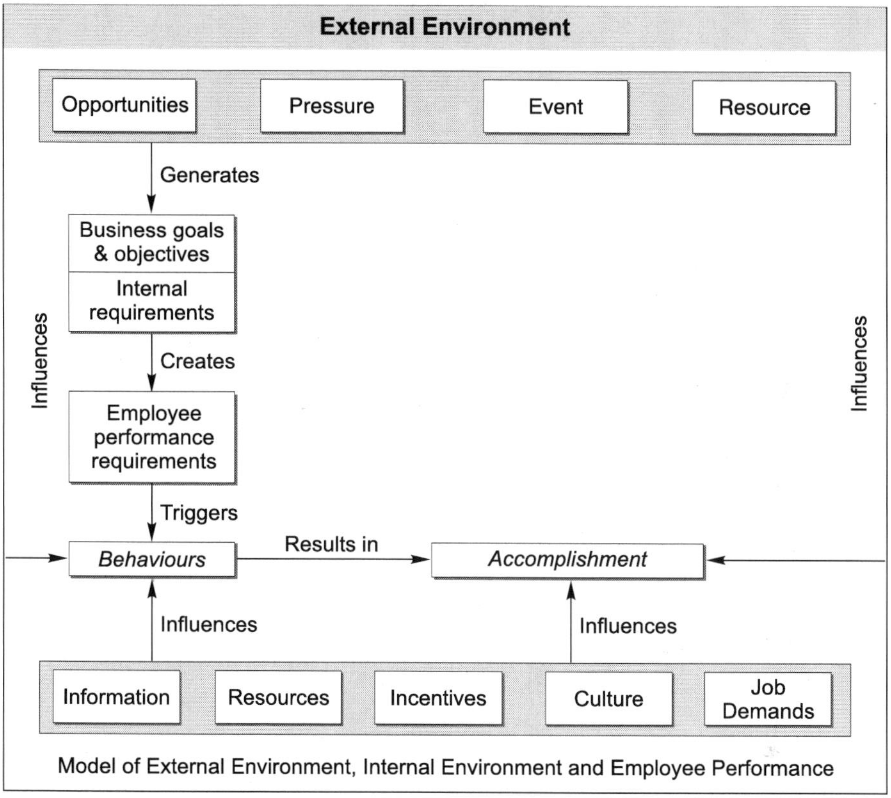

Source: Stolovitch and Keeps, 2004

Fig. 1.2 The Performance Model.

1.4 Basic Concept of Performance Management

With globalization of world economy, the business landscape has changed forever. This has led to increased pressure on bottom-line of the organization as physical or natural resources can no more assure them business success. Technology, products and financial capital are increasingly prone to duplication by competitors. Therefore, organizations need those resources which are not prone to emulation by competitors. The search for such resource has finally centred on the employees of the organization who are now increasingly valued for their talents, skills, motivations and commitment for improving performance both at individual and group/team level which is capable of increasing an organization's competence and performance.

Improved organizational performance is critical for competing effectively in the marketplace characterized by Olympian competition.

A Football Team

Which football team would win a single game if the players competed with each other for the ball; if most players rested on the efforts of the few; if the captain was mistrusted and the coach was the only person who knew the location of the goals?

Amazing! However this seems to be corporate reality with employees competing with each other for managerial favours and organizational rewards. This is because their performance goals have not been either properly identified or are misaligned with organizational goals and objectives. The result is that all employees are not moving in the same direction as that of the organization. This implies that performance management is often not understood properly or is ineffective. This makes the study of performance management all the more important otherwise the situation of organizations will be similar to the football team.

People have limitless capacity and capability to think, innovate and act in differentiating ways. This calls for astute management of human resources so that they are able and willing to put their best efforts and contributes to the success of their organizations. Once human resources are proactively managed as a scarce resource and competency of an organization, optimum organizational outcomes are expected. But as once management doyen *Peter F. Drucker* said, "What Gets Measured, Gets Done". Therefore, organizations need to devise, implement, monitor and develop contributions of human resources through a systematic and coherent approach. One such approach is performance management. Although the evolution of performance measurement can be attributed to industrial revolution time as it is inherently a human nature to judge oneself and others. *Beer and Ruh* (1976) used the term for the first time and popularized the concept of performance management. Today's business complexities and competitive priorities makes it more than judging people, it is essentially now developing people through their work performance. Performance management therefore plays a crucial organizational and individual function of motivating people for better performance for sustainable and sustained competitive advantage.

Performance management is a strategic approach to management, which equips leaders, managers, employees, and stakeholders at different levels with a set of tools and techniques to regularly plan, continuously monitor, periodically measure and review performance of the organization in terms of indicators and targets for efficiency, effectiveness and impact. Performance management places emphasis on the fact that it is a system that ensures organizational performance through the alignment and integration of all the organizational actions such as the vision, mission, values and culture of the organization through cooperation and support of employees. When implementing performance management system, it is necessary to address the cultural beliefs, values and norms to identify issues which can either hinder or facilitate the implementation process.

Noe, Hollenbeck, Gerhart and Wright (2000) state that a highly committed workforce is the source of an organization's sustainable competitive advantage. A well-designed and developed performance management system can ensure worker commitment to the organization's goals. Performance management will only be able to achieve the above if the organization also implements a sound job analysis and design procedure, effective recruitment policy, good training and development programmes, competitive pay structure and incentives, with good labour and employee relations. All these coupled with a well-developed performance management helps to ensure a culture of effectiveness. Therefore, a mechanism is required to give direction, coordinate, organize and implement efforts of employees towards productive goals. It is in this context that performance management assumes the role of integration mechanism. *Amstrong and Baron* observes four types of integrations namely, vertical, functional, human resource and goals as described below:

1. ***Vertical integration*:** Aligning objectives at organizational, individual and team levels and integrating them for effective performance. The individuals and teams agree upon to a dialogue to work within the broad framework of organizational goals and values.
2. ***Functional integration*:** It deals with focusing several functional energies, plans, policies and strategies onto tasks in different levels and parts of the organization.
3. ***Human resource integration*:** This ensures effective integration of different sub-systems of human resource management to achieve organizational goals with optimum performance. These subsystems include people management, task monitoring, job design, motivation, appraisal and reward systems, and training and empowerment.
4. ***Goal integration*:** It focuses on arriving at congruence between the needs, aspirations and goals of the managers with that of the goals and objectives of the organization.

To summarize, performance management refers to the comprehensive system of:

(*a*) Developing employee performance plans, including the key result areas and indicators of performance;

(*b*) Communicating to the employees in clear terms the performance plan at the commencement of the period of performance;

(*c*) Monitoring and supporting employees for moving effectively towards attainment of performance goals;

(*d*) Evaluating the performance of each employee on the basis of the performance plan during the period of performance;

(*e*) Recognizing and rewarding those employees whose performance has meet/exceed the performance plan;

(*f*) Enabling the employees to improve the unacceptable performance; and

(*g*) Reassigning, reducing in grade or removing those employees who could not improve their performance even after providing adequate opportunities to improve.

Thus, the management principle underpinning performance management is that performance management is a management 'tool' that integrates the business operations with the strategic intent of the organization. The success of any organization is said to depend on its ability to execute its functions against its strategies. Strategies within the organization must ensure that all efforts are made in the same direction, and that every person within the organization is contributing to the organizations objectives via their daily activities in support of measurements as contained within the performance management. A measure then of how effectively performance management has been implemented is the degree to which synergies in organizational performance are achieved because all employees are working towards the same objective or goal.

Implementing Performance Management

Most experts agree that a successful system of performance management involves four basic components:

- A clear organizational definition of performance;
- A training and development programme that focuses on improving performance;
- An objective evaluation system to review employee performance; and
- A method of recognizing and rewarding performance.

Source : Subramanian, Iyer, "Performance Evaluation", *Business Manager*, Vol. 11, No. 9, March 2009, pp. 24-28

1.5 Definitions of Performance Management

A few noteworthy definitions of performance management are as follows:

1. *"Performance Management is the process through which managers ensure that employee's activities and outputs are congruent with the organization's goals."*

— De Cieri et al.

2. *"Performance Management is about applying processes, techniques and systems which maintain and improve individual's performance whilst simultaneously aiming to improve the performance of the organization."*

— Hale and Whitlam

3. *"Performance management is the process that begins with translating the overall strategic objectives of the organization into clear objectives for each individual employee."*

— Amos, Ristow and Ristow

4. *"Performance Management is the process through which managers ensure that employee's activities and outputs contribute to organizational goals."*

— Gomez & Mejia

5. *"Performance Management is defined as a process of defining, monitoring, and using objective indicators of the performance of an organization and performance on a regular basis".*

— Poister

6. *"Performance Management is an interlocking set of policies and practices which have as their focus the enhanced achievement of organizational objectives through a concentration on individual performance."*

— Storey and Sisson

7. *Performance Management is an ongoing communication process, undertaken in partnership, between an employee and his or her immediate supervisor that involves establishing clear expectations and understanding about:*
   - *the essential job functions the employee is expected to do;*
   - *how the employee's job contributes to the goals of the organization;*
   - *what doing the work will mean in concrete terms;*
   - *how employee and supervisor will work together to sustain, improve or build on existing employee performance;*
   - *how performance management will be measured; and*
   - *identifying barriers to performance and removing them.*

— Bacal

From an analytical study of the above definitions, we may conclude that:

- Performance management ensures congruence of individual and orgnizational goals;
- Performance management is a process involving planning, reviewing, developing and enhancing performance;
- Managers are catalyst of employee performance through effective policies and practices; and
- Employees get an opportunity to seek organizational support and resources for overcoming barriers to performance.

1.6 PHILOSOPHY OF PERFORMANCE MANAGEMENT

It includes the following:

- Support management philosophy and contribute to the business plan achievement;
- Emphasize personal development;
- Improve communication;
- Develop leadership;
- Foster teamwork;
- Facilitate succession planning;
- Improve organization's effectiveness and bottom-line performance;
- Achieve results while modeling, reinforcing Core Value behaviours;
- Communicate clear objectives for reinforcing excellence;
- Setting challenging, yet achievable performance expectations;
- Continually developing personal management skills;
- Concern for both internal and external customers;
- Providing coaching, counseling and career development; and
- Providing ongoing feedback.

1.7 PRINCIPLES OF PERFORMANCE MANAGEMENT

The major principles of performance management are as follows:

1. **Principle of outcome orientation**: Performance management from a system's perspective consists of inputs (performance expectations), throughputs (performance development and performance appraisal) and outcomes (rewards and recognition). It is crucial to understand that there is a difference between outputs and outcomes. Output is concerned with only result whereas outcome is concerned with results and behaviour that drives results. Often performance management emphasizes inputs (moderately), throughputs (high) and outputs (high) without adequately focusing on outcomes, that is, behaviour that drives results as also the impact of outcomes on overall organizational strategy, processes and procedures. An effective performance management emphasizes inputs, throughputs and outcomes and utilizes a balanced set of means and measures for fostering performance excellence through employees.
2. **Principle of evidence**: Since performance management is a mechanism that utilizes sets of data, measures and decisions, therefore all managerial decisions must be based upon good quality, reliable, valid, relevant and timely data pertaining to business, environment, organization, system and employees.

3. **Principle of transparency**: Performance management is a participative HR strategy which requires that relevant information necessary for enabling employee performance must be objective and readily accessible to all concerned. This will enable performance management to be viewed as objective, fair, reliable and meaningful for all the stakeholders including management/leadership, shareholders, customers, employees and society at large.
4. **Principle of focus**: Performance management should be based upon strategic plans of the organization and must be periodically reviewed to ensure continuing relevancy. Organization's competitive priority must be reflected in individual performance plans and accomplishments.
5. **Principle of ownership**: Performance management must ensure that employees have a say in setting performance expectations, evolving robust performance plan and access to data, information, resources, support and managerial guidance to effectively achieve their performance expectations. Employee's involvement and participative decision-making will ensure that employees accept the system and strive to contribute to organizations bottom-line and take measures for improving performance continuously.

1.8 FEATURES OF PERFORMANCE MANAGEMENT

The major features of performance management are as follows:

1. The organization develops a vision, mission and ethical values that is being communicated to all employees for seeking employee commitment;
2. Employee performance is viewed as consequence of integration of individual objectives with organizational goals and objectives;
3. Performance expectations is established against which individual achievements can be measured and developed further;
4. Tracking of employee's progress towards performance expectations is regular with feedback provided to the employee on one-to-one basis;
5. Review of progress of employee's performance leads to identification of areas of competency development;
6. Measuring performance of employees against individual, team, departmental and organizational performance expectations is linked to reward outcomes;
7. Propels employees to continually improve performance; and
8. The organization evaluates the effectiveness of performance management as a system so that modifications and improvements can be made.

1.9 SIGNIFICANCE OF PERFORMANCE MANAGEMENT

Some of the major significance of performance management is enlisted below:

1. **Clarifies organization's strategic plans**: It helps in clarifying the mission, vision, strategy and values of the organization to the employees in order to motivate them for effective achievement;
2. **Business process improvement**: It helps in improving various business processes because the deficiencies are highlighted;
3. **Talent management**: It helps in attracting and retaining talents in the organization and helps in establishing robust talent management system;
4. **Personnel development**: It aids in competency development and training and development needs identification and implementation as part of individual development tool;
5. **Validation of talent acquisition**: It helps management in validating HR processes such as recruitment, selection, socialization, training, career and succession planning;
6. **Work-life balance**: It helps employees to attain their full potential and attain a balance between professional demands with personal life effectively;
7. **Improved adaptability**: It helps in identifying the gap between organization's performance expectations and employee's actual performance for developmental intervention;
8. **Individual relationship management**: It fosters a strong individual relationship even at grass root level against traditional industrial relations which is marked with conflicts and clashes;
9. **Sustainable competitive advantage**: It enables sustainable competitive advantage through high performance employees; and
10. **Culture building**: It helps in creating and/or sustaining a performance oriented work culture and proactive practices.

1.10 THE PERFORMANCE MANAGEMENT MODEL

The performance model is depicted in Fig. 1.3 which will help us to understand the framework of monitoring and improving performance of employees in the organizational context.

Performance management model comprises of organizational goals and objectives, human capital, contextual factors, situational factors and competitive advantage. In other words, performance management entails linking human capital to competitive advantage through organizational goals and objectives. The details are as enumerated below:

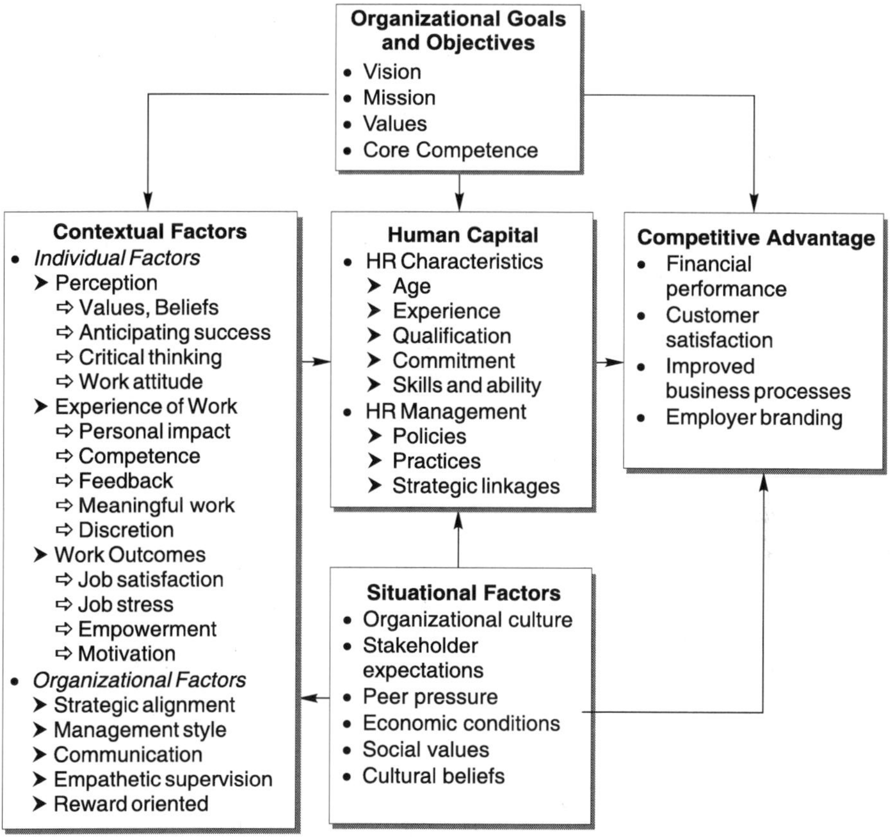

Fig. 1.3 Performance Management Model

A. **Organizational goals and objectives**: The starting point of performance management is vision, mission, values and core competence of the organization. The vision lays down the ultimate goal of the organization, mission elaborates the path or strategy to reach the vision, value indicates the business ethics core to the organization and core competence exhibits the specified area of business where organization has better ability and high confidence.

B. **Human capital**: Performance management essentially entails performance through human capital of the organization. The nature and quality of the human capital plays a decisive role in the success of performance management. The characteristics of human resources and the way they are managed play a pivotal role in leveraging skills and abilities of employees effectively. Employee characteristics such as age, experience, qualification, organizational commitment and individual skills and ability provide the ground for effective job performance. On the other hand, nature and extent of human resource management helps to maximize utilization of employee characteristics successfully. HR policies and practices help to maintain a productive workforce necessary for effective performance. However, in the absence of linking human resource management to strategic goals and objectives of the organization, performance management is likely to produce sub-optimal results.

C. **Contextual factors**: Contextual factors are internal to an employee and significantly impact his job performance and effectiveness. Consider the following dependent factors as follows:

(*a*) *Individual factors* that include issues of individual perception (values, beliefs, critical thinking, anticipation of success and work attitude), experience of work (needs, self-concept, personal impact, skills, competence, feedback, incentives and rewards) and individual work outcomes (job satisfaction, empowerment, motivation, worker capability and achievement).

(*b*) *Organizational factors* that include issues of manager's support and performance management, organizational culture, norms and standards used at work, communication, supervisor and peer support. All these factors affect the capability of employees to perform certain task positively or negatively.

D. **Situational factors**: Various intra and inter organizational factors also impacts both contextual factors as well as employee's job performance. Intra organizational factors such as its culture, stakeholder expectations, peer pressure etc. tend to influence the efforts, motivation and outcomes of employees. Inter organizational factors such as economic conditions, social values and cultural pressures also impact employee's perception, motivation and work outcomes.

E. **Competitive advantage**: The ultimate results of organizational goals and objectives, human capital, contextual factors and social factors culminate into organizational competitive advantage. It results in financial success, higher customer satisfaction, improved business process and employer branding.

Hence, we may conclude that performance management shall be effective and help to attain competitive advantage for the organization provided it has excellent human capital and favourable contextual and social factors.

Day-to-Day Performance Management

These five steps will guide your day-to-day performance management:

- Plan what needs to be done, involve the employee in the planning process to encourage ownership of the tasks, and set expectations for the job;
- Monitor and periodically evaluate each employee's performance;
- Develop the individual's skills through training, challenging work, and opportunities for advancement;
- Review the employee's performance during quarter or annual reviews using a rating scale or other form of objective measurement; and
- Reward good performance with positive reinforcement.

Source: Subramanian, Iyer, "Performance Evaluation", Business Manager, Vol. 11, No. 9, March 2009, pp. 24-28.

1.11 Strategic Implications of Performance Management

De Waal (2002) emphasizes the strategic nature of performance management and defines it as "the process that enables an organization to deliver a predictable contribution to sustained value creation. A world-class performance management process consists of excellent strategy development, budgeting/target setting, performance measurement, performance review, and incentive compensation sub-processes". The effective management of individual performance is critical to the execution of strategy[1] and the organization achieving its strategic objectives. *Golden and Ramanujan* has given four different levels of linkage as follows:

Administrative linkage	No linkage between HRM and organizational strategies. People management function has a traditional role, dominated by day-to-day administrative concerns.
One-way linkage	A one-way linkage between people management and strategic planning, either people management taking a more active role or strategic planning process taking a more active role in the integration process.
Two-way linkage	There is a reciprocal and interdependent relationship between strategic planning process and people management.
Integrative linkage	Dynamic and multifaceted linkage that is based on an integrative relationship between people management and strategic management process.

1. Strategy is the pattern or plan that integrates an organization's major goals, policies, and action sequences into a cohesive whole. A well formulated strategy helps in appropriate allocation of an organization's resources into a unique and viable posture based on its relative internal competencies and shortcomings, anticipated changes in the environment and contingent moves by intelligent opponents.

Thus, it is clear that for organizational effectiveness, a clear linkage between organizational strategy and people management is necessary. In other words, the management of performance of employees must be driven by organizational goals and objectives. Strategic planning constitutes an important element of performance management; as it is through this process that the foundation of performance management namely the vision, mission and values of the organization are determined. Strategic planning process should begin with a dream, a notion or an idea. This notion or blueprint should act as the driving force in making the corporate leader's dream become a reality. Hence, many organizations have some means of looking to the future through strategic planning at corporate level. This can include a description of the general mission of the organization and its goals for the long-term. That plan can then be translated into year-by-year plans that are aligned with the longer-term strategic plan. Both long and short-term goals must be translated into goals and objectives for each smaller work unit and then into goals and objectives for each employee. This translation from organization goals to individual responsibility is done through the performance planning process. That process should align the work of each employee to the organizational goals and objectives. Therefore, performance management has to be seen as a system within a larger system, which linked to other organizational processes.

However, in order to enable an organization to motivate performance, it should be able to identify and measure the performance that it wants to motivate and reward. The key issue is finding the best way to measure the performance of individuals and aligning these measurements with the strategic objectives of the organization. To be motivating, these measures must be seen to be credible and susceptible to the influence of those individuals whose performance is being measured and whose pay or reward is being determined. The "influenceability" of a measure is often referred to as the line of sight or line of influence. Both terms capture the idea of individual ability to affect their performance measures through behaviour. Therefore, strategy should drive decisions about the kinds of performance to reward and about how to measure performance. Therefore, reward and compensation plans that are tied to performance are another way in which organizations can recognize and motivate employees. Employees must be able to see a direct connection between their rewards and their accomplishments, and they must believe that the standards by which they are measured are fair. The key is to set goals that can be quantified and measured objectively.

The primary focus of reward and compensation systems is how organizations define their reward schemes and communicate this in a manner that employees clearly understand the link between reward and performance in the light of strategic goals and objectives of the organization. Moreover, organizations should periodically gauge if employee's performance is still in line with the organization goals and rewards. For this reason, the performance management and reward systems are linked to goals that are in turn linked to organization vision and strategy. Communication is a key aspect in the performance management process, from clarifying the rewards system, to how the organization should communicate it and most important how employees see the link between performance goals and rewards. The aspects of job performance that have an impact on success, that differentiate between successful and unsuccessful performers, and are at least partially within the control of the person being rated should be identified as performance measures. These performance measures are also the factors that establish the reason why an individual has received the reward. The performance management process determines that managers monitor performance and provide ongoing feedback, both positive and negative. This process encourages managers to break away from their desks, observing performance, comparing it to standards or expectations, and intervening in the ongoing process using behaviour-based language to reward, recognize or improve performance. Problem-solving, coaching, counseling, developing, and removing obstacles to success, rewarding and recognizing may all be required during the performance management process.

1.12 Performance Management Strategy

Performance management is not just a HR strategy but a key organizational priority to attain and sustain competitive advantage through commitment, competence and performance of its employees. Since it is the employees who create competitive advantage for organizations, therefore performance management strategy needs to be designed and developed by organization in order to attain its goals and objectives both successfully as well as in a sustainable manner. Therefore, performance management strategy must be in tight fit with organizational strategy. Broadly performance management strategy can be categorized as: cost driven strategy, quality driven strategy and innovation driven strategy as enumerated below:

1. **Cost driven performance management strategy:** In today's globally competitive business scenario, cost is a major determinant of organizational success or failure. Producing goods or services at lowest possible cost holds key to organization's sustained competitiveness. It is important to understand here that cost cutting and cost containment are not necessarily the same term. Cost cutting may lead to reduction in expenditure on certain parameters or business aspects which may prove detrimental to organizational competitiveness in the long-term. Cost containment on the other hand emphasizes eliminating non-essential expenses and wastages in all forms.

   Performance management strategy focuses upon improving individual productivity, keeping strong performance linked incentive systems in place and encouraging employees to generate and actively work upon cost saving ideas. Employees make maximum utilization of available resources, optimizes operational processes and procedures and expenses are kept under tight monitoring and control. Thus, a cost-driven performance management strategy focuses upon cost saving, improving individual productivity, optimizing resources and business processes and continually working on reducing operational costs.

2. **Quality driven performance management strategy:** Besides cost, quality is equally important for organizations intending to compete in globalized economy. Quality is first and foremost determinant of acceptance of a product or service by the customers. Quality needs to be ingrained into the organization's management style, business processes, work culture and practices. Various quality tools and techniques like TQM, Kaizen, 5S, quality circles, etc. are the competitive priority of the organization. Since these tools and techniques require total involvement and commitment of the employees, therefore it can be integrated with performance management.

   Quality driven performance management strategy emphasizes that work efforts, behaviour and outcomes must be quality driven. Employees are trained, developed and motivated to internalize various quality tools in their day-to-day working and mindset is attuned to quality outcomes only. A quality driven performance management strategy encompasses inculcating quality culture, quality efforts, and quality outcomes.

3. **Innovation driven performance management strategy:** Innovation refers to creating new ideas, processes, products, systems and tools by making significant improvisation of existing things. Organizations cannot just thrive on cost and quality parameters unless they unleash innovation in their products and services. Since human minds are prime sources of innovation therefore nurturing an innovation driven performance management strategy helps to attain organizational effectiveness.

   An innovation driven performance management strategy encompasses nurturing employees for thinking, analyzing and delivering innovative ideas which can be transformed into profitable and viable business solutions. Employees are motivated and supported for assuming the role of intrepreneur in their respective work domains and with the help of available resources, develop systems that can provide sustained competitive advantage to their organizations.

   Hence, we may conclude that a cost driven performance management strategy emphasizes cost containment, a quality driven performance management focuses upon quality systems and finally an innovation driven performance management strategy seeks to tap limitless human talents through involvement, participation, commitment and contribution of the employees. In reality, these three strategies operate seldom in isolation; rather they work effectively in combination in our dynamic, uncertain and competitive business world.

We may summarize our discussions as follows:

Performance Management Strategy	Performance outcomes entail:
	• Cost containment • Rewards and compensation linked to performance • Optimum compensation ratio • Quality efforts and outputs • Ingraining quality work practices and mindset • Quality is part of organizational culture • Innovative products and services • Managerial nurturing of ideas • Employees are intrepreneurs • Talent is competitive advantage

1.13 Approaches to Performance Management

The various approaches to performance management are as follows:

1. **Performance driven integration**: This approach emphasizes the role of performance management on changing organizational behaviour and tends to undervalue the part played by other human resource development activities. It focuses on the planning (goal alignment and setting performance expectations), appraisal and rewards processes with secondary attention to employee development.
2. **Development driven integration**: This approach stresses the importance of ensuring the appropriate human resource development (HRD) activities are in place to meet the long-term objectives of the organization and to ensure that business needs and HRD are coordinated. Performance based pay may operate in these organizations but it is perceived to be complimentary to HRD activities rather than driving it.
3. **Team oriented**: This describes the organization's design, culture and processes including performance management. These organizations will either adopt either a performance-driven integration or development-driven integration approach. The main difference is in the implementation which emphasizes team setting of performance expectations, development feedback, and rewards, and requires a significantly different role of managers as facilitators.

A concern with certain approaches to performance management could reinforce the predisposition to short-term orientation and set back organizational effectiveness in the long term. This is based on the use of performance management to micro-manage and/or reward people for short-term thinking and deliverables. This is reinforced in organizations which tend to move people before there has been sufficient time to see the results of their action.

1.14 PERFORMANCE MANAGEMENT PROCESS

Performance management embraces all aspects of the organization including organizational strategies, environmental responsiveness, business processes, and innovation with employees and managers at the epicenter of the process. It is a competitive strategy of the organizations to continuously and continually enhance the competitiveness and performance of the organization by fostering employee commitment towards organizational goals and objectives, developing employees through work, providing direction to channelize work efforts and improve employee productivity and competence. Performance management seeks to integrate employee's work efforts with organizational development initiatives. This integration involves a process, a series of activities, for seeking its aims. It involves the following sub-processes or activities as discussed below (*see* Fig. 1.4):

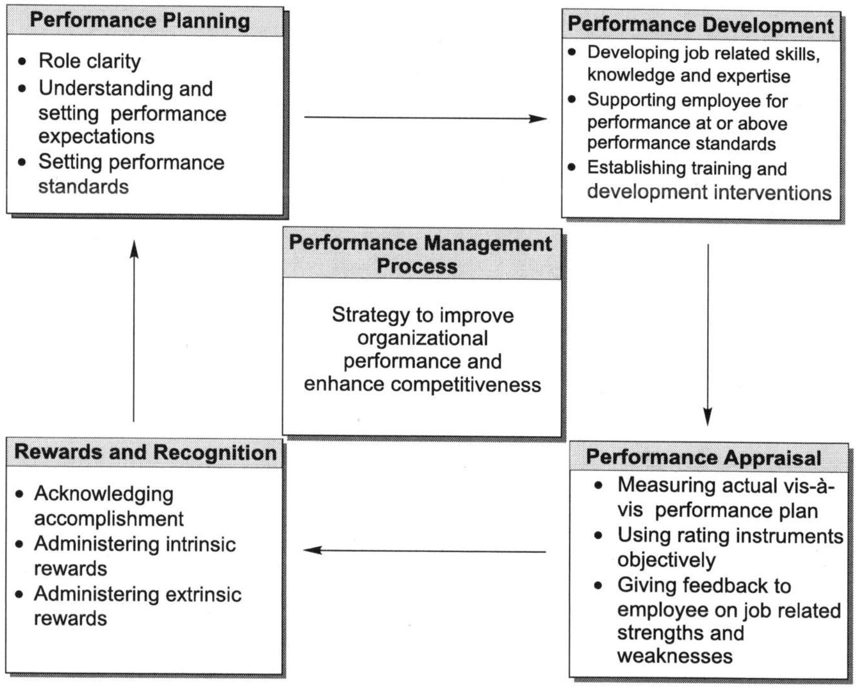

Fig. 1.4 Performance Management Process

Cycle 1: Performance Planning

Performance planning means setting performance expectations for groups and individuals to channel their efforts toward achieving organizational goals and objectives. Performance planning starts with role clarification in order to align an individual's objectives with the goals and strategic plan of the organization, as well as the clearly defined needs of his internal and external customers. This is designed to meet a clear understanding of what the individual is expected to achieve and how he is expected to achieve it.

Once the individual has clarified his role, the next step is to develop performance expectations and action plans for the coming year in support of this defined role. Performance expectations should focus on the high priority, high added value, and high improvement potential areas and the primary aim is to pave the way for personal and organizational development. Performance expectations can be classified into three categories as under:

1. ***Operating***: Tangible, measurable and challenging performance expectations that connect directly to the implementation of the operating plan, budget and departmental plans.
2. ***People Development***: Tangible, measurable and challenging performance expectations which enhance the capabilities, skills, and future contributions of the individual.
3. ***Strengthening the Business***: Tangible, measurable and challenging performance expectations which will position the business for greater competitive and operational strength in the future.

The requirements for planning employee's performance include establishing the elements and standards of their performance. Performance elements and standards should be measurable, understandable, verifiable, equitable, and achievable. Through critical elements, employees are held accountable as individuals for work assignments or responsibilities. Employee performance plans should be flexible so that they can be adjusted to changing objectives and work requirements. When used effectively, these plans can be beneficial working documents that are discussed often, and not merely paperwork that is filed in a drawer and seen only when ratings of record are required.

Cycle 2: Performance Development

An important component of the performance management process is development of employee's work related skills, knowledge and experience. Performance development is a process of promoting a climate of continuous learning and professional growth, helping to sustain employee performance at a level which meets or exceeds expectations, enhancing job or career related skills, knowledge and experience thereby making the employee competitive for employment opportunities within the organization. Managers are expected to diagnose the employee's career stage and to identify the source of the individual's performance problems in order to develop a personal development plan (PDP).

Development of performance of employees is essential in today's rapidly changing workplace so that the organization remains competitive and enable the organization to retain its reputation for excellence. Employees too recognize that it is essential for them to continue to learn so that they will be effective in their current jobs and able to move into other positions or accept new responsibilities as circumstances demand.

Performance development entails evolving a plan for improving employee competitiveness. Performance development plans should be considered with the needs of the organization and the needs of the employee in mind. Performance development entails:

- The employee's need for training.
- The employee's career plan.
- The needs and strategic goals of the organization.
- The affirmative action objectives of the organization.
- The resources of the department.
- Advantages of one type of training over another.
- The effect of the determination on workload and other employees.

Assessment tools such as 360 feedback instruments and peer reviews can be used at this phase. Development areas are then identified specific learning activities targeted at each competency area.

Mentoring At Sona Koyo

In the company, employees are asked to identify people from senior management who can solve the problems of their mentees- either personal or professional. The people from senior management acts as a coach and mentor to them.

Emotions influence all aspects of one's life. It's almost impossible to separate personal life from professional life. It one's professional life is not sunning smoothly, an employee is suffering from an issue, and all these will ultimately affect the personal life of an employee. In the company, and effort is made to balance professional as well as personal life by organizing *"spouse mentoring programme"*, where the spouses of the employees are invited to the plant. They come to know about eh working conditions, work stations of their better halves. When they the plant as well as the workstations they realize the work pressure that they handle.

Source: Nair, Hari, "Employee's Emotional Intelligence: Pragmatic Approach", Business Manager, Vol. 11, No. 9, March 2009, pp. 10-11.

Cycle 3: Performance Appraisal

Performance appraisal is the most crucial phase of the performance management process. Performance appraisal is a systematic and objective way of judging the relative worth or ability of an employee in performing his job and administering rewards in accordance with exhibited performance. This phase is described as the process of providing ongoing feedback and coaching to employees, as well as evaluating the performance at year ends. Specific minimum requirements are defined which include a mid-year review intended to:

- Review and discuss progress on each performance expectation;
- Review the conditions that may have an impact on the performance expectations and develop plans to overcome problems or obstacles;
- Discuss the possibility of adding, eliminating or modifying some performance expectations;
- Noting any "special" performance expectations that were assigned after consensus was reached on the original performance plan; and
- Review and discuss the employee's behaviours without rating them.

The performance appraisal phase emphasizes the role of the manager in driving the process. At year end, the manager is expected to evaluate both the employee's performance against performance expectations and his behaviours against a defined set of criteria which is the same for all employees at all levels in all jobs. Performance is evaluated using "sound judgment" and a rating instrument with scale ranging from "inadequate" to "outstanding" and behaviours are rated using "sound judgment" as "needs development", "satisfactory", or "superior". The combination of these two ratings determines the employees overall performance rating.

This phase is very performance-oriented with determination of factors that have influenced the individual's performance as performance can be explained by a combination of role perception, skills, motivation and organizational support systems, as well as other disrupting factors such as personal trauma. However, it is clearly implied that the key focus of this phase of the performance management process is on performance in terms of actual results achieved by the employee.

Cycle 4: Rewards and Recognition

Rewards acknowledge the performance of employees. Financial rewards like compensation is an extrinsic motivation for the employees performing well and induces other employees to perform better due to grant of differentiating pay and benefits to best performers. Providing people with an opportunity to learn and grow is also important motivator of performance. Rewards and recognition programmes provides a rationale, transparent, open and legally defensible mechanism to improve employee performance.

Is Performance Management Effective?

There are a few things you can do to ensure your performance management policies remain current and effective:

- Measure improvements in retention rate, productivity, employee morale, competency level, and employee advancement;
- Regularly reassess performance standards to make sure you are keeping up with the demands of the workplace; and
- Encourage employees to comment on performance evaluation standards. This makes for a motivated, empowered workplace.

Source: Subramanian, Iyer, "Performance Evaluation", Business Manager, Vol. 11, No. 9, March 2009, pp. 24-28.

1.15 Employee Motivation and Performance Management

Motivation is defined as "a set of processes concerned with the force that energizes behaviour and directs it towards attaining some goal" (*Baron*, 1983). *Kreitner and Kinicki* (1992) postulate that motivation represents, "those psychological processes that cause the arousal, direction and persistence of voluntary actions that are goal directed." Since the role of managers to successfully guide employees toward accomplishing organizational objectives, therefore it is crucial for them to understand these psychological processes in order to ensure that all employees performance their tasks and exhibit appropriate behaviours for effectively attaining goals and objectives of the organization. *La Motta* (1995) views job performance as the result of motivation and ability. Ability includes training, education, equipment, and simplicity of task, experience and both inborn mental and physical capacity. Given all of these factors at their peak, an employee may still not perform well on the job if the motivation is not directed at that particular task. *Lawler* (2003) argues that people need both motivation and ability. Highly motivated employees will not achieve results if they do not have the necessary skills, expertise and attitude that the organization requires of them. Similarly, employees with expertise, knowledge and skills will not do well if they are unmotivated. This implies that motivation to perform well is crucial for the success of performance management.

Motivation is intentional and directional. The word 'intentional' refers to personal choice and persistence of action, whilst 'directional' denotes the presence of a driving force aimed at attaining a specific goal. This implies that employees have personal goals and managers need to align these personal goals with organizational goals and objectives. Performance management helps employees in setting performance expectations in tandem with their managers which is both fulfilling for that employee and beneficial for business. Managers should ensure their support, guidance and coaching to the employees so that their efforts are reflected by job involvement and commitment towards individual performance plans at micro-level, departmental goals at meso-level and organizational goals and objectives at macro-level. In other words, employee's performance is both intentional and directional in the context of performance management.

Employee motivation is a process that an organization can foster and nurture so that it can occur spontaneously. If organizations believe that people are naturally motivated, they must simply provide the environment and atmosphere that fosters and supports their motivation. This will help in channelizing efforts and talents of the employees towards performance management in such a way that their commitment to strategic plans reaches highest level of excellence.

La Motta (1995) posits that managers have to learn to motivate people. He believes that employees bring their own motivation, and what they need from work is to be liberated, to be involved, to be accountable and to reach their full potential. This will assist in transforming every employee into an independent performance manager who is committed to deliver excellent results and also induces co-workers to follow suite. Such high levels of organizational commitment, job involvement and performance orientation will help in realizing a highly engaged workforce. Employees who are engaged and self-motivated do not have to be managed, as they are motivated by doing a job they believe in, in a constructive direction. In order words, performance management ceases to become a controlling tool but a commitment seeking system.

Also, better job performance also entails better rewards. *Baron* (1983) posits the view that if successful performance leads to organizational rewards, such performance could be a motivational factor for employees. Under such conditions, they can see that their efforts result in rewards. Consequently they may be motivated to exert higher levels of effort on the job. Thus, not only can motivation influence performance, but also that performance if followed by rewards can influence motivation. Hence, employees who are motivated and committed make their performance management system succeed thereby sustaining organization's competitive advantage in the marketplace.

Dealing with Underperformers

Terminations are always difficult, even when they are clearly necessary. These points are worth remembering:

- Termination may be especially traumatic for junior employees because it could be their first experience of losing a job;
- Mid-level employees might be qualified for lateral transfers;
- Termination of senior executives affects the whole organization;
- When senior people are terminated, other employees want to know how they will be affected; and
- Severance pay should always be commensurate with the individual's year of service.

Source: Subramanian, Iyer, "Performance Evaluation", Business Manager, Vol. 11, No. 9, March 2009, pp,. 24-28.

1.16 LEADERSHIP'S ROLE IN PERFORMANCE MANAGEMENT

Leadership can be defined in terms of behaviours, traits, competencies and results. In the organizational context, leadership refers to top or senior management personnel. Their behaviours and competencies decide the quality of organizational outcomes. The successful leader is able to manipulate the present to create the future, and therefore is able to 'see the whole' (*Follet*, 1933). According to *Giamatti* (1982, cited in *McLarney*, 2009), "Leadership is an essentially moral act not, as in most management as essentially protective act. Leadership is the assertion of *qa vision*, not simply the exercise of style. It is the moral courage to assert a vision of the institution in the future, and the intellectual energy to persuade the culture of the wisdom and validity .... And such assertion of leadership. By speech, by deed, by decisions large and small, have been largely missing". Thus, leadership is more about establishing direction, aligning people, and motivating and inspiring others. Leadership is concerned with long-term outcomes and future goals of the organizations.

Top management is primarily responsible for creating vision, mission, strategy and core values which is used to motivate employees to achieve them. The process of realizing organizational vision, mission, and strategy entails utilization of performance management. Performance management is a management tool for realizing organizational goals and objectives through the talents, ingenuity and commitment of the employees by providing right leadership to them. The success of performance management is heavily dependent upon the commitment, support, guidance, cooperation and push. In other words, since performance management is a commitment oriented mechanism to seek, nurture, develop and align appropriate employee behaviours necessary for achieving effective results, therefore top management's or leadership's capability or competencies in ensuring the success of performance management is of paramount importance for the organization as a whole. Since leadership is more about people and less about tasks, therefore leadership through its own competencies can ensure success of performance management with commitment, cooperation and collaboration of the employees (*see* Fig. 1.5).

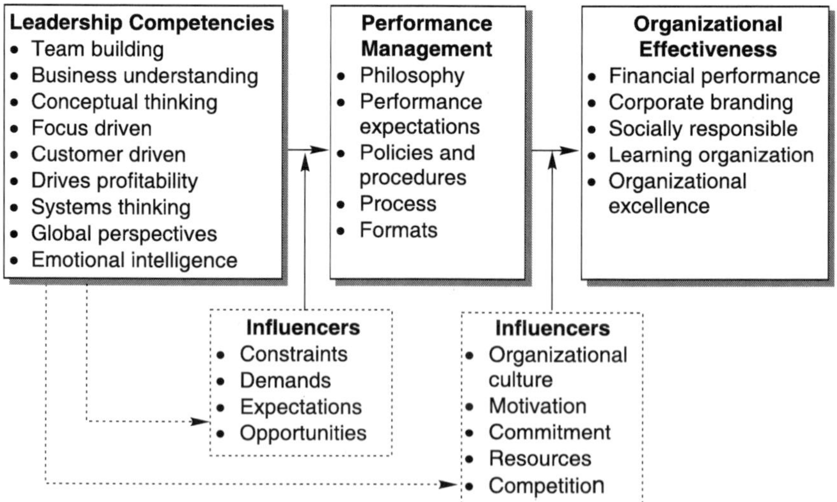

Fig. 1.5 Leadership Driven Performance Management.

Kotter's Management and Leadership Grid

	Management	Leadership
Creating an agenda	Planning and budgeting-establishing detailed steps and timetables for achieving needed results and then allocating the resouces necessary to make that happen	Establishing direction-vision of the future, the distant future and strategies for producing the changes needed to achieve that vision.
Developing a human network for achieving the agenda	Organizing and staffing-establishing some structure for accomplishing plan requirements, staffing that structure with individuals, delegating responsibility and authority for carrying out the plan, providing and procedures to help guide people and creating methods or systems to monitor implementation.	Aligning people-communicating the direction by words and deeds to all those whose cooperation may be needed so as to influence the creation of teams and coalitions that understand the vision and strategies and accept their validity.
Execution	Controlling and problem solving-monitoring results versus plan in some detail identifying deviations and then planning and organizing to solve these problems.	Motivating and inspiring-enegizing people to overcome major bureaucratic and resource barriers to change by satisfying very basic but often unfulfilled human needs.
Outcomes	Produces a degree of predictability and order and has the potential of consistently producing key results expected by various stakeholers.	Produces changes, often to a dramatic degree and has the potential of producing extremely useful change.

Source: Cited from: Dr. Jain, Mahaveer, "Definition of Leadership", Developing Behavioural Skills on Leadership for Trade Union Leaders, Readings, January 12-17, 2009, V. V. Giri National Labour Institue, Noida, pp. 8.

The roles of leadership in ensuring effective performance management are as under:

- **Builds teamwork**: Leaders should build effective teams committed to organizational goals and results in order to ensure that the employees 'buy-in' performance management;

- **Understands the business**: Leaders must know the organization and stay abreast of business and competitive trends. This will ensure that performance expectations set for the employees are linked and responsive to these business and competitive trends;
- **Conceptual thinking**: Leaders should conceive and select innovative strategies and ideas for the organization thereby encouraging innovation and big-picture thinking amongst the employees. This will help in motivating employees to become strategically agile and develop a broad-based performance plan;
- **Customer driven**: Leaders should strive to create value for the customer resulting in mutual long-term success. This will motivate employees to serve their internal and external customers well and develop a deep-rooted customer oriented work culture;
- **Focus drive**: Leaders must focus on a goal and prioritize and harness employee's energy to meet that goal, balances focus and drive them towards excellence in performance;
- **Drives profitability**: Leaders achieve shareholder and/or stakeholder benefit by securing cost-effective and efficient operations through strategy driven performance management system;
- **Systems thinking**: Leaders connects processes, events, and structures through performance management and balances people orientation with task discipline;
- **Global perspective**: Leaders addresses cultural and geographic differences in driving corporate strategies for competitive advantage through a performance management that is adapted to meet cultural aspirations and norms and aligned with organizational strategy;
- **Emotional intelligence**: Leaders understand and master one's own emotions (and those of employees) in a way that instills confidence; balances perception and emotional maturity. This will facilitate operation of a performance management system that is both objective and result focused.

Four Common Performance Management Routines of Great Managers

- The routine is simple. Simple formats allow manager to focus on what to say and how to say.
- The routine forces frequent interaction. Meaningful feedback happens whether it follows on the heels of an event.
- The routine is future focused. Postmortems can lead to recriminations. Positive energy comes for discussing the future.
- The routine lets employees keep track of their performance and learning. Creates more employee ownership of the self-discovery process.

Source: Branham (2005), pp. 83

1.17 National Culture and Performance Management

National Culture refers to values, beliefs, and assumptions learned in early childhood that distinguishes people in one society from those in another. National culture is not a characteristic of individuals; it encompasses a number of people who were conditioned by the same education and life experience. Culture is a collective social phenomenon. For instance management communicates organizational work culture through practices of recruitment, performance management, reward management and flexible work arrangements. All these practices are aspects of social interactions. Organizational culture can, therefore, be created, rather than just inherited by employees. Once in existence, it subtly influences perception, thought, action, and feeling of the employees in ways that are consistent with their cultural reality. It guides the selection, interpretation, and communication of information in ways that are meaningful to the employees.

To successfully implement performance management the cultural values of the employees need to be identified to ensure that there is a fit between the culture and the performance management system being implemented. *Hofstede et al.* (1990), states that these are five dimensions based on a continuum on which one can explore or understand how a culture functions. These are:

- **High power distance versus low power distance:** In a high power distance culture, key factors inter-alia are such that authority cannot be challenged, hierarchy is seen as necessary and beneficial, management style is too autocratic and close supervision is expected. A low power distance culture is characterized by authority being questioned, hierarchy is minimized, and the management style is consultative and participative. *Kakar* (1978) observes that the Indian social systems are steeply hierarchical and that Indians are highly status conscious. They feel easier to work in superior-subordinate roles rather than with equals (*Kothari*, 1970). This implies that performance management in the Indian context shall follow a top down approach. Managers decide the performance expectations of the employees and employees are happy working towards attaining manager initiated performance plans.
- **Individualistic versus collectivist cultures:** In an individualistic culture, the values of independence and privacy, where the management style is often directive with rewards and punishment, is linked to individual achievement. In an individualistic culture, management's job is to ensure that the individual and organization's interests coincide. In a collectivist culture, loyalty to the group is important, and the management style is seen as participative, and an employee is not

dismissed for poor performance. The organization is seen as a family. *Kakar* (1971) observes that a highly controlling superior has a positive effect on subordinate performance and job satisfaction. This implies that employees are dependent upon their managers for performance guidance, removing performance deficiencies and working successfully through performance plans. In other words, performance management is a managerial activity rather than a joint or participative activity between the manager and his employees.

- **High uncertainty avoidance versus low uncertainty avoidance:** It deals with the focus on the means used to adapt and cope with uncertainties. In a low uncertainty avoidance culture, there is a minimization of rules and rituals that govern interaction, dissent is encouraged, and openness to change and conflict is regarded as normal. In high uncertainty avoidance, dissent is not tolerated, there is a resistance to change, stability is valued and conflict is not regarded as natural. Indian society is rigid and any move towards change meets with stiff resistance. This implies that performance management philosophy, systems and procedures are traditional and accepted by all employees whether old or new without any resistance. This is a major reason causing many Indian organizations still adhering to performance appraisal system although some organizations have tactfully renamed it as performance management system.
- **Masculine/achievement culture versus feminine/nurturing culture**: In an achievement orientated culture, ambition is seen as important and people are judged on the basis of their performance. The management style is more achievement orientated where those who perform are praised and rewarded. In a nurturing orientated culture, emphasis is placed on the importance of life choices and the improvement in the quality of life. The management style is more consultative and participative in nature.
- **Long-term versus short-term orientation**: Where a long-term orientation is characterized by the sparing use of resources and value is attached to future rewards. Traditions are adapted and modernized as required. The short-term orientation is characterized by respect for tradition and the fulfillment of social obligations. Indian businesses have often long-term orientation. This implies that performance management is driven by long-term goals and objectives of the organization. Future rewards are valued by the employees. Fig. 1.5 summarizes the above discussions.

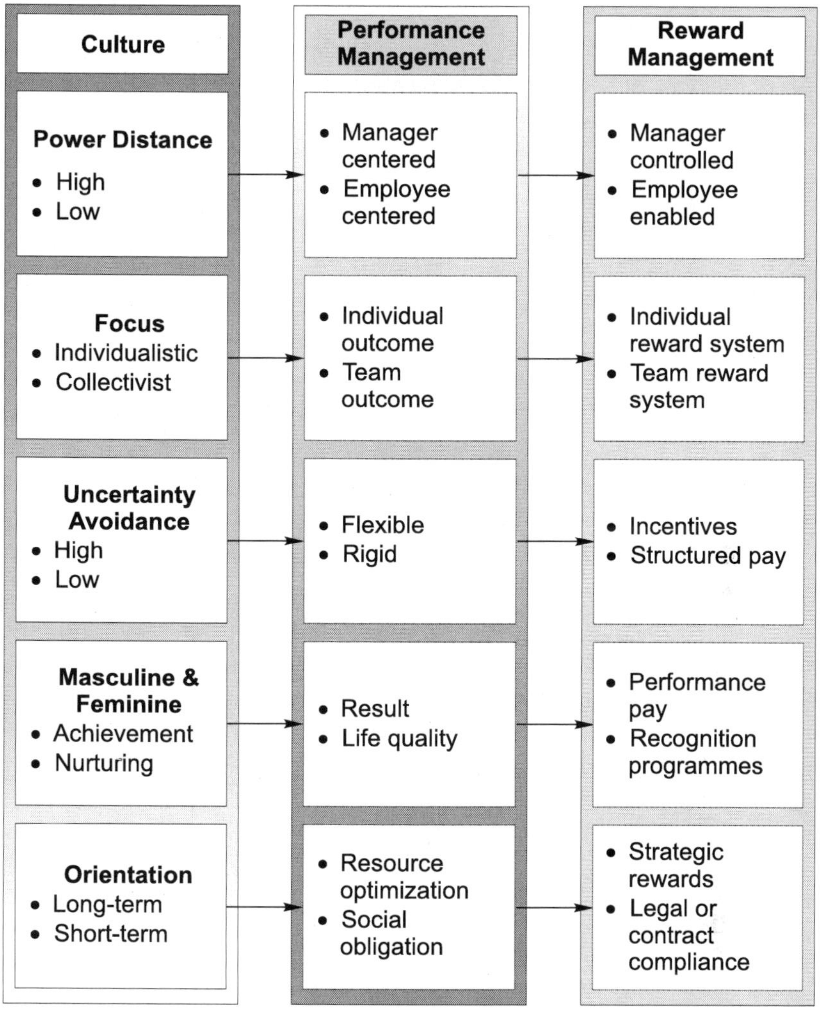

Fig. 1.5 Summarizes the above discussions. Impact of Culture of Performance and Reward management

1.18 Organizational Culture and Performance Management in Mergers and Acquisitions

The influence of mergers or acquisitions on organizations culture and its impact on performance management is depicted in Fig. 1.6.

In today's globalized economy, competitiveness and competitive advantage have become the buzzwords for organizations around the world. Organizations have been aggressively trying to build new competencies and capabilities to remain competitive and to grow profitably. In the Indian context, organizations are increasingly using mergers and acquisitions for one or more of the following reasons:

- To improve revenues and profitability;
- Faster growth in scale and quicker time to market;
- Acquisition of new technology or competence;
- To eliminate competition and increase market share;
- Tax shields and investment savings;
- Acquiring new customers or expanding the customer/market/product / service portfolio;
- Enhancing infrastructure base through acquisition of undervalued infrastructural assets or brands or additional manufacturing capacities from weaker competitors; and
- Creating new synergies through product market efficiencies and/or economies of scale.

Mergers and acquisition deals worldwide have reached an all time high in 2006, with a total value of $3.7 trillion, surpassing the 2000 high of $3.4 trillion. This implies that mergers and acquisitions have been a new business reality which also impacts HR policies, strategies and programmes of the organization.

Organizational culture represents a set values, beliefs, assumptions, perceptions and common norms. Organizational culture according to *Schein* (1992) "is a pattern of shared basic assumptions that the group learned as it solved its problems of external adaptation and internal integration that has worked well enough to be considered valid and therefore to be taught to new members as the correct way to perceive, think and feel in relation to those problems". *Barney* (1996) argues that culture of an organization can be a source of competitive advantage if it is valuable, rare and imperfectly imitable. Organizational culture is characterized by the following metaphors:

- **Who we are**—the organizational identity.
- **What we believe**—about others and ourselves.
- **What our capabilities are**—what assets and resources we possess.
- **How we behave**—how we use the assets and resources to demonstrate our beliefs.
- **Where we operate or have impact**—the way we interact with the environment.

Kotter and Heskett (1992) argue that:

- Organizational culture can have a significant impact on an organization's long-term economic performance;
- Organizational culture will probably be an even more important factor in determining the success or failure of organizations in the next decade;
- Organizational cultures that inhibit strong long-term financial performance are not rare; they develop easily, even in organizations that are full of reasonable and intelligent people; and
- Although tough to change, organizational cultures can be made more performance enhancing.

Perspectives of Organizational Culture

Perspective	Organizational Paradigm	Organizational Culture
Rationalism	Organization is the tool of efficient performance	Organizational culture serves as a tool to achieve organizational targets
Functionalism	Organization is community that seeks for survival by performing the necessary functions	Culture is a common system of shared values and basic assumption that carries out functions concerning external adaptations and internal integration
Symbolism	Organizations is a human system that expresses the complex pattern of symbolic activities	Organizational culture is a system of symbols and meanings created by the society.

Source: Scott (1992)

Hence, organizational culture is a powerful determinant of an organization's sustained competence and performance. In mergers or acquisitions, the following key elements of organizational culture are influenced as follows:

- Rules and policies
- Performance management system
- Reward and recognition programmes
- Recruitment and selection
- Training and development
- Ceremonies and events
- Leadership behaviour
- Communications
- Organizational structure

According to *Habeck, Kroger and Tram* (2000), the most important step in the mergers and acquisitions pertains to the choice of organizational culture. The authors elucidate three basic cultural approaches for execution. These three strategies or approaches are: cultural imposition, culture remains separate and creating a compound culture. The choice of organization culture is crucial because it influences employee's behaviours which in turn impact their performance. In other words, culture influences performance management in post merger and acquisition scenario. We will discuss these three approaches alongwith their impact on performance management as follows:

- **Cultural imposition**: Under this approach, organization culture of one organization is imposed on another organization if there are clear and logical reasons behind this. The new culture needs to be noticeably more appropriate to the business environment than the old one, and the imposition must furthermore take place quickly, explicitly and completely. In addition, it needs to be effectively communicated, and supported systems must be established to help employees to adapt to the new culture.

Performance management in cultural imposition approach entails implementing the performance management system as it is to the acquired organization. The assumption, values, philosophy, process and expectations associated with performance management are clearly communicated to the employees of the acquired organization. Decisive action is taken to ensure that performance management is understood and accepted by the employees of the acquired organization as it is understood and accepted by the employees of acquiring organization.

- **Remain cultures separate**: Simply because a culture is successful in one market does not automatically mean that it is profitable in another. Mergers or acquisitions between businesses in different kinds of sectors should preferably be left separate. This is because maintaining different cultures is a less traumatic and risky way to change the culture than the more forceful interventions. However, maintaining different cultures inevitably reduces the possibility for effective communication, and makes synergistic benefits difficult to realize.

  Performance management in remain cultures separate approach entails continuing with two different performance management system often with different assumption, values, philosophy, process and expectations associated with performance management. This makes strategic integration of employee performance with organizational goals and objectives as one corporate entity difficult and troublesome. The interpretation of individual, team and organizational performance remains different to the two employee groups. Hence, performance management is an integrating mechanism remains highly limited in scope and effectiveness.

  However, the situation can be very successful if both the organization in mergers or acquisitions has highly effective performance management system. In such an event, both performance management systems will continue to deliver effective outcomes individually. But this could be short-term success formulae as in the long-term integration of both these performance management systems shall be necessary for ensuring competitiveness of the merged organization as one corporate entity.

- **Creating a compound culture**: Often the most difficult but valuable approach for choosing an organizational culture is to create a compound culture. This means creating a new and better culture with a common set of beliefs, assumptions, and rules of behaviour that take advantage of the strengths of both of the parent organizations. Therefore, it is important to build communication channels between the organizations. A mutual respect must be established between the cultures of the two organizations. The objective is to understand what the most appropriate cultures should be and to build it from the elements available from both parts to the future organization.

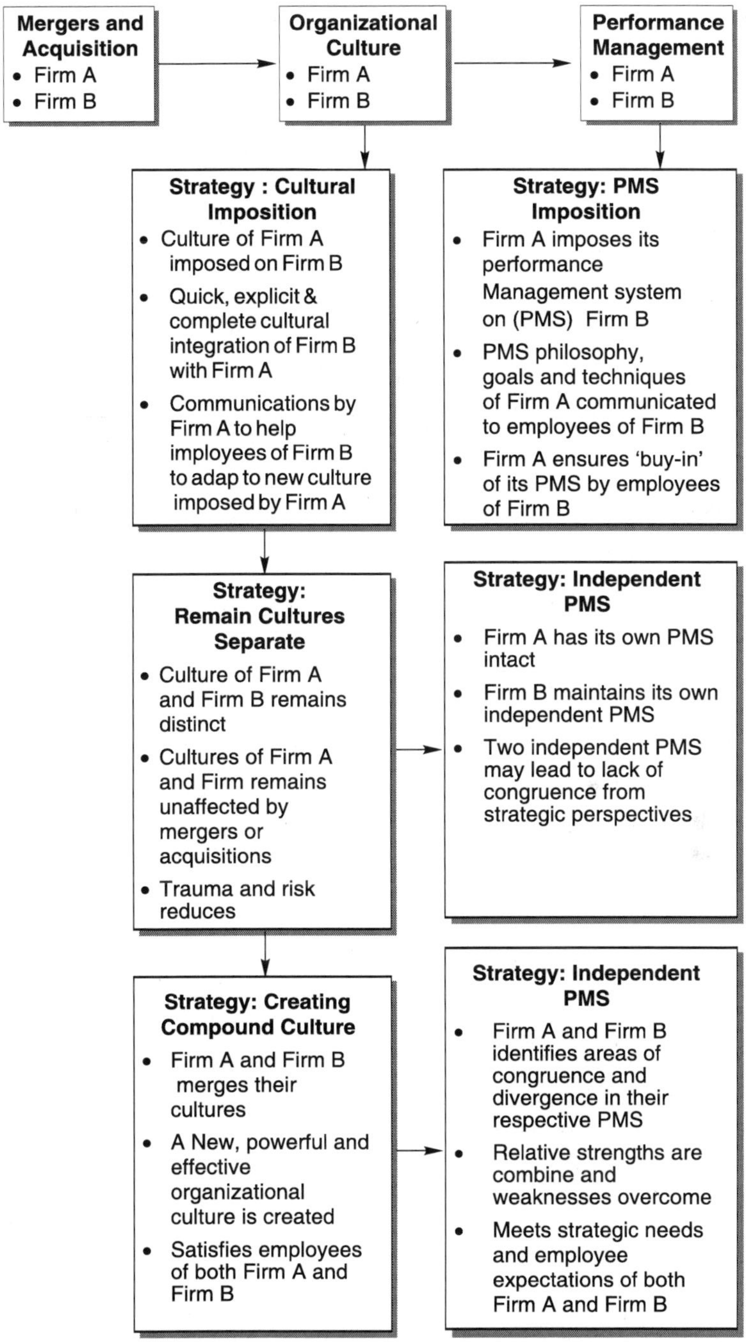

Fig. 1.6 Influence of Organizational Culture on Performance Management in Mergers and Acquisitions

In creating a compound culture approach, the performance management systems of both parent organizations should be understood, analyzed and compared rationally. This will allow the organizations to define areas or aspects of performance management that can be readily handled, areas where significant differences can appear or exists, and the positive areas where the performance management system shows a strong similarity in orientation and approach at a high level. By capitalizing on the relative strengths of performance management systems of parent organizations, a powerful, integrative and new performance management system can be created which meets needs, demands and aspirations of all employees of parent organizations, to move the organizational performance and competitiveness forward.

Irrespective of approach, one most important factor to consider is to keep valuable employees for sustaining competitive advantage. In order to ensure that the appropriate employees are retained, a reward strategy and system should be considered, for example, finding incentives in the work situation viz. providing challenge, autonomy, variety and meaningfulness or in career management viz. development opportunities, personal growth and training. In most cases, retention bonuses and deferred cash accounts are preferable to inflated compensations.

1.19 Implication of Performance Management on Learning in Organizations

The potential for an organization's performance management system to influence learning is significant. Simply the enormity of scope and the degree to which it integrates and has an impact on organizational processes would indicate that there is tremendous potential for both positive and negative results.

At the level of individual learning, behaviour is directly influenced by the quality and the content of the feedback and review process as well as performance development discussions. Effectively linking rewards to performance outcomes can further influence behaviour as well, a variety of role models are provided such as coaches, mentors, managers, and superior performers, who reinforce the desired behaviours.

Team learning can be reinforced by an effective team-based approach to performance management that includes team-based reward systems. However, the potential negative consequences of imposing a traditional approach in a team situation are enormous. Instead of fostering collaboration, an individualistic system can create competition among team members that undermines team effectiveness and even its survival. On the other hand, team-based approaches can facilitate team learning by developing the dialogue, feedback and coaching skills that will enhance team and organizational effectiveness.

Performance management systems can also enable or hinder the organization's capacity to continually learn and reinvent itself. In part, this is a direct outcome from individual and team learning but there are also other factors to consider. One of the most important is the degree to which the organization examines and renews itself-the way in which it learns, in whole and in part from the external environment as well as its own successes and failures. It also includes the extent to which the system supports and promotes innovation and continual improvement, as well as the acquisition and development of new skills and knowledge.

1.20 Divergent Thoughts on Performance Management

It is difficult to define performance management and its precise meaning could vary between organizations. It should be viewed as a management philosophy or belief as opposed to a distinctive body of management techniques. Some interpret performance management as an evolutionary extension of traditional appraisal practice or performance based pay, taking the view that it is merely an old wine in a new bottle approach. Others argue that performance management is more than a singular practice. They note that it consists of a range of activities engaged in by an organization to enhance the performance of a target person or group.

Apart from the variations on what the critical ingredients of performance management are, perspectives on the level of measurement are also varied. There are three different models to determine "what to measure". One is about managing organizational performance through various organizational strategies such as structure, technological change, and procedures. The second model focuses on individual performance, which places objective setting and formal appraisal systems as the centerpiece. The third model is considered a combination of the other two, with an emphasis on integration. Of these three models, the trend over the past 20 years seems to be moving towards the integrative and strategic model in defining performance management.

The diversity in perspective on what should be part of performance management and at what level of performance the system should operate inevitably create difficulty in understanding the meaning and purposes of performance management. Performance management should be selectively reinvented. The challenge is to develop effective approaches that will both meet individual needs (individuals need to be guided and encouraged to develop particular skills and to direct their performance toward critical organizational outcomes) and fit the increased use of teams and total quality management system.

1.21 Basic Concept of Performance Appraisal

Performance appraisal enables to determine whether the employee's performance is in accordance with performance expectations and it is primarily based on the appraisal of employees work results and activity (behaviour), and potential (skills, abilities and characteristics). Performance appraisal is a necessary part of an organization's quality control process to ensure that customers get the services they deserve. Well designed performance appraisals should:

- Provide employees with adequate feedback concerning their performance;
- Serve as a basis for modifying or changing behaviour toward more effective working habits;
- Provide managers with data which they can use to judge future job assignments and compensation; and
- Provide a profile of the organization in terms of its human resources strengths and weaknesses, an inventory of employee's skills and experiences and an evaluation of the organization's human capital.

To determine the performance, diverse appraisal methods and their combinations are used. During the appraisal process work results are valued that create preconditions for improvement in the future and enables managers to differentiate rewards by diminishing equalisation and increasing rewards. There is a tendency to give too much credit to circumstances that are dependent on different situations, regardless of whether we are evaluating our own activities or the activities of others. This is especially true when the results are not satisfactory. In order to avoid such a result, more appraisal interviews should be used and special computer programmes could be useful in order to document and evaluate information obtained during appraisal more efficiently and accurately. Decisions based on evaluations can be backed up by properly documented performance appraisals, which can also include additional documentation in the form of journal, notes, diaries etc.

A performance appraisal is designed to record the quantity and quality of work performed by employees. At its best, performance appraisal can accomplish a variety of functions as under:

- Communicating work standards.
- Enhancing employee motivation.
- Encouraging increased performance and productivity.
- Conducting workforce planning, such as layoff determination.
- Conducting succession planning, including termination, promotion, demotion, and lateral reassignment.
- Identifying training needs.
- Serving as a criterion data collection device for selection test validation.
- Defending employment actions in the case of litigation.

1.22 Definitions of Performance Appraisal

A few noteworthy definitions of performance appraisal are as follows:

1. *"Performance Appraisal is the systematic evaluation of the individual with regard to his or her performance on the job and his potential for development."*

   —Dale S. Beach

2. *"Performance Appraisal is a method of evaluating the behaviour of employees in the workspot, normally including both the quantitative and qualitative aspects of job performance."*

   —Carrell and Kuzmits

3. *"Performance Appraisal is a process by which an organization measures and evaluates an individual employee's behaviours and accomplishments for a finite time period."*

   —Johnson

4. *"Performance Appraisal is a process of systematically evaluating performance and providing feedback upon which performance adjustments can be made."*

   —Schermerhorn, Hunt and Osborn

5. *"Performance Appraisal may be defined as any procedure that involves (i) setting work standards; (ii) assessing the employee's actual performance relative to these standards; and (iii) providing feedback to the employee with the aim of motivating that person to eliminate performance deficiencies or to continue to perform above par."*

   —Gary Dessler

6. *"Performance Appraisal is a system of review and evaluation of an individual's (or team's) performance."*

   —Mondy, Noe & Premeaux

7. *"Performance Appraisal involves the identification, measurement and management of human performance in organizations."*

   —Gomej-Mejia, Balkin and Cardy

8. *"Performance Appraisal is a measurement of actual results achieved within those areas for which the employee is held accountable and for the competencies deemed critical to job and organization success."*

   — Berger

From an analytical study of the above definitions, we may conclude that:

- Performance appraisal is a systematic evaluation of employee performance;
- It is a tool of assessing potential for future development;

- It involves quantitative and qualitative aspects of performance; and
- It facilitates sharing of feedback with employees for enabling them to overcome performance deficiencies.

1.23 Features of Performance Appraisal

The major features are:

- Performance appraisal provides reassurance to employees that they are contributing and doing the right things;
- Performance appraisal creates awareness of the impact on desired results such as customer satisfaction;
- Performance appraisal reveals the adequacy of performance in terms of quantity, quality, speed, timeliness, etc.;
- Performance appraisal provides means for recognition of the importance and value of performance of employees;
- Performance appraisal provides opportunities for self-development of employees;
- Performance appraisal provides for administrative decisions and reward management of employees;
- Performance appraisal is a critical tool for training and development of employees;
- Performance appraisal is a foundation of career and succession planning;
- Performance appraisal is a basis for legally defensible management actions; and
- Performance appraisal is valuable source of talent management.

1.24 Significance of Performance Appraisal

The significance of performance appraisal is as follows:

1. **Feedback:** Performance appraisal provides feedback to employees on their performance. The feedback is given in a positive environment by the manager with a view to let the employee know the areas of job where he excels and areas which needs immediate improvement. This also helps clarifies an employee the level of performance expected from him and is therefore mentally prepared to align his efforts, skills and commitment in the desired direction at the required pace with appropriate quality of delivery.
2. **Self-evaluation:** Every person is interested to know he is performing on his job. This is a natural human tendency. Performance appraisal provides a mirror to an employee about his own job related strengths and weaknesses. Once an employee knows his areas of improvement, he seeks avenues, means and measures for developing his ability and commitment. Thus, performance appraisal helps in self-evaluation.

3. **Performance expectations:** Performance appraisal is conducted on the basis of agreed performance expectations. It is a reflection of the quality and judiciousness of setting performance expectations by the managers and employees. A poor performance need not necessarily be the result of individual inability but at times it may be the consequence of lack of proper performance expectations. For example, if performance expectations are too difficult to achieve given the competencies of an employee and they are established even knowingly, then appraisal will only show the failure to accomplish the targets. Thus, performance appraisal also helps in setting correct and relevant performance expectations.
4. **HR decision-making:** In order to enhance the performance, productivity and commitment of employees, organizations needs to review various employee related decisions particularly on compensation management, career development, training and mobility and knowledge management initiatives. Performance appraisal provides an objective basis for taking employee related decisions.
5. **Fairplay and justice:** Performance appraisal helps in identifying better performers from marginal performers. Based on this differentiation, decisions on an employee's compensation review/increase, promotions, transfers, re-assignments, overseas placements, training needs, and other administrative decisions are taken. The use of performance appraisal for HR decision-making tends to create a sense of fairplay and organizational justice in the minds of the employee.

   However, managers often view fairness over accuracy as the most vital issue in performance appraisal. Indeed, Slaughter *et al.* (2003) observed that managers escalated (were more lenient) to a greater extent than team members on the promotability variable. This effect may be due to persons described as managers demonstrating more felt responsibility than persons described as being part of a team, or actually placed in a team to make evaluation decisions.
6. **Identifying potentialities:** Performance appraisal helps in identifying the potential of individual employees for shouldering higher level roles and responsibilities in the organization. This helps an organization to meet its human resource needs in a cost effective manner as hiring from external labour market is costly and time consuming.
7. **HR policies and practices:** Performance of employees are affected by number of intrinsic factors such as individual motivation, commitment, knowledge, skills and ability, relevant experience, communication and interpersonal skills, etc. and extrinsic factors such as organizational culture and climate, human resource policies and practices such as employment security, promotion opportunities, equitable pay, adequate fringe benefits, etc. Thus, performance appraisal is not only a reflection of an individual employee or a manager but the influences of organization's policies and practices on human resources.

Thus, it can help to set correct various deficiencies and locunaes in employee related policies and practices.

8. **Retaining top talents:** Performance appraisal help reward an organization's top performers with increased compensation, promotions, leadership grooming opportunities, job rotations, etc. and helps retain top talents in the organization by satisfying their growth and development needs.
9. **Team spirit:** Performance appraisal brings a sense of opportunity of purpose between the employees and organizational goals and objectives. This is because all jobs in an organization are not only interlinked but also inter-dependent on each other. Collaboration is the only way through which every employee can achieve his performance expectations and effectively accomplish his work. Thus, performance appraisal fosters a collaborative work culture in the organization.
10. **Accountability and ownership:** Performance appraisal places high responsibility on the individual employees to accomplish their work objectives effectively. It induces an employee to put his heart and soul into improving performance for which he is accountable to his manager. Since he is clear of performance expectations and standards, therefore ownership of the performance appraisal system is significantly increased.

1.25 Performance Appraisal Process

A systematic performance appraisal process is depicted in Fig. 1.7.

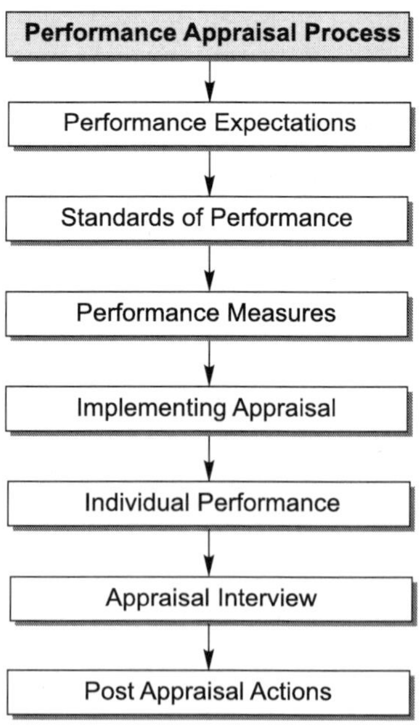

Fig. 1.7 Performance appraisal process.

1. **Performance expectations:** is the identification and setting quantifiable (measurable) targets so that the individual employee has greater clarity of the activities in which he needs to put in more efforts. Generally, performance expectations are set jointly by the employee (appraisee) and his manager (appraiser).
2. **Standards of performance:** are the established based on job description (role description) and job specification. The standards should be clear, concise and incorporate all relevant factors.
3. **Performance measures:** is the communication of standards of performance to the employee by the manager. It clarifies to the employee as to what will be acceptable and what will be unacceptable level of performance.
4. **Implementing appraisal:** is the conducting of appraisal by the manager, including conducting of interview, scrutiny of records & reports, etc. Also, the facilitating and inhibiting factors need to be noted.
5. **Individual performance:** is finding out the actual performance of the employee against standards of performance for finding out deviations. Deviations may be in the form more than required by the standards of performance or vice-versa. Also, the employee performance is compared with his past performance and that with other employees to find out where the employee stands.
6. **Appraisal interview:** The manager should start the appraisal interview with the agreed and documented performance plan of the employee. He should clearly communicate to the employee as to what will take place and why in the appraisal interview and fix up a specific date, time and venue for the purpose. Keeping the focus on performance plan, the employee's performance should be assessed in an objective manner. Specific instances are best because the employee can easily relate to the situation.

   Giving feedback to the individual employee is one of the major objectives of appraisal interview. Feedback facilitates an individual's performance by providing the information necessary to improve his or her development of an effective work process or procedure (*McAfee, Quarstein, and Ardalan*, 1995). Feedback has both informational value in terms of promoting learning and motivational value in terms of promoting efforts. For feedback to be effective, it must consist of the following characteristics as under:

- Address relevant performance, achievements, needs and interests;
- Provided immediately as soon as information is available;
- Factual based on actual performance;
- Provide suggestions for improvement of performance;

- Given directly to the individual involved;
- Given in a way that the respect, needs and integrity of the individual is maintained;
- Tailed to meet individual's specific needs and circumstances;
- Motivate the individual to continue and to increase efforts;
- Realistic and based upon established measurement standards;
- External evaluations should be congruent with the personal standards of the individual being evaluated; and
- Evaluation standards should be clear, descriptive, specific and developed;

However, positive feedback should come first so that the appraisal interviews can begin on a positive note. When reviewing performance deficiencies, the manager and the employee should jointly try to determine the reasons for performance plan not being achieved. Then, both should work to establish some type of new performance expectations to focus upon until next cycle. The more the feedback is given, the better. The appraisal interview is a good opportunity for the employee to voice concerns about his position and about performance barriers. Successful managers use good listening skills, ready to relinquish control when needed, being sensitive when providing negative feedback and not putting the employee on the spot.

Guidelines for Using Feedback: An Example

In one group George, intending to compliment Marie, says to her, "I wish I could be more selfish, like you". Marie might respond, "why you insensitive boor, what do you mean by saying I'm selfish? George might then get defensive and retaliate and both people would become involved in the game of "who-can-hurt-whom-the-most". That is, she could say "when you said, I wish I could be more selfish like you: I feel angry and degraded". This second method of giving feedback contains positive elements that the first does not.

Source: Cited from: Dr. Jain, Mahaveer, "Feedback: An Art of self and Organizational Excellence", Developing Behavioral Skills on Leadership for Trade Union Leaders, Readings, January 12-17, 2009, V.V. Giri National Labour Institute, Noida, pp. 96-97.

7. **Post appraisal actions:** is the means for identifying various human resource decisions in respect of the employee by taking appropriate actions based on the information as revealed by the appraisal. Finally, the appraisal records are consigned to the personal file of the employee for future reference.

Responsibilities in Performance Appraisal System	
The Company	• Creates the strategic plan • Provides support and resources
The Manager	• Identifies job requirements • Observes and documents performance • Provides ongoing feedback to the employee • Provides support and resources
The Manager and the Employee together	• Identify job goals • Create action plans for how to meet requirements and goals • Engage in ongoing development about improving performance
The Employee	• Listens to and acts on feedback from the manager • Perform by meeting requirements and goals • Provides feedback to the manager about the work environment

Source: Delpo (2007), Pp. 19

1.26 Performance Coaching

Performance coaching means a collaborative solution-focused, result-oriented and systematic process in which the manager facilitates the enhancement of job performance and goal attainment of the employees. "Performance coaching involves establishing a collegial partnership between managers and their staff for the purpose of improving performance" (*Gilley*, 2007). Performance coaching is a continuous process of equipping employees with the tools, knowledge and opportunities they need to develop themselves and to be more effective in a current job. Through the process of performance coaching, empsloyees deepen their learning, improve their performance and enhance their quality of life. Usually, performance appraisal is followed with performance coaching to facilitate improved performance and productivity of the employees.

Why Employees Don't Do What They are Supposed To Do

Ferdinand Fournies offers the following sixteen reasons:

1. They don't know that they are supposed to do;
2. They don't know how to do it;
3. They don't know why they should do it;
4. They think they are doing it (lack of feedback);
5. They are obstacles beyond their control;
6. They think it will not work;
7. They think their own way is better;
8. They think something is more important (priorities);
9. There is no positive consequence to them for doing it;

10. There is a negative consequence to them for doing it;
11. There is a positive consequence to them for not doing it;
12. There is negative consequence to them for not doing;
13. Personal limits (incapacity);
14. Personal problems;
15. Fear (they anticipate future negative consequence); and
16. No one could do it.

Source: Branham, 2005, Pp. 81-82

There are two types of performance coaching:

1. **Targeted performance coaching**: Under this type of performance coaching, manager provides a one-on-one focused, practical, skill-oriented, custom designed to meet the employee's needs for performance improvement through personalized instruction, practice and feedback. This type of coaching is most popular wherein the manager assumes a centre-stage in the whole performance coaching programme.
2. **Intensive performance coaching**: Under this type of performance coaching, complex performance problems and issues are addressed. Complex performance problems and issues are discussed both elaborately as well as thoroughly with the employees with an intention to arrive at a solution which is acceptable, viable and cost effective.

Performance coaching is essential for ensuring success of performance management process. According to *Gilley* (2007), the performance coaching process involves five strategies:

(*a*) Building trust and understanding so that employees are willing to work manager;

(*b*) Inspiring commitment so that employees focus their energy on goals that matter;

(*c*) Building new competencies to ensure that employees know how to do what is required;

(*d*) Developing persistence amongst employees and their managers; and

(*e*) Creating conditions that foster growth and development.

Performance coaching involves the following steps:

1. **Preliminary meeting**: Manager initiates a meeting with specific date, time, venue and agenda with an employee to discuss issues and aspects connected with his performance. The idea is to understand the employee's perspectives and views on his areas of excellence and improvement in performance. This discussion aims to provide preliminary data and information on performance strengths and weaknesses of the employee.

2. **Joint action planning**: At this stage, manager and employee arrive at some conclusions regarding the issues, factors and causes of employee's performance deficiencies with a purpose to evolve a joint action plan for performance improvement. The action plan for improvement incorporates specific means and measures of overcoming performance deficiencies and identification of managerial support, guidance and organizational resources for realizing the goals of the action plan. Participation of the employee along with the manager is necessary for subsequent ownership of the action plan for improvement by the employee.
3. **Performance improvement contract**: Once the joint goal setting for performance improvement has been jointly agreed, the next step is to document it with signature of the manager and the employee so that employee's accountability can be ensured.
4. **Formal monitoring**: Manager needs to review the progress of the employee against the goals and objectives enumerated in the performance improvement action plan. This helps the manager to keep track of the employee's efforts and commitment to overcome his performance problems and work successfully towards realizing performance improvement action plan.
5. **Feedback**: Manager on the basis of formal monitoring must provide feedback on employee's progress so that deviations, if any, can be corrected and remedial measures be taken.
6. **Termination**: Once the employee overcomes his performance problems or deficiencies and achieves the goals and objectives of the performance improvement plan, the performance coaching relationship comes to an end. However, the performance coaching relationship between the manager and his employees really never comes to an end because another performance concern needs to be addressed which invariably reinstates the performance coaching relationship between the two.

1.27 Methods of Performance Appraisal

There are broadly two methods of performance appraisal. One is called past-oriented approach and other is called future-oriented method. Past-oriented methods include rating method, essay method, graphic rating scale method, forced choice method and critical incidents method while future-oriented methods include MBO method, BARS method, Assessment Centre, 360-degree method, and Balanced Scorecard as discussed below.

1. **Rating Scale:** Under this method, managers grade employees on a pre-determined scale. Information gained through rating scales provided more precise information to managers because it is based on pre-determined standards of performance. Scales can be constructed by using numbers, adjectives or both for rating performance of the employees. Rating by

numbers seems to be impersonal and easy to administer. Rating by adjectives can provide feedback which an employee can relate easily to his specific job objectives. Rating scale method allows rating to be consistent as employees performance is observed and recorded according to a pre-determined format. The two most effective methods are simple ranking, alternation and paired comparison ranking.

(a) ***Simple ranking:*** Employee's overall performance is assessed in comparison with other employees using identified performance traits, the result of which is the production of a list of employees in order of their level of performance. This can be done either by listing from best to marginal or identifying the best performer and putting him at the top and then identifying the marginal performer and putting him at the bottom. The same process is followed for the other employees to fit them in between these two extremes.

(b) ***Alternation ranking:*** In this method, the names of employees are listed on the left-hand side of a sheet of paper preferably in random order. If the rankings are for compensation purposes, a manager is asked to choose the "most valuable" employee on the list, cross his name off, and put it at the top of the column on the right-hand side of the sheet. Next, he selects the "least valuable" employee on the list, crosses his name off, and puts it at the bottom of the right-hand column. The ranker then selects the "most valuable" person from the remaining list, crosses his name off and enters it below the top name on the right-hand list, and so on.

(c) ***Paired comparison:*** One employee's performance is compared with that of other employees. Two employees are taken at a time and a decision is made on who is more competent. Then another pair is compared and the same process is repeated until all are compared and ranked.

Merits:

1. Simplest method.
2. Needs no specialist knowledge or skill.
3. Complete ranking of all employees.

Demerits:

1. Time consuming and cumbersome for appraisers.
2. Suitable for small organization with limited number of employees.

2. **Essay or Narrative Method:** Under this method, performance of specific job role and responsibilities are observed and described by the manager/appraiser in narrative or essay form in a log book on regular basis. This helps the manager to evaluate how well the employee is carrying out job responsibilities in terms of strengths and weaknesses, achieving specific results or any other performance criteria vis-à-vis some standard of

performance. The skills of the manager in accurately and appropriately describing the performance of the employee are crucial for the success of this method of performance appraisal.

Often this method us used for the purpose of fostering employee development and performance improvement and is extensively used in appraisal interview and discussions by the managers. Such discussions can motivate employees for learning, development and growth.

Merits:

1. More closed evaluation of employee work and performance.
2. Employee performance and work behaviours are documented in detail.
3. Facilitates design of performance improvement programmes with ease given ready availability of performance records.

Demerits:

1. Incorrect sentence construction can give a different impression.
2. Maintaining a diary for noting performance of employees on regular basis increases cost of supervision and reduced for performing critical managerial activities.
3. Honesty of appraiser in recording and reporting employee performance is central to the effectiveness of this method.

3. **Graphic Rating Scale Method:** Under this method, employee characteristics and performance are evaluated through a graph. This technique is more consistent and reliable. Typically, a graphic scale assesses an employee on the quality and quantity of his work (is he outstanding, above average, average, or unsatisfactory) and on a variety of other factors that vary with the job but usually include personal traits like reliability and cooperation. It may also include specific performance items like oral and written communication.

Merits:

1. Easy and less costly.
2. Categorizes employee's performance clearly and specifically.
3. Facilitates easy linkage to compensation increases.

Demerits:

1. Lacks validity of rating.
2. Lacks reliability of rating.
3. Subject to managerial and employee manipulations.

4. **Forced Choice Method:** This technique was developed to reduce bias and establish objective standards of comparison between individual employees. Although there are many variations of this method, the most common one

asks raters to choose from among groups of statements those which *best* fit the individual being rated and those which *least* fit him. The statements are then weighted or scored, very much the way a psychological test is scored. Employees with high scores are, by definition, the better employees; those with low scores are the poorer ones. Since the rater does not know what the scoring weights for each statement are, in theory at least, he cannot play favourites. He simply describes his employees, and someone in the human resource development department applies the scoring weights to determine who gets the best rating.

Merits:

1. Easy and less costly.
2. More objectivity in evaluation.
3. Involvement of impartial HR functionary.

Demerits:

1. Irritates managers.
2. Lacks managerial acceptability.
3. Subject to managerial manipulations.

5. **Critical Incidents Method:** TUnder this method, the work behaviours leading to outstanding success or failure are evaluated. The manager as appraiser observes and records in a log book the employee's work behaviour from time to time. Both positive and negative behaviours of the employee are noted by the manager.

   The observed and recorded work behaviours of the employee are compared with the work behaviours expected from the employee's job performance, which helps the manager to evaluate the actual performance of the employee vis-à-vis expected work performance. Also, the recorded positive and negative work behaviours serve as specific and measurable example of performance of the employee and are often relied upon for providing feedback to the employee. Additionally, with this type of documentation done of a regular basis, noting success and failures, manager can actually formulate some kind of chart to visually present employee's work progress to him for facilitating performance improvement.

Merits:

- Avoids manager–employee conflict due to sharing negative feedback.
- More objective and documented performance.
- Factual in nature.

Demerits:

- Additional chore of maintaining performance log book.
- Subjective in nature.
- Lacks measurement performance.

6. **Management by Objective Method :** Under this method, manager and the employee set performance goals on mutually acceptable basis. At the beginning of an appraisal year, managers and employee agree upon the employee's performance goals for that year. While setting performance goals, organization's goals an objectives are taken into consideration so as to align employee's effort with organization's business plans. This requires that each employee must be aware of the organization's goals and objectives. These goals then serve as standards for the employee's achievement of performance. Upon conclusion of the year, the two will meet again to compare performance goals with actual results. This requires managers to drive employees to write a brief statement of results against performance goals. During the meeting set to review this statement, the manager should look for variances. With the discovery of any area of performance deficiency, possible solutions to correct problems should be discussed and it necessary, a check point meeting could be set to make sure that the employee is working in the right direction and is making desired progress. With the information and feedback gained through evaluation of performance and appraisal meeting for the previous appraisal year, performance goals for the next year can again be jointly decided upon by the manager and the employee.

   Levinson (1990), a critique of MBO, says that employee's personal goals should be taken into account while setting performance goals as the highest point of self-motivation arises when there is complementary conjunction of the employee's needs and the organization's requirements. He further observes that care must be taken also that the goal setting process does not become a static and sterile one with little room for creativity and spontaneity of service and self-assumed responsibility.

Merits:

- Establishes link between organizational and individual performance.
- Easy to implement and measure.
- Measures performance and not personality of employees.

Demerits:

1. Emphasizes job completion rather than the quality of a job.
2. Setting targets and objectives may not be possible for certain jobs.
3. Teamwork suffers.

7. **Behaviourally Anchored Rating Scales (BARS) Method:** A much more detailed form of rating scales which is commonly used is BARS. This method has been chosen by many organizations over MBO because it provides more opportunity for managers to advise employees on how their performance can be improved. BARS are based on actual observed behaviour. This helps the employee to distinguish between effort exerted and the result

achieved. This method enables the manager to more easily offer solutions to specific behaviours that might be deterring job performance.

BARS involve the following two steps:

- The job or jobs to be evaluated should be defined clearly as within a work unit/department several jobs may overlap which could pose understanding problems for the employees.
- Scale should be assigned to the observable behaviours by both the manager and the employee. Numbers are then assigned to how well the task should be performed and how pertinent the success of the job task is to the overall requirement of the position.

Merits:

1. High participation and hence acceptance of the technique by superiors and subordinates.
2. Differentiates among behaviour, performance and results.
3. Technique is valid and reliable as it identifies observable and measurable behaviours of specific jobs.

Demerits:

1. Identified critical behaviours are activity directed rather than result directed.
2. Construction of BARS is expensive and time consuming.
3. Research does not support the high gain claims of BARS.

8. Assessment Center: An assessment center is a comprehensive, standardized procedure in which multiple assessment techniques are used to evaluate individual employees for a variety of decisions. Under this method, various experts using various techniques do assessment of several individual employees. A technique can be considered as assessment centre only if it meets the following requirements:

1. Multiple assessment techniques must be used, one of which must be a simulation.
2. Multiple trained assessors must be employed.
3. Judgments must be based on pooled information from all assessors.
4. Evaluation must be made at a time separate from the observation of behaviour.
5. The dimensions, attributes, characteristics, or qualities evaluated by the programme must be determined by an analysis of relevant job behaviour.

The procedure followed at assessment center is elaborate and as follows:

- During exercise the one assessor observes and records the behaviour of the employee/participant and no final interpretations are arrived at.

- Once the individual assessors have prepared the reports, they are followed by assessor discussion to carry out a comparative analysis. After the discussions, final rating (average) is arrived at.
- The role of facilitator in assessment center technique is critical to the success of the technique. He provides inputs on various areas such as job competencies, training on the assessment center technique, assessor's selection, etc.
- CEO plays a vital role in supporting and propagating the concept and ensuring that it is in line with the organization's objectives.

9. **360-Degree Method:** The 360-degree feedback can be used as a tool for assessment. This technique was first developed and administered by General Electric Company (GEC) of USA in 1992. It is a process of giving performance feedback that combines self-appraisal with ratings made by co-workers at the same level, above, and below the target person in the managerial hierarchy and customers.

    Milliman et al. (1994) are of the opinion that traditional performance appraisal systems are subjective, simplistic and political. They advocate for 360-degree appraisal system, which requires obtaining information from all sources–internally as well as externally, with whomever the employee has interacted. Internal parties include managers, top management, subordinates, co-workers and representative from other department who interacts with the employee. On the other hand, external parties include clients, suppliers, consultants, and community officials. In short, anyone who has useful information on how the employee does the job may be a source in the 360-degree appraisal. According to *Edwards and Sproull* (1987) "When many individuals rate an employee's performance; the consensus they reach is more reliable, credible, and defensible (and often less biased) than the supervisor's sole judgment."

    Feedback is not only important for clarifying individual weaknesses and strengths, but also ensures that those being assessed understand how the process is in fact operating. "360-degree feedback reveals how successful an individual is in all-important work relationships" (*Sheal*, 1999). The 360-degree appraisal takes information from more than one source, that is, superiors, subordinates, peers, customers, and oneself in order to get a 360-degree view of an individual's performance. Evaluation includes both the ratings of individual employee (appraise) by superiors on elements in an employee's performance plan and the evaluation of programmes and teams by senior managers. Subordinates can provide valuable insight into various aspects of working such as leadership style, subordinate development initiatives, planning and organizing of work, reports and documents, etc. Peers have a unique perspective on a co-employee's job performance and employees are generally very receptive to the concept of rating each other. Peer ratings can be used when the employee's expertise is known or the performance and results can be observed. Since customers now occupy the centre stage of business today, therefore they can provide valuable developmental inputs. Customers may be both internal as well as external. The employee himself identifies the key accomplishments which best represents his performance in critical and non-critical performance elements. The cumulative result of multi-source feedback is consolidated and given very carefully to the appraisee/manager as development input. Generally, 360-degree method is used for developmental appraisal purpose and not for evaluative purpose.

The 360-degree performance appraisal system is based on the following four key principles as follows:

1. ***Principle of performance enhancement*:** The nature and speed of feedback which is key element in enhancing individual, team and organizational performance.
2. ***Principle of validity & reliability*:** Use of multiples sources for assessment results in higher quality, valid and more reliable information than single source assessment.
3. ***Principle of change*:** It provides increased level of insight that individual employees have of their own attitudes and behaviours. This enables employees to understand their strengths, development areas and weaknesses to enable them to modify and change their behaviour and improve performance.
4. ***Principle of participation*:** It fulfills the desire of the employee in participate and learn.

The procedure for conducting 360-degree appraisal is as under:

(*a*) A questionnaire is developed which includes from 50 to 100 items to measure different dimensions of job performance such as communication, teamwork, leadership, initiative, judgment, etc.

(*b*) Steps must be taken to maintain strict confidentiality of feedback results. For example, feedback ratings from several subordinates may be combined (averaged) to mask the identity of an individual subordinate.

(*c*) Training on 360-degree appraisal is to be given to all employees and why it is being implemented in an organization.

(*d*) Feedback to employees could be provided through printed forms or post the form in company's website for easy access to employees.

(*e*) Analysis of data may include performance dimension summary, summary-performance vs. expected, individual item ratings, item ratings-performance vs. expected (normed), highest or lowest rated items (shows individual's strengths and weaknesses), and recommendations for development.

(*f*) Feedback should be shared with the employee. It should not be mandatory that the employee share the results with their managers.

The following guidelines should be used while employing 360 feedback and performance appraisal that can help organization to improve performance and achieve success:

- *Use performance appraisal to:*
  - Set clear, specific goals.
  - Establish measurements to determine outcomes and results.
  - Evaluate the degree to which outcomes and results were achieved.
  - Determine, based on performance, what reward is to be given.
- *Use 360 feedback to:*
  - Identify the skills, competencies, behaviours, and practices needed to successfully achieve performance criteria.
  - Measure proficiencies in skills, competencies, behaviours and practices.
  - Assess where improvement is needed to achieve performance criteria.
  - Create targeted development plans that increase capabilities and performance.
  - Assess what environment will bring out the best results from the employees.

Merits:

1. Provides a well-rounded view.
2. Avoids individual bias.
3. Can have more impact than a single source.
4. Can establish consensus.

Demerits:

1. Responses from colleagues and external customers may be biased or simply the result of trade-offs (give and take).
2. It ignores performance in terms of achieving goals.
3. The rate may deny the truth of negative feedback.

10. **Balanced Scorecard Method:** The balanced scorecard approach has been developed at the Harvard Business School by Kaplan and Norton at the beginning of the 1990s. It is essentially a multi-dimensional approach to performance management that is linked to organizational strategy. They devised the balanced scorecard (BSC) framework which complements the financial measures with operational measures on customer satisfaction, internal processes and the organization's innovative and improvement activities. These perspectives are described below:

(*a*) **Financial perspective** measures indicate whether an organization's strategy, implementation and execution are contributing to bottom-line improvement.

(*b*) From the **customer perspective**, managers identify the customer and market segments in which the business will compete and the measures of the business unit's performance in these targeted segments.

(*c*) In the **internal business process perspective**, managers identify the critical internal processes that will have the greatest impact on customer satisfaction and achievement of the organization's financial objectives in which organization must therefore excel.

(*d*) The **learning and growth perspective** identifies the infrastructure (people, systems and organizational procedures) that the organization must build to create long-term growth and improvement.

Factors contributing to successful implementation of Balanced Scorecard include:

1. Gaining and maintaining top management commitment;
2. Involving employees in the development process;
3. Agreeing strategy before developing the scorecard;
4. Focusing the scorecard on strategic objectives;
5. Avoiding focusing on worthless measures such as tracking output/ outcome metrics that cannot be influenced or controlled;
6. Failure to adapt the scorecard to meet local requirements;
7. Using terms consistently;
8. Utilizing pilot projects in the implementation process;
9. Using experienced consultants to support implementation process;
10. Avoiding misusing the Balanced Scorecard as a means of imposing unnecessary control;
11. Constructing and understand the cause-and-effect map;
12. Using the Balanced Scorecard to drive the compensation process;
13. Using the Balanced Scorecard to support organizational learning;
14. Ensuring a proper understanding of Balanced Scorecard issues within the organization;
15. Avoiding over-complex and lengthy development; and
16. Establishing clear objectives for Balanced Scorecard programme.

While implementing the Balanced Scorecard, the following are the key issues:

1. Incorporating strategy into the scorecard and using it as a means of internal communication;

2. Defining a balanced set of specific performance indicators, both leading and lagging, that guide and drive the organization to achieve the strategy;
3. Ensuring that the system of reward is clearly linked to strategy in order to drive behaviour that will help achieve the strategic aims;
4. Using the scorecard for external communication only where this provides advantage, and avoid revealing strategy outside the organization when disclosure would enable competitors to undermine or frustrate the objectives;
5. Building business plans unpinning the scorecard to manage the implementation of the strategy;
6. Aiming for breakthrough performance to transform the business rather than seeking incremental improvement rather than copying other organization's processes, e.g. through benchmarking; and
7. Linking the Balanced Scorecard to the resourcing and management processes to ensure that there are no other processes that will detract or undermine the Balanced Scorecard process.

Kaplan and Norton (2001) found a degree of reluctance among organizations to replacement of existing reward systems that were fairly simple and easy to operate, as well as being well understood by employees. Introducing a new reward system linked to the Balanced Scorecard will be difficult because:

(*a*) It will be complex and thus difficult and expensive to administer;

(*b*) Uncertainty on the part of the organization on the benefits and impact, including cost of bonuses, resulting from the new system; and

(*c*) There is likely to be resistance from employees because of a dislike of change, uncertainty over the likely rewards, uncertainty of the linkage between action and reward, perceptions of reduction in the ability to manipulate the system in order to gain reward.

Success of Balanced Scorecard Technique

A study by the Metrus Group Inc. that compares companies using measurement with those that does not. Organizations with "Balanced Measurement" were perceived as performing better:

- 83% *"had financial performance in the top third of their industry"*;
- 74% *"were perceived as industry leaders by their peers"*; and
- 97% *"were perceived as pioneers or leaders on changing the nature of their industry"*.

Source: Quoted from Kaplan and Norton (2001)

Merits:

1. It allows managers to look at the business from four important perspectives simultaneously.

2. It minimizes information overload by limiting the number of measures used to those that are the most critical.
3. It guards against sub-optimization by forcing managers to consider all the important operational measures together.
4. It demands that managers translate their general mission statement into specific measures that really matter.

Demerits:

1. Actual data for each metric can be difficult, sometimes even impossible to reasonably track.
2. It is relatively complex and costlier measurement system.
3. Finding cause-effect linkages between four perspectives could prove difficult.
4. The inter-relationships of the selected measures need to be well understood and the efforts to improve them well coordinated; otherwise the organization will be pulled in different or even competing directions.

Methods of performance appraisal employed by organizations depend to a large extent on the cultural context. Different organizations in different cultural setting use differing methods. For example, in India the most common appraisal tool is graphic rating scales. *Rao* (1982) conducted a survey of appraisal practices in 45 different organizations (34 private sectors and 11 public sectors). From the results, he observed that about 50% of the organizations seem to profess the purpose of their appraisal as regulating employee behaviours as well as developing employee capabilities. About 30% of them still used appraisals only for controlling and regulating employee behaviours whereas only about 10% seem to use appraisals mainly for development purposes. Moreover, in a large number of organizations (71%) the final assessment is of confidential nature. *Vallance* (1999) describes the performance appraisal methods used in Singapore, Thailand and Philippines (in the context of appraising civil servants) and examines the role of organizational culture on the appraisal process in those countries. Singapore adopts the Potential Appraisal System (PAS) developed originally by Shell Petroleum Company in 1960s. In its present form, it has the following criteria: 'helicopter quality' (meaning that an individual's ability to examine the problems or issues taking all important factors into account), 'intellectual qualities' (power of analysis, imagination and sense of reality), 'results orientation', 'leadership quality' (capacity to motivate, delegate and communicate). In the Thai context, the criteria used are: output of work in terms of quality, quantity and application of work outputs; the ability to manage and perform the work in terms of planning and implementation; the ability to direct and make decisions including meeting deadlines, taking control, coordinating efforts with other organizations, solving problems and resolving conflicts and helping to accomplish the goals of the organization; ability to improve work and services, demonstrating new ideas and solutions, identifying and addressing problems and performing work efficiently and effectively. In the Philippines setting, the criteria consist of six areas: management of work, management of people, management of resources, management of linkages, management of constraints and innovativeness.

1.28 Common Errors in Performance Appraisal

Performance appraisals are subject to a wide variety of inaccuracies and biases referred to as 'Rating Errors'. These errors occur due to the rater's own framework of observation, judgment, and information processing. Many HR Heads frequently complain about the fact that performance appraisal ratings are notoriously inflated and that people simply are not being told the truth about just how they are doing. Many of these HR heads had distasteful experience of talking to a line manager who has finally made the decision to fire a poor performer after years only to discover that the individual has a drawerful of performance appraisals in his file, all with stellar ratings.

Common rating errors are as discussed below:

1. **Halo Effect:** A halo error takes place when a particular aspect of an employee's performance influences the evaluation of the entire performance of the employee. For example, an employee working in late hours in the organization might be rated high on productivity and commitment.
2. **Horn Effect:** A horn error takes place when a particular negative aspect of an employee's performance overshadows the evaluation of the entire performance of the employee. For example, an employee leaving office consistently in time in the organization might be rated low on commitment.
3. **Central Tendency:** A central tendency error takes place when all employees are rated as average instead of 'outstanding performance' and 'below average performance'. The rater indiscreetly rates everyone and avoids being confronted for justification for differential ratings to employees.
5. **Strict Rating:** A strict rating error takes place when there exists a strong tendency amongst appraisers to be overly harsh while judging performance of employees. This may be a case where the standards of performance may be too high or unrealistic.
6. **Lenient Rating:** A lenient rating error takes place when rater has the tendency to be overly generous while judging performance of employees. By this way such appraisers avoids conflicts with employees. This situation is just reverse of error due to strict rating.
7. **Status Effect:** A status effect takes place when employees in higher level job are overrated or held in high esteem and employees in lower level job are underrated or held in low esteem.

8. **Spillover Effect:** A spillover effect takes place when past performance appraisal ratings unjustifiably influence current ratings. Past ratings, good or bad, result in similar rating for current appraisal although demonstrated behaviour does not deserve the rating, good or bad.
9. **Initial Impression:** Initial impression error takes place when an employee's performance appraisal unjustifiably gets influenced by the initial impression of the employee–good or bad. It is a classic case of 'first impression is the last impression'.
10. **Latest Behaviour:** Latest behaviour error takes place when an employee's overall performance evaluation gets unduly influenced by latest behaviour, good or bad, of the employee.
11. **Same as Me:** This error takes place when an employee's performance appraisal gets unjustifiably influenced by the presence or absence of certain behavioural characteristics or traits in the employee which is same in nature to the appraiser/rater.
12. **Different from Me:** This error takes place when an employee's performance appraisal gets unjustifiably influenced by the presence or absence of certain behavioural characteristics or traits in the employee which is contradictory in nature to that of the appraiser/rater.
13. **Sympathy Effect:** This error takes place when an employee's performance appraisal gets unjustifiably influenced by sympathy factor such as personal hardships faced, troubled marriage, financial crunch, etc. because of which rater tends to assign higher ratings to the employee than what is warranted by demonstrated performance.

1.29 Limitations of Performance Appraisal

According to *Lawler* (1994), "The problem and it is well documented is that most performance appraisal systems do not motivate individuals nor guide their development effectively. Instead they cause conflict between supervisors and subordinates and lead to dysfunctional behaviours. These dysfunctions are often exaggerated when performance appraisals are tied to traditional merit pay systems. They are particularly severe when the system the system forces supervisors to compare subordinates evaluating some of them favourably and some unfavourably creating the classic forced distribution problem".

Resistance to performance appraisal system does not come from employees only but also from managers. Manager's resistance arises due to their normal dislike of criticizing an employee, lack of skill, dislike of changes accompanying a new procedure and mistrust of the validity of the appraisal instrument. Both managers and employees are often uneasy about performance appraisal. Some of this unease is a function of the perception that conventional appraisal processes smack of product inspection and conflict with convictions about the worth and dignity of the human personality.

The major limitations of performance appraisal are as follows:

1. **System vulnerability**: Performance appraisal is subject to various biases and prejudices. Also, since it is often linked to rewards and compensation therefore there is a natural urge or tendency to manipulate the system for getting maximum rewards. Rather than improving performance of employees, it tends to reward system manipulators.
2. **Self-defeating**: Performance appraisal as a vital component of performance management system seeks to improve performance and commitment of employees for effectively achieving organizational goals and objectives. However, often it becomes a painful experience for the managers as well as the employees owing to complicated and long forms and formats, lack of time and commitment to exchange views and feedback, dynamic and uncertainties associated with organization's environment and other similar factors. Therefore, under such circumstances instead of rational evaluation it gets reduced to judgment based on perceptions.
3. **Inconsistent with team work**: Performance appraisal evaluates and reward individual contributions rather than team achievement. Since often rewards and compensation issues are associated with performance appraisal, therefore there is always competition between employees, leaving behind team working.
4. **Acts as a substitute for proper management**: Performance appraisal evaluates performance of employees by the mangers on periodic basis. However, many experts questions this very premise on the ground that management must evaluate and assess the performance of employees on direct basis rather than asking the employee to document and share his own work performance.
5. **Inherently unfair**: Performance appraisal often distrubs the harmony amongst employees by facilitating administration of differentiating rewards and compensation to employees. This is not to be misunderstood as with objective appraising no employee will have any problem with differentiating rewards and compensation but in reality many differentiating rewards and compensation are the result of system manipulations by both employees and managers.
6. **Complex in nature**: Performance appraisal is complex and requires time and effort. Managers seeking to institute fair and efficient performance appraisal will find themselves having to continuously consult, communicate, modify, and train. Many managers do not collect data on how the performance appraisal systems they use affect their employees. Therefore, they are unaware of the importance of these systems as a management tool.

7. **Poor appraisal system**: Performance appraisal should be able to answer to pertinent questions viz. whether people know 'what is expected from them' and 'how well they are doing'. If the system is unable to answer these two vital questions they such a performance appraisal system can be safely labeled as poor appraisal system. Poorly designed performance appraisal system may be used as a short-term control system rather than long-term strategic source of information for planning may be ineffective in identifying work habits or behaviours that need to be changed and will provide data that are invalid for deciding on promotability or compensation. Such systems can create fear and mistrust, lowering employee's self-esteem and productivity, and hindering the organizational effectiveness.
8. **Lack of appraising skills:** If there is one thing that an organization could do to significantly improve their existing system, it would be to train managers in how to effectively implement performance management and performance appraisal. If an organization decides to do traditional performance appraisals, it is critical that it invests its considerable time in the training of appraisers so that they can develop the skills that are not a natural of the management repertoire (Lawler, 1994). This statement should also be expanded to include training and education on the planning, development and recognition components of the process.

1.30 Emerging Concepts of Performance Appraisal

Performance appraisal has been in existence for long-time in the organizational context to judge human performance. However, amidst global competitive scenario, the concept of performance appraisal has been gradually undergoing dynamic changes. According to *Gupta and Joseph* (2008), following are the emerging concepts of performance appraisal:

(*a*) It is an instrument of assessing the performance of individuals and teams and to take decisions to enhance their effectiveness and efficiency within current environment and available resources;

(*b*) It is a system derived on the basis of strategic, perspective and tactical plan of the organization to develop the capacity and capability of employees to implement the organizational plans to achieve its goals and objectives;

(*c*) It is a tool to give rewards and create opportunities for the employees to develop themselves to their full potential;

(*d*) It is a tool for deciding and organizing development programmes and creating attractive rewards for well performers;

(*e*) It is a process of learning from feedback of the self and stakeholders on the quality of performance with the objective of improving performance;

(*f*) It is a process of mutual, collaborative, cooperative and action learning in which all the employees participate with positive attitude to learn and enhance the academic climate of the institution, to face challenges and competitions; and

(*d*) It is a pre-requisite process performed by the organization that becomes base for taking significant decisions such as training, counseling, coaching and mentoring of individuals and teams.

1.31 Competency Based Performance and Reward Management

Competency refers to the knowledge, skills, attitude and behaviours necessary for effective job performance and the possession of the same by the individual employee. *Meyer* (1996) defines competency as the "integration of knowledge, skill and value orientation, demonstrated to a defined standard in a specific context". Moore *et al.* (2002) states that an individual's competency "becomes a combination of relevant attributes that underlie aspects of successful professional performance". A competency therefore describes a feature of a person's ability to perform job effectively. Thus, competency relates to the attributes and characteristics displayed by an individual to achieve effective performance in relation to a defined standard. An individual demonstrating behaviour to support the relevant area of work, in which he is seen to be competent in, would be 'exhibiting competency'.

Competency based management is increasingly becoming popular these days given the renewed emphasis on gaining and sustaining competitive advantage by organizations in a marketplace characterized by Olympian competition. Performance, by definition, is concerned with human behaviour that drives the individual for attaining desired outcomes. An employee may have number of skills and abilities but he may not all at the same time while meeting his performance expectations. This could be due to low motivation, poor organizational culture, poor leadership, unfair reward systems and so on and so forth. Further, even if the employee is motivated has favourable organizational climate, culture and fair systems in place particularly reward systems, the employee may not apply his skills and abilities in a proper manner focusing on competitive priorities emphasized by the organization. This often occurs due to lack of individual and organizational focus on competency.

The organization particularly managers must be aware of what are the key competency requires for successful accomplishment of job related tasks, activities and roles and then matching them with the individual competencies. The gaps so identified must be first addressed through various training and development interventions. Once the individual employee is fully ready to accomplish performance expectations from his job (or position), performance expectations should be identified, agreed and set up. Often managers set performance expectations from an individual job holder rather than the job itself and such misperception creates gap in expectations from the job and expectations from the individual employee. Competency based approach to performance management overcomes this problem by aligning job requirements with individual performance goals. The congruence between job requirements and individual skills and abilities create the right momentum for effective delivery of desired results in tandem with organizational goals and objectives. In simple words, competency based approach to performance management ensures that the employee delivers outcomes as per requires of his job.

Another problem pertains to the fact that performance management tends to look at individual activities without attention to their impact on other activities. This makes performance management an isolated and insulated mechanism which often becomes a human judgment tool. A competency based performance management ensures that there is a strategic link between organizational goals and objectives to the jobs and finally to individual performance expectations and subsequent achievement. This results into clear relationship between the budgeted performance promises and the actual performance report in annual reports. In other words, performance management under a competency based approach assumes the role of an integrating mechanism which links people, processes, activities, resources, strategic objectives, and environmental factors for effective results.

Since reward is the outcome of performance management, therefore competency based approach also applies to reward management. The reward systems should be so designed as to reward employees for their performance and contributions to the organizational goals and objectives. Rewards should not be granted for being good performer but more for achieving the strategic objectives of the organization in order to improve bottom-line of the organization. The idea is to motivate employees to connect their performance expectations, achievements and motivation with organization's competitive priority. Thus, competency based reward management should elicit enhanced level of individual contribution to organizational success. This will also help to ensure that performance and reward management should not get reduced to mere judgment oriented activity but a strategic priority of every manager, employee and the organization. A competency based performance and reward management is characterized by the following attributes:

(*a*) Align and link organizational goals and objectives with people, processes, activities, resources and environmental demands;

(*b*) Translate strategic goals into operational objectives;

(*c*) Effectively communicate the strategy, objectives, job goals, and performance expectations to all employees;

(*d*) Prioritize and align new and existing initiatives to the organizational strategy;

(*e*) Establish measures and targets that drive performance and behaviours;

(*f*) Establish a strategic and performance management process that is based on facts and data;

(*g*) Align budgets to the strategic direction;

(*h*) Establish effective HR management processes;

(*i*) Establish reward systems that induces employees for continuous and sustainable improvements; and

(*j*) Recognize and address the change management issues that will arise in implementing performance management.

To summarize, we may conclude that competency based performance management approach is based upon three elements as depicted in figure 1.8. Firstly, the job's demand element refers to "what a person in the job is expected to do" and relates to assigned tasks and duties (*Boyatzis*, 1982, in *Spangenberg*, 1990). Clearly defined job descriptions provides the basis for defining the work activities an employee is expected to perform in order to justify the existence of a particular job in an organization. It also aids in setting effective performance expectations which are based on the job demands and not what the job holder is capable to do or expects to do. Job demands sets the periphery or boundary within which the employee has to establish his performance plan and achieve performance expectations in order to support organizational goals and objectives.

Secondly, the organizational environment element "reveals how a person is expected to respond to the job demands" (*Boyatzis*, 1982, in *Spangenberg*, 1990). Organizational environment comprises of culture, climate, managerial support and feedback systems. Organizations characterized by a participative and proactive environment tend to motivate employees to set specific and measurable performance expectations with the commitment to achieve it successfully. Organizational environment therefore acts as a facilitator to employee performance and enables imbibing a performance oriented work culture and practices.

Thirdly, "the individual's competencies" element entails "what a person is capable of doing" (*Boyatzis*, 1982, in *Spangenberg*, 1990). Employee's knowledge, skills, attitude and behaviour plays a pivotal role in his job performance. Employees with higher competencies coupled with right motivation, enabling organizational environment and supported by job demands helps in excelling in individual and ultimately organizational performance.

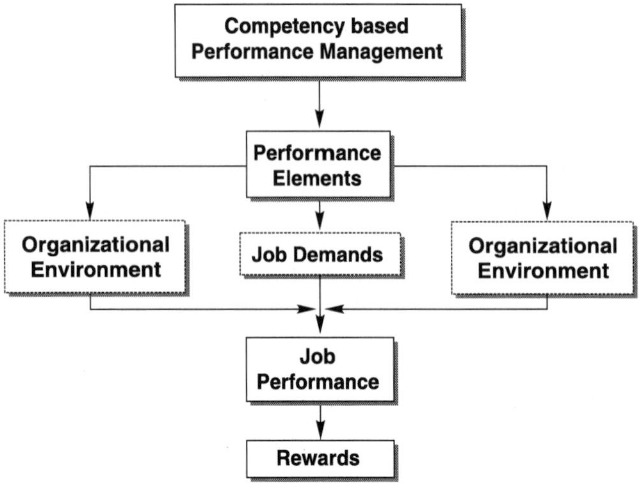

Fig. 1.8 Competency-based performance management.

CHAPTER REVIEW

- Performance means both behaviours and outcomes of that behaviour. In other words, performance has both qualitative (behaviour) and quantitative (result) dimensions.
- Performance Management is a continuous process of steering the organization through the systematic determination of mission, strategy and objectives of the organization, making these measurable through key performance metrics, in order to be able to take corrective actions to keep the organization onto the path of excellence and success.
- Performance management is a process involving planning, reviewing, developing and enhancing performance in order to ensure congruence of individual and organizational goals for individual excellence and organizational success.
- The three major purposes of performance management are as follows:
  (*a*) It is a process for strategy implementation;
  (*b*) It is a vehicle for culture change; and
  (*c*) It provides input to other human resources systems, such as reward and compensation systems.
- Performance management is driven by organizational goals and objectives by emphasizing the vision, mission and values of the organization.
- There three approaches performance management viz. (i) performance driven integration which emphasizes changing organizational behaviour (ii) development driven integration which stresses the formulation of

HRD activities for attaining strategic plans of the organization and (iii) team oriented integration which adopts either a performance-driven integration or development-driven integration approach.

- Performance planning is a systematic outlining of activities the employee is expected to undertake during a specified period so that he is able to make his best contributions to the developmental and organizational outcomes.
- Performance development is a process of promoting a climate of continuous learning and professional growth, helping to sustain employee performance at a level which meets or exceeds expectations, enhancing job or career related skills, knowledge and experience thereby making the employee competitive for employment opportunities within the organization.
- Performance appraisal is a systematic and objective way of judging the relative worth or ability of an employee in performing his job and administering rewards in accordance with exhibited performance.
- Rewards and recognition entails promotion, increments, re-assignments, etc. being given to employees for performance exhibited.
- Performance coaching is helping technique by which manager provides systematic and result focused solutions to performance problems or deficiencies of the employee in order to improve overall performance and contributions of the employee.
- Leadership plays a crucial role in success of performance management through their leadership behaviours and competencies.
- Employee's job performance is defined as ability and motivation. Without motivation, employee's performance is likely to be sub-optimal.
- National culture has profound influence on performance management. In a high power distance culture, hierarchy is seen as necessary and beneficial, management style is too autocratic and close supervision is expected, in an individualistic culture, the values of independence and privacy, where the management style is often directive with rewards and punishment, is linked to individual achievement. In uncertainty avoidance cultures, rules, rituals and dissent govern interactions. In an achievement orientated culture, ambition is seen as important and people are judged on the basis of their performance. Where a long-term orientation is characterized by the sparing use of resources and value is attached to future rewards. Traditions are adapted and modernized as required. The short-term orientation is characterized by respect for tradition and the fulfillment of social obligations.
- Organizational culture plays a crucial role in performance management during mergers and acquisitions. In cultural imposition strategy, performance management system is transferred from one parent

organization to another, in remains cultures separate performance management of parent organizations continues to exist and function independently and finally in creating a compound culture, performance management of parent organizations are combined to form a robust system.

- There are three divergent views on performance management viz. (i) managing organizational performance through various organizational strategies such as structure, technological change, and procedures, (ii) focuses on individual performance, which places objective setting and formal appraisal systems as the centerpiece and (iii) a combination of the other two, with an emphasis on integration.
- Reward and recognition is the outcome of the performance exhibited by the employees versus their performance plans. The objective is to motivate employees perform better.
- In ranking method, employee's overall performance is compared with other employees based on identified performance traits.
- In essay method, impression of employee's performance and behaviours are recorded for analyzing actual performance.
- In graphic rating scale method, employee's performance is assigned a position on the graph or scale based on pre-determined personal characteristics or traits.
- In field review method, a neutral person interviews employees and impressions on performance noted for comparing with manager's rating for normalization.
- In forced choice distribution method, two types of statements: best fit and least fit are designed and employee's performance marked accordingly.
- In critical incident method, critical behaviours that ensure effectiveness or non-effectiveness on job are focused, observed and recorded.
- In management by objective method, clear and precise performance expectations are set with the employee and compared with actual achievements.
- In behaviourally anchored rating scales method, behavioural dimensions required for job success are determined and assigned numerical value. These dimensions provide the criteria for assessing employees.
- In Assessment Center method a multiple assessment of several individuals performed simultaneously by a group of trained evaluators using a variety of group and individual exercises.
- In 360-degree method, performance feedback given by superiors, subordinates, peers, customers, and one-self.
- In balanced scorecard method, performance is evaluated in four perspectives viz. financial, customer, business processes and learning and growth metrics.

- Common errors in rating include halo effect wherein a particular aspect of an employee's performance influences the evaluation of the entire performance of the employee. In horn effect a particular negative aspect of an employee's performance overshadows the evaluation of the entire performance of the employee. Central tendency error takes place when all employees are rated as average instead of 'outstanding performance' and 'below average performance'. A strict rating error takes place when appraisers are overly harsh while judging performance of employees. A lenient rating error takes place when rater has the tendency to be overly generous while judging performance of employees. A status effect takes place when employees in higher level job are overrated or held in high esteem and employees in lower level job are underrated or held in low esteem. A spillover effect takes place when past performance appraisal ratings unjustifiably influence current ratings. Initial impression error takes place when an employee's performance appraisal unjustifiably gets influenced by the initial impression of the employee–good or bad. Latest behaviour error takes place when an employee's overall performance evaluation gets unduly influenced by latest behaviour, good or bad, of the employee. Sympathy error takes place when an employee's performance appraisal gets unjustifiably influenced by sympathy factor.
- Competency based approach to performance and reward management seeks to ensure that all performance expectations set are directly linked to organization's competitive priority and contribute to bottom-line. Job performance priorities must take precedence over individual discretion. A competency based performance management approach consists of three elements viz. job demands, organizational environment and individual competencies.

A. Conceptual Review Questions

1. What do you understand by the term 'performance'? Discuss the concept and model of performance.
2. Define and explain the concept of performance management. Enlist its features and significance.
3. Design a performance management model for your organization.
4. Why is performance management crucial for attaining the goals and objectives of the organization?
5. How does leadership influences performance management in the organizational context?
6. Does motivation of employees affect performance management?
7. Explain impact of national culture on performance management.
8. Illustrate the impact of organizational culture on performance management post mergers and acquisitions.

9. Discuss the concept and perspectives of performance appraisal. Give suitable examples.
10. What are the methods of performance appraisal? Explain in detail any two methods.
11. What are the merging concepts in performance appraisal?
12. Write short notes on:

    (*a*) 360-degree appraisal

    (*b*) Balanced scorecard appraisal

    (*c*) Ranking method

    (*d*) Forced choice distribution method

    (*e*) Impact of performance management on learning

    (*f*) Divergent Thoughts on Performance Management
13. Why performance appraisal is often a discredited management tool in the organizations?
14. Discuss the concept of competency based performance management with suitable examples.

B. Analytical Questions

1. Performance management is often misunderstood as performance ap praisal. What are the possible reasons behind this and how can these constraints be removed?
2. "Performance Management cannot remove effective management supervision of the work of the employees. Do you agree? Why or why not?
3. "Performance management is a panacea but a tool to seek employee commitment towards organizational goals and objectives". Critically evaluate the statement.

CASE INCIDENT

Performance Appraisal at The General Hospital

Dr. Manoj Sharma, a highly qualified Doctor, has recently joined at the General Hospital as the mental health educator under Dr. A.S. Billimoria. Manoj liked his boss not only because he was always kind and considerate but also because of his high professional standards. Manoj's job involved giving lectures to schools, business organizations and NGOs upon request and conducting training programmes on mental health education for new teachers, nurses and social workers. He was proud of his performance record which contained mainly excellent ratings and nothing below excellent ranking.

Dr. Billimoria recently resigned from General Hospital on getting a prestigious overseas assignment. His position was filled-in by Dr. Ganesh Kumraj. Dr. Kumraj was chosen carefully by the hospital panel from a pool of highly qualified applicants. Dr. Kumraj is known for his brilliant academic record and is considered as a hard task master. Mr. Manoj gets along with Dr. Kumraj pretty well until a few days ago. It was the result of the annual performance appraisal that made Manoj antagonized with Dr. Kumraj.

Performance appraisal at the General Hospital was made every 12 months and the customary procedure was for the reports to be prepared and placed in each employee's mailbox. Employees could discuss them with their supervisors if they wished to do so, but they were expected to sign them. One day Manoj found his appraisal in his mailbox and became very upset over it. Instead of excellent rating on the scale, he found very good rating. There was no explanation given for the drop in ratings only the statement that 'Mr. Manoj continues to do good work' was mentioned. Manoj asked to see Mr. Kumraj immediately.

The interview between Dr. Manoj and Dr. Kumraj took place that morning. Manoj was quite blunt and wanted to know what was wrong with his work. Dr. Kumraj explained that his work was fine and he would not understand why he was upset. Manoj pointed out the difference in his current rating and the rating given to him in the past by Dr. Billimoria and asked Dr. Kumraj to explain the difference. Dr. Kumraj said that he thought it was good appraisal. He refused to explain further, but assured Dr. Manoj that his work was good and encouraged him to maintain his high standard. Manoj did not want to sign the appraisal but later conceded, inserting 'signed under protest' under his name. He then made plans for appealing against the rating to the Medical Superintendent and if necessary the President.

Dr. Kumraj failed to understand the reaction of Dr. Manoj to his performance appraisal. He never had a chance to see Dr. Manoj's past appraisals. To him good and excellent means the employee is a category 'A' employee. He is in a state of utter confusion.

QUESTIONS

1. Why is Dr. Manoj Sharma upset?
2. Is it correct for Dr. Manoj Sharma to compare performance ratings given by two different supervisors? Why or why not?
3. Did Dr. Ganesh Kumraj handle the situation effectively?

EXPERIENTIAL EXCERCISES

1. Working individually or in groups, interview five HR Managers at firms in your locality. Prepare a brief report for presentation to the class or submission for critique outlining the ways in which the HR department there handles performance management process.
2. Prepare a brief report describing three Indian organizations that have recently adopted a new approach to performance management and appraisal. Explain the changes made and elucidate their impact on employee morale, performance, productivity and organizational effectiveness.

❑❑❑

Learning Objectives

At the conclusion of this chapter, you should be able to:

- ❒ Understand the concept elements and types of rewards
- ❒ Discuss the concept, objectives and theoretical framework of reward management
- ❒ Develop reward system
- ❒ Explain approaches to reward system
- ❒ Describe the concept, features, significance, significance and philosophy of compensation management
- ❒ Design a compensation management model
- ❒ Assess factors contributing to inter and intra industry compensation differentials

2

Reward Management

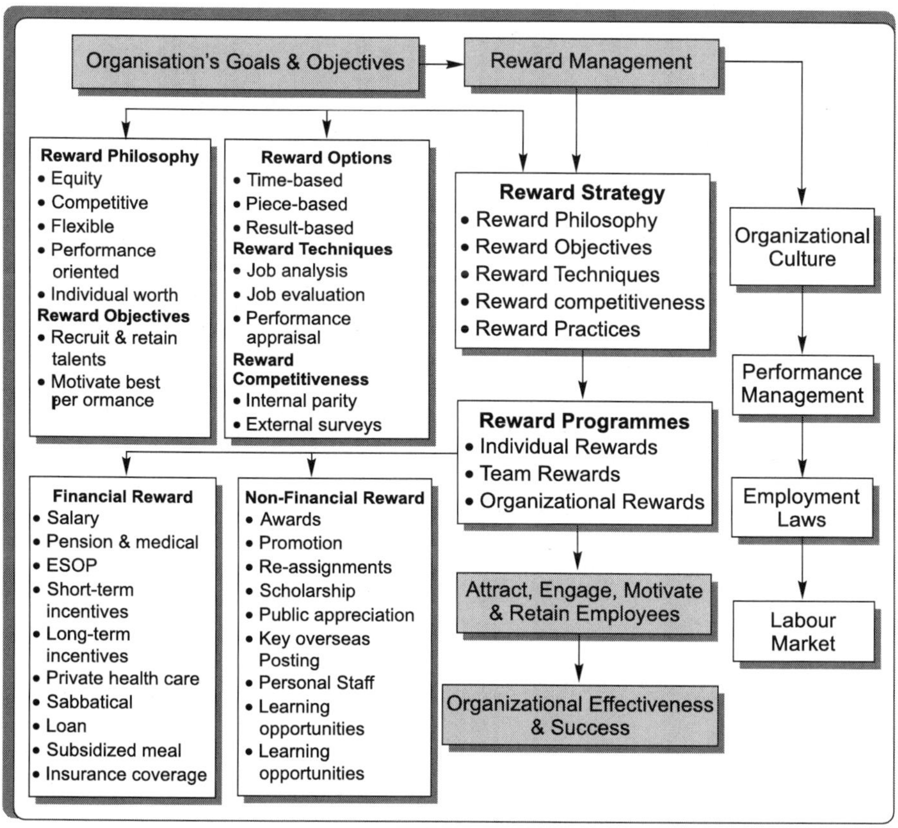

2.1 MEANING OF REWARD

Performance management is directly or indirectly connected to reward systems as well as other components of performance management. However, performance management can mean different things in different situations. Formal and informal approaches which may have a multiplicity of purposes, including: evaluation, auditing, succession planning, training, controlling, development and motivation. Competency-based performance management focuses on both training to address short-term issues and on long-term career needs. In contrast, the performance-based performance management approach focuses on managerial control and judgment. A range of methods of appraisal also exist, from managerially defined behavioural traits and performance criteria, measurement against achievement of objectives.

Organizations must reward employees because, in return, they are looking for certain kinds of behaviour: they need competent individuals who agree to work with a high level of performance and loyalty. Individual employees, in exchange for their commitment, expect certain extrinsic rewards in the form of promotions, salary, fringe benefits, bonuses, or stock options. Individuals also seek intrinsic rewards such as feelings of competence, achievement, responsibility, significance, influence, personal growth, and meaningful contribution. Employees will judge the adequacy of their exchange with the organization by assessing both sets of rewards. Reward is concerned with intrinsic as well as extrinsic motivation, the non-financial as well as the financial rewards. The reward management system can therefore be seen as a set of relationships between the various reward management processes and the organizational strategy. Reward management strategy and policy is thus driven by organizational and human resource management strategies, such as employer of choice. Effective reward management can help an organization to achieve its business objectives by attracting and retaining competent employees.

For effectiveness of reward management, reward should be:

- **Personal** by determining whether they prefer private or public recognition and communicating with the individuals involved to see what they prefer, whether it is an award, a gift, time-off or money;
- **Proportional** by balancing the size of type of reward with the individual or group contribution and accomplishments as it relates to organizational goals and objectives;
- **Pleasurable** by making things fun and entertaining through the event in which rewards are given or by the selection of a creative reward;

- **Precise** by giving individual or group detailed information on relevancy of what was done, as well as acknowledging when, where, why, and how it was done;
- **Principled** by showing sincere and honest acknowledgement of an individual or group that supports organizational beliefs and values through their commitment and accomplishments; and
- **Prompt** by giving well-timed acknowledgement as soon as possible after the event has occurred or action has been completed.

2.2 Elements of Rewards

According to *McCormick and Tifflin* (1979), rewards can be either intrinsic or extrinsic. Individuals engage in work-related activities to attain some variety and magnitude of rewards. Certain rewards, including pay, promotions, and organization status are extrinsic since they are provided by the organization.

Cash Rewards

- Purely an extrinsic motivator with little emotional involvement;
- Does not provide lasting satisfaction and long-term performance stimulation;
- Receiver attaches no greater emotional or inspirational value to cash.
- No trophy value to be a constant reminder and continue to motivate.
- Difficult to target a particular behaviour because of the lacking association with particular achievement;
- Recipients often can't recall what they purchased with cash reward which further diminishes its impact;
- Not cost effective as it requires three times the incentive investment compared to non-cash, on average; and
- Usually spent on necessities thus lacking a positive association with the targeted accomplishment or behaviour.

Surce: "Recognition and Rewards: The Changing Face", Cover Feature, *Business Manager*, Vol. 11, No. 6, December 2008, pp. 20-26.

Rewards such as feelings of achievement, accomplishment and self-satisfaction are intrinsic. Intrinsic rewards stem from Maslow's higher level needs. It proposes that employees can give themselves rewards in the form of self-esteem as well as in feelings of achievement and growth. Individuals can literally reward themselves for certain kinds of behaviour because they feel they have accomplished something of worth, achieved a personal goal, learnt a new skill, or experienced excitement or intellectual stimulation.

Tangible Rewards

- Carry a significant trophy value thus continue to reinforce the good performance and behaviours;
- Provide tangible symbol of achievement and serve as an encouragement to other employees;
- Reinforce the association with the organization and thus increase loyalty;
- Provide guilt-free enjoyment of reward thus increase the motivating impact;
- Both extrinsic and intrinsic motivators; provide strong emotional appeal to participant's personal wants and interest;
- Carry a higher perceived value because of the increased emotional attachment; therefore stimulate performance better than cold cash;
- Can be attached to a particular behaviour thus stimulating a specific response in a long term;
- Receiver's family is involved in sharing awards thus multiplying the emotional value of the reward and its impact on the participant; and
- Do not become an expected part of an employee income or an entitlement; always seen as a reward for a particular accomplishment or perforance

Surce: "Recognition and Rewards: The Changing Face", Cover Feature, *Business Manager*, Vol. 11, No. 6, December 2008, pp. 20-26.

The greatest amount of motivation is present when employees perform tasks that are both intrinsically and extrinsically rewarding. The types of rewards available to employees and the manner of their distribution can have a striking impact on both employee satisfaction and organizational effectiveness. Although a variety of purposes may potentially be served, rewards are most typically used to motivate employees or induce some desired action or behaviour.

2.3 Types of Rewards

Top management and HR Heads who are primarily responsible for creating reward programmes should start by thinking about what make employee's chest swell with pride, and then to creatively translate these good feelings to the working context. Managers should make an effort to get to know their employees, and then to tie the rewards and recognition to what they know the employee will appreciate and value. The best way of knowing how to meet employees' needs is by asking them how they want to be rewarded and recognized and what the elements are that they value.

Various categories of reward programme that commonly exist are as follows:

Type	Description	Examples
Cash awards	Programmes that provide either a fixed cash award or are based on a percentage of the employee's pay.	• Lump-sum bonus • Cash incentive • Additional paid time off • Paid trips • Gift certificates • Specialized training • Prize programme tied to earning points
Spot programmes	Recognition programmes that have low or minimal cost and do not require a formal plan document or extensive administration.	• Movie tickets • Paid meals • Flowers • Tickets to special events
Symbolic awards	Recognition programmes designed to provide a tangible award or memento.	• Movie tickets • Service award • Quality award· • Recognition • Certificates • Plaques and trophies
Verbal recognition	This approach provides praise directly to the individual or team.	• Thank you card • Testimonies from senior leadership· • Customer feedback • Written congratulations • Public recognition

Nelson (1994) sums it up very well when he says "you get the best effort from employees not by lighting a fire under them, but building a fire within them." In his book "1001 Ways to recognize employees" he makes the following suggestions for informal recognition. These types of rewards would fit into the above category of informal recognition, such as spot programmes or verbal recognition and are generally low cost in nature.

- Buy "welcome to the team" flowers for a new employee on their first day;
- Put gold stars on employees' name badges;
- Give out "time off" certificates;
- Create a "hall of fame" for top employees;
- Hand out thank you cards with flowers or candy;
- Give movie tickets;
- Take a employee out to lunch;
- Wash a employee's car, or have it washed;
- A personal note of thanks;
- Spoken 'thank you';
- Revolving trophy;
- Birthday day or half day off;

- Plaque or certificate;
- Achievement acknowledged at staff meetings;
- Volunteer to do a colleague's least desirable work task for a day;
- Pay for a magazine subscription;
- Give CD or dinner vouchers;
- Bake a batch of the person's favourite cookies;
- Pay for a housecleaning service for a employee's home;
- Give sticky notes with a saying appropriate to their personalities; and
- Send a thank you note to the employee's spouse for their support during the employee's overtime.

Although compensation is a key factor in retention, but lack of recognition is one of the primary reasons for top talent leaving their organizations. The challenge of informal rewards is to find the right match between the individual and the recognition given, as the psychic income of being openly acknowledged and appreciated equals or exceeds the material, monetary income. Leaders who recognize the power of the emotional appeal of informal forms of recognition can more easily motivate employees to higher levels of performance, often for much lower costs than monetary rewards.

2.4 Basic Concept of Reward Management

Reward management refers to the process of formulation, implementation, maintenance and communication of strategies and policies with the purpose of rewarding people fairly, equitably and consistently in accordance with their relative contribution to the organization and to help the organization to achieve its goals and objectives. It is a mechanism by which employee performance is defined, evaluated and rewarded. Essentially reward management deals with reward systems comprising–reward processes, practices and procedures which meet the needs of both the organization and its stakeholders, that is, shareholders, customers, employees and society at large.

Reward management is intended to motivate certain performance from the employees. It sends a powerful message to employees of an organization as to what kind of organization management seeks to create and maintain and what kind of behaviour and attitudes management seeks from its employees. It is, therefore, based on the following premise:

- Employees must believe that effective performance will lead to certain rewards. For example, attaining certain results that will lead to a bonus or recognition from others;
- Employees must feel that the rewards offered are attractive. Some employees may desire promotions because they seek power, but others want a fringe benefit such as a pension because they are older and want retirement security; and

- Employees must believe that a certain level of individual effort will lead to achieving the organization's standards of performance.

Reward strategies flow from business strategies of the organization as reward management addresses strategic issues relating to how employees should be valued for what they do and what they achieve. To improve the effectiveness of the rewards and recognition system, the focus should be on supporting the business strategies and organizational goals, and providing a meaningful return on investment rather than on attracting and retaining employees. This includes programmes that fit into three main categories. These are broad-based group incentive programmes including profit sharing and gain sharing plans, special individual-team contribution approaches, which tend to vary depending on the perceived value of the contribution and reward-recognition schemes for employees, which recognize contributions of significance. There is no standard approach, however, it is important to build in diversity to involve employees and recognize and reward their achievements.

Reward management is an integral part of human resource management and is closely linked to performance management in cause (performance management) and effect (reward management) relationship framework. Linking reward to performance also potentially induces equity and consistency in the reward structure and enables the organization to attract and/or retain talents given current trends toward job hopping in search of better rewards.

2.5 Definition of Reward Management

A noteworthy definition of Reward Management is as follows:

"Reward Management is about the development, implementation, maintenance, communication and evaluation of reward processes. These processes deal with the assessment of relative job values, the design and management of pay structures, performance management, paying for performance, competence or skill (contingent pay), the provision of employee benefits and pensions, and management of reward procedures."

—Michael Armstrong & Helen Murlis

2.6 Objectives of Reward Management

Reward management needs to embody following objectives as under:

- High performance and productive contributions towards attaining the goals and objectives of the organization by individuals and teams are recognized and rewarded;
- Teamwork and efforts to eliminate internal competition are encouraged by recognizing and rewarding successful practices;
- Clear and specific performance improvement objective are included in performance management and reward system;

- Promotion criteria include the action and activities create and sustain competitive advantage by organizations;
- Develop a positive employment relation and psychological contract;
- Align reward practices with business strategy of the organization and communicate business values and direction to employees; and
- Operate in ways that are fair, equitable, consistent and transparent.

2.7 Theoretical Fraemwork of Reward Management

Employees can make difference between success and failure of an organization. Simply designing jobs as efficient as is possible will not ensure success of an organization as once though under Taylorism. Employees are more likely than other forms of competitive advantage to lead to a sustainable competitive advantage in rapidly changing environments. This is because economic changes and globalization weakens other traditional sources of competitive advantage including market, financial capital and economies of scale.

The reasons what motivates employees to perform well has been a subject of great interest and deliberations amongst the practitioners as well as academicians. Managers in every kind of organization have made generalized assumptions about what motivates their employees. Motivation is the single most important determinant of performance. Job performance is the result of motivation and ability. Ability includes training, education, equipment, simplicity of task, experience, and both inborn mental and physical capacity. Motivation makes an organization more effective because motivated employees are always looking for better ways to do a job, generally are more quality-oriented and are more productive, so it is important for management to understand how organizations influence the motivation of their individual employees.

Motivation refers to the internal forces arouse, direct and maintain an individual's voluntary choice of behaviours. Motivation can be broken down into two elementary forms viz. extrinsic motivation and intrinsic motivation. Individuals who are extrinsically motivated work on tasks because they believe that participation will result in desirable outcomes such as rewards, praise and avoidance of punishment. Intrinsic motivation is a process of arousal and satisfaction in which the rewards come out from carrying an activity rather than the result of that activity.

There are three levels of employee's motivation as follows:

1. The direction of an employee's behaviour. It relates to those behaviours which the individual chooses to perform.
2. The level of effort. It refers to how hard the individual is willing to work on the behaviour.
3. The level of persistence. It refers to the individual's willingness to pursue the behaviour despite obstacles or roadblocks.

Thus, we may conclude that performance is dependent upon motivation also. There are number of theories underpinning what motivates employees to perform well including the goal setting theory. Three primary goals that motivate employees at work are as follows:

1. **Equity:** Employees would like to be treated justly in relation to the basic conditions of employment. These basic conditions include physiological needs, that is, safe working conditions, reasonable workload and comfort, economic needs of job security, satisfactory remuneration and benefits and psychological needs of respect, good interpersonal relations and credible management.
2. **Achievement:** Employees want to take in their accomplishments by doing a job that matters to them; to receive recognition for their accomplishments and take pride in the organization's achievement.
3. **Camaraderie:** Employees wish to have warm, interesting and cooperative relations with others in the workplace.

Thus, it is clear that motivation, a prerequisite of performance, is concerned with equity, expectancy and job characteristics. The characteristics of the job and related context are also crucial for ensuring that employee perform well in addition to motivational content. In this regard, we shall first discuss equity and expectancy theories with job characteristics model to crate an integrated model to understand the linkages between motivation, performance and rewards sequence.

1. **Equity Theory:** The Equity theory of job motivation was put forward by *Adams* (1963). The theory postulates that individuals are concerned not only with the absolute amount of rewards they receive for their efforts, but also with the comparison of this amount to what others receive. Equity theory states that employees make comparisons of their job inputs and outcomes relative to those of others. Employees perceive what they get from a job situation (outcomes) in relation to what they put into it (inputs), and then compare their outcome/input ratio with that of relevant others. Evidence suggests that the referent with which an individual compares himself is an important variable in equity theory. There are four referent comparisons an employee can use are:
   - (i) **Self-inside:** An employee's experiences in a different position inside his current organization.
   - (ii) **Self-outside:** An employee's experiences in a situation or position outside his current organization.
   - (iii) **Other-inside:** Another individual or group of individuals inside the employee's organization.
   - (iv) **Other-outside:** Another individual or group of individuals outside the employee's organization.

When people perceive an imbalance in their outcome/input ratio relative to others, tension is created. This tension provides the basis for motivation, as people strive for what they perceive as equity and fairness. Equity theory proposes that when employees perceive an inequity they can be predicted to make one of six choices:

(i) **Change their inputs:** An individual may decrease the amount of effort they are willing to exert.

(ii) **Change their outcomes:** Individuals paid on a piece-rate basis can increase their pay by producing a higher quantity of units of lower quality.

(iii) **Distort perceptions of self:** Individuals may decide that they actually work harder than other colleagues.

(iv) **Distort perceptions of others:** An individual may decide that a colleague's job is not as desirable as they originally perceived it to be.

(v) **Choose a different referent:** An individual may decide to compare himself with a friend in a lesser job rather than a more successful work colleague.

(vi) **Leave the field:** Employee look for a job in another organization.

Thus, equity theory establishes four propositions relating to inequitable pay:

(*a*) *Given payment by time*, over-rewarded employees produce more than equitably paid employees. Hourly and salaried employees generate high quantity or quality of production in order to increase the input side of the ratio and bring about equity.

(*b*) *Given payment by quantity of production*, over-rewarded employees produce fewer, but higher quality, units than equitably paid employees. Individuals paid on a piece-rate basis increase their effort to achieve equity, which can result in greater quality or quantity. However, increases in quantity only increase inequity, since every unit produced results in further over-payment. Therefore, effort is directed toward increasing quality rather than increasing quantity.

(*c*) *Given payment by time*, under-rewarded employees produce less or poorer quality of output. Effort is decreased, which brings about lower productivity or poorer output quality than equitably paid employees.

(*d*) *Given payment by quantity of production*, under-rewarded employees produce a large number of low-quality units in comparison with equitably paid employees. Employees on piece-rate pay plans can bring about equity because trading off quality of output for quantity results in an increase in rewards with little or no increase in contributions. Quality of output for quantity results in an increase in rewards with little or no increase in contributions.

2. **Expectancy Theory:** Expectancy theory, first formulated by *Vroom* (1964), rejects the idea that people have fixed sets of needs and attempts to take into

account human variability and complexity. The assumptions of expectancy theory are as follows:

- People make conscious decisions about their own behaviour in organizations, especially with regard to the amount of effort they are prepared to direct towards performing their jobs.
- Different people have different attitudes and orientations towards work, which are expressed as different needs, desires and goals, and which can be systematically analyzed.
- People make choices between the possible alternative modes of behaviour of which they are aware. They consider the degree to which a particular course of action will lead to outcomes they desire, or at least which they think are likely to lead to such outcomes.
- Essential to understanding human motivation in work organizations is the need to discover the different meanings people attach to work and their working environments.

Expectancy theory argues that the strength of a tendency to act in a certain way depends on the strength of an expectation that the act will be followed by a given outcome and on the attractiveness of that outcome to the individual. The theory states, therefore, that an employee is motivated to exert a high level of effort when he believes effort will lead to a good performance; a good performance will lead to organizational rewards like a bonus, a salary increase, or a promotion; and the rewards will satisfy the employee's personal goals.

The theory, therefore, focuses on three relationships:

1. **Effort-performance relationship:** The probability perceived by the individual that exerting a given amount of effort would lead to improved performance.
2. **Performance-reward relationship:** The degree to which the individual believes that performing at a particular level will lead to the attainment of a desired outcome.
3. **Rewards-personal goals relationship:** The degree to which organizational rewards satisfy an individual's personal goals or needs and the attractiveness of those potential rewards for the individual.

The concepts of expectancy and valence are central to the understanding of expectancy theory. Expectancy is defined by Vroom as the "beliefs an individual holds about the outcomes likely to result from a given work behaviour or performance". The individual must subjectively assess the rewards receivable for achieving different levels of output and the expected necessary effort to reach those levels. The individual's prior experience of the interaction between actions and outcomes, as well as the individual's level of self-esteem, influences his subjective appraisal of these relationships and his subjective estimation of the probability that a particular course will lead to particular outcomes.

Valence describes the level of satisfaction or dissatisfaction an individual expects to receive from various outcomes resulting from different actions and behaviour. Once again, expectancy theory does not assume that people's perceptions of desirable outcomes (positive valence) and undesirable outcomes (negative valence) will be universal. The individual's attitudes and orientations towards work will be a large influence on their perceptions of desirable and undesirable outcomes.

Generally, there to be two types of rewards available to individuals in work environments: intrinsic and extrinsic rewards. Intrinsic rewards are the rewards that an individual receives subjectively from actually doing the job, such as feelings of achievement, challenge, competence and self-worth. Organizations are unable to give these rewards directly, but they are able to develop a structure and culture that makes them more likely. Extrinsic rewards are rewards administered by agents external to the individual and include payment systems, promotion, fringe benefits and job security. The interaction of the two types of rewards may not produce a simple, linear relationship with satisfaction and motivation.

3. **Hackman and Oldham's Job Characteristics Model** The Job Characteristics Model by *Hackman and Oldham* (1976) focuses on the interaction between the psychological states of employees, the job characteristics that are believed to determine these states and the attributes of individuals that determine how positively a person will respond to a complex and challenging job.

   The core job dimensions are seen as prompting three psychological states that, in turn, lead to a number of beneficial personal and work outcomes. The critical psychological states are defined as follows:

   (*a*) **Experienced meaningfulness of the work**: The degree to which the individual experiences the job as generally meaningful, valuable and worthwhile.

   (*b*) **Experienced responsibility for the work outcomes**: The degree to which individuals feel personally accountable and responsible for the results of their work.

   (*c*) **Knowledge of results**: The degree to which individuals continuously understand how effectively they are performing.

   The theory proposes that employees who experience these states at sufficiently high levels are likely to feel good about themselves and respond favourably to their jobs. The model suggests that five core job dimensions can be seen as determining the extent to which employees experience the three critical psychological states:

   (*a*) **Skill variety**: The degree to which the job requires a variety of activities that involve different skills and talents.

   (*b*) **Task identity**: The degree to which the job requires completion of a 'whole' and identifiable piece of work, that is, a job that has a beginning and an end with a tangible outcome.

(*c*) **Task significance**: The degree to which the job affects the lives or work of other people, both in the immediate organization and in the external environment.

(*d*) **Autonomy**: The degree to which the job allows the individual substantial freedom, independence and discretion to schedule the work and determine the procedures for carrying it out.

(*e*) **Feedback**: The degree to which the job activities give the individual direct and clear information about the effectiveness of his performance.

Skill variety, task identity and task significance are seen combining to form the experienced meaningfulness of the work. Therefore, jobs that require the use of several different skills, allow employees to complete a substantial piece of work (as opposed to the continuous repetition of a simple task) and are seen as having an impact on other people will be thought of as worthwhile and meaningful by the employees in those jobs. Job autonomy is seen as determining experienced responsibility for the outcomes of the work and feedback is seen as determining knowledge of the actual results of the work activities.

The three psychological states are then seen as combining to determine various personal and work outcomes such as high internal work motivation (*i.e.* intrinsic motivation), high-quality work performance, high satisfaction with the work, and low absenteeism and turnover. Hence, the model postulates that an individual experiences positive affect to the extent that he/she learns (knowledge of results) that he personally (experienced responsibility) has performed well on a task that he cares about (experienced meaningfulness). Summary of the above discussions is given in Fig. 2.1.

2.8 Reward Oriented Performance Management

There are ten drivers to develop reward oriented performance management as follows:

1. **Setting objectives**: Which are clearly articulated and acceptable to all levels of employees.
2. **Tracking past and present**: The past and present strategies are studied to develop and optimize reward system for performance.
3. **Determining and application of methodology**: The existing gaps are analyzed and new objectives are identified, external and internal business environment is considered along with job profile and employee focus.
4. **Determining components**: The components include monetary, indirect monetary and non-monetary reward. The composition of each component is determined based on the type of industry it works and with employee consent.
5. **Determining the monetary reward**: This includes pay for position, pay for person and pay for performance.
6. **Design reward system**: To design the system, assimilate the reward data, design the policy and determine employee compensation.

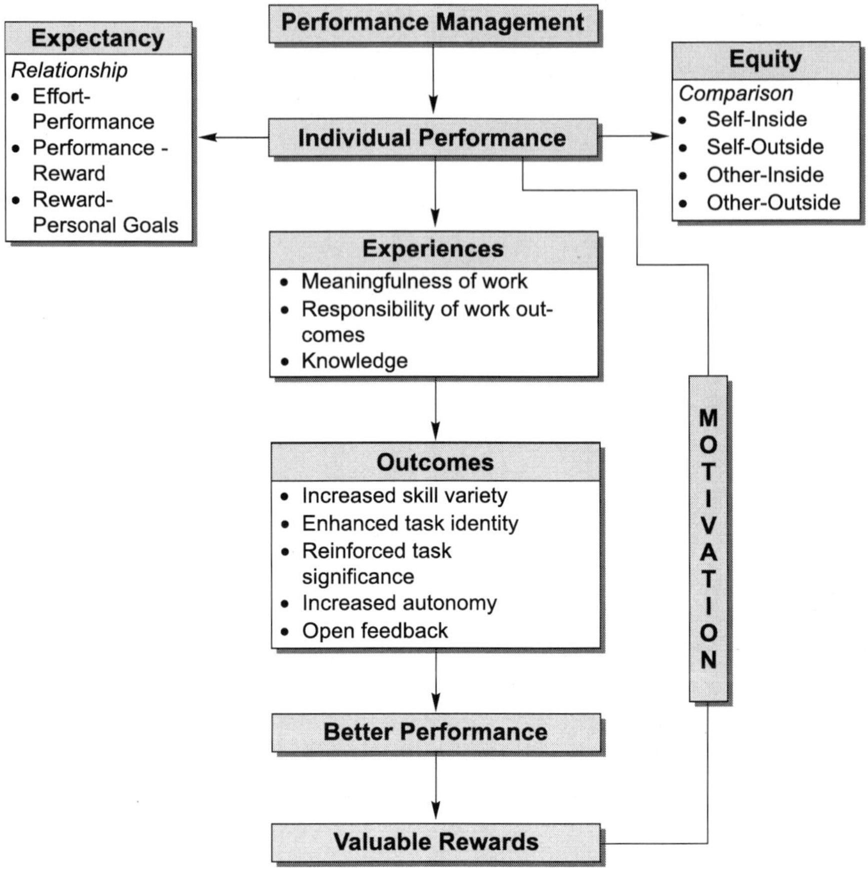

Fig. 2.1 Theoretical Framework of Reward Management.

7. **Communicating about the reward strategy:** Publish about the proposed reward system and hand over to employees in the organization and consult with the trade unions.
8. **Implementation of reward strategy:** Incorporate the suggestions which are feasible, choose the appropriate time for launch, create a centre of responsibility and give notification for implementation and its processes.
9. **Evaluating reward strategy:** To be reviewed on a periodic basis. Reviewed on an organizational and employee level. To check the benefits at both levels and measures to overcome, if any.
10. **Refining reward strategy:** This has to be done from time-to-time to match industry standards and remain competitive in the market.

To capitalize on the drivers of development of this strategy, there are ten drivers of intervention which help to institutionalize this strategy. They are:

1. **Rewards to institutionalize performance management**: Reward is an attractive tool and effective in institutionalization of performance management. It should be demonstrated, that is, monetary or non-monetary and not just on paper.
2. **Reward as perk**: Reward should be given to performers. This will motivate performers and differentiate the non-performers.
3. **Act as centre of institutionalization**: Reward should be the centre point for the strategies of integrated performance management. This will make performance management effective.
4. **Integrate reward with measurement**: To provide the appropriate reward, measurement of performance is essential. Measurement takes into consideration the quality and quantity aspects of the performance.
5. **Integrate reward with competency**: Competency of the employees has to be updated from time-to-time, with the changing demands. Reward will reinforce the competence among the employees and will continue with the urge to upgrade the competency levels.
6. **Integrate reward with culture**: Culture and reward are interdependent. Though there are rules and regulations for the implementation of reward strategy, its culture will enable a smooth implementation and acceptance among all the stakeholders.
7. **Leadership as reward**: Leadership is an opportunity for all the employees. Leadership is not a single person activity anymore, it has transcended into group activity. Giving the opportunity to lead is a reward in itself.
8. **Growth in career as reward**: Careers as reward is enriching and motivating for employees. Job enrichment is in the form of more responsibilities, authorities and multiple tasks. Along with that increment in salary and perks also should follow.
9. **A strategy for employee involvement**: The reward strategy can inspire employees and make them participate voluntarily. If they are rewarded appropriately they will be motivated to participate more actively.
10. **Process centric reward for institutionalization**: This aspect takes into consideration the amount of hard work, risk and efforts put in by employees for the results. They should be rewarded for their hardwork, and then only an organization can retain hardworking and efficient employees within its vicinity.

2.9 Designing Reward System

Reward means money or honour that is distributed as a sign of appreciation for a job well done. Developing a reward system is crucial for organizations in order to induce employees to perform well. However, every individual employee responds to different kinds of rewards depending on their life circumstances. However, the connection between an employee's performance and the reward given to him is not entirely controlled by the employee. This is because an employee may have control over his efforts but not fully over the outcome of his efforts, which is influenced by a number of facilitating and inhibiting factors. This makes design of reward systems a necessity.

Following are the steps of designing a reward system:

1. **Develop list**: A list of all rewards the organization offers to the employees should be developed and compiled. The rewards should then be categorized as monetary and non-monetary.
2. **Comprehend rewards**: How financial and non-financial rewards will influence an employee's performance should be comprehended. Monetary rewards have value both as for what it is worth and can buy, but it also has value as it can be used as an instrument to communicate with the employees;
3. **Benchmark reward**: Conduct a survey of the employees to find out how they perceive each reward in terms of value, equity, and behaviour contingent. This will provide feedback on employee perception of different rewards offered by the organization. Also, an external survey should be conducted to analyze current trends and best practices in reward management. This will provide vital information to the organization to fine tune its reward strategies and systems;
4. **Value proposition**: Rewards identified for administration to employees should be of reasonable value;
5. **Different approaches**: The organization should try to vary the compensation, try to have both individual and group based rewards;
6. **Performance expectations**: The performance expectations should be kept easy and exercise restriction over number of measures, mainly because they can be complicated to measure and therefore also time consuming; and
7. **Communication**: Employees should be continuously informed about the reward system. Communication is a keyword for a well functioning reward system. This will let the employees know how they are doing-by-doing continuous comparisons with the target result and today's result.
8. **Review reward system**: Reward system designed should be periodically reviewed for improvement and effectiveness.

2.10 Approaches to Reward System

The major approaches to reward system are as follows:

1. **Individual reward system**: Under this approach, individual employees are rewarded based on their individual performance, contributions and results. Employees exhibiting better performance tend to get better financial rewards (higher compensation raises) and non-financial rewards (promotion, public acknowledgement). Generally individual rewards are linked to performance appraisal and is undertaken on yearly basis. The idea is to differentiate better performers from average performers. Thus, average performers are also enticed by higher value

of rewards given for better performance. In other words, it acts as an inducement for both performers and non-performers. However, such rewards (financial and non-financial) motivate employees for a short-term as the charm vanishes quickly since the need for higher rewards has been fulfilled.

How to Implement a Pay for Performance Plan?

1. Get your CEO's financial commitment;
2. Know your organization;
3. Know what your organization objectives are;
4. Bring your Managers on board;
5. Get your house in order;
6. Data, Data, Data: financial modeling is a must;
7. Create a plan and document it; and
8. Track and monitor results from the plan.

Source: Martinez, Ester, "Pay-for-performance: Retaining the Crown Jewels", People and Management, Inaugural Issue, March-April 2009, Noida, Pp. 32-35.

2. **Team reward system**: A team can be described as a group of individuals working together for the same goals and objectives. Under this approach, the entire group of employees is rewarded instead of one individual. This encourages teamwork and employees collaborate more frequently with each other to attain the organizational goals and objectives. In other words, organization's collective performance improves due to teams getting rewarded for their accomplishments. Also, team based reward system is easier to measure and therefore also easier to evaluate.

However, as to which approach is best has been a matter of intense arguments as discussed below:

(*a*) *Competition versus cooperation*: Individual reward system promotes individual conflict while team reward system promotes cooperation. The better way to balance conflict and cooperation is to reward individually for motivating well performed efforts and at the same time advocate cooperation and team-work by rewarding well performed results on this level also.

(*b*) *Connection between job design and reward system*: The choice between a job design and reward system organized along individualistic versus group based lines may be less important than ensuring that the job design and reward system are aligned with one another and consistent with other HR practices. With better job designs, monitoring of individual performance is easier and hence individual reward system is better while where job design is not perfect, group based rewards are better.

(*c*) *Contingencies*: Where the contingency between the outcomes and the behaviours of the individual employee are stronger, outcomes are more valued by the individual. But often the willingness to work together as a team is very low amongst individual employees which adversely affect team performance. This implies that individual should be rewarded on the basis of individual performance that is relevant for fulfilling the team tasks.

4. *Team cohesiveness*: Teams with strong group identity and membership can contribute to better performance and hence seek higher rewards. This is because in cohesive teams, individuals do not escape from their role expectations. In a non-cohesive team, individual members of the team would decrease their efforts when working together with others with collective tasks, which can result in a substantial loss for the organization. They have tendency to compare their own inputs and outcomes with other team member. When individual employees are rewarded in team based approach, with a reward based on the outcome of the group tasks, they feel that the performance and outcome of each team member should be relatively equal; otherwise this is by those who perform well, considered unfair and has adverse impact on motivation. This implies that team based reward system ultimately gets reduced to individual reward system.

2.11 Basic Concept of Compensation Management

Compensation refers to all the ways in which an organization may reward employees for the services that they render. These rewards could include compensation payments, fringe benefits, such as vacations, pensions, and medical aid, status symbols, promotion and security. Compensation is the primary inducement offered to employees in exchange for the contributions of labour services in the employment contract. Examples of various compensation forms are as under:

1.	**Base Pay**	Salary and wages for being at work
2.	**Increases for demonstrating new skills**	• Performance based pay • Skills and competency based pay • Job progression
3.	**Increase for results**	• Incentive *Short-term Incentive* • Retention bonus • Signing bonus • Referral bonus • Guaranteed annual bonus • Gainsharing • Cash incentive programmes • Vacation awards *Long-term Incentive* • Stock options • Employee stock ownership

		• Restrictive stock • Manager bonus plan • Ownership stake • Retirement plan • Deferred compensation • Gainsharing • Profit sharing
4.	**Pay for working more hours**	• Overtime pay • Premium pay
5.	**Increases not dependent on anything else**	• Fringe benefits • General increase
6.	**Increase based on the organization's financial success**	• Profit sharing • Market adjustment

Performance-related compensation has been described as the explicit link of financial reward to individual, group or organization performance and part of a re-orientation of pay and reward systems away from traditional methods of job evaluation and time-based pay, often carried out on a collective basis, to a more individualized approach which recognizes employee contributions. Three forms of performance-related pay exist. First, individual merit and performance-related systems based on appraisal, making a payment which is consolidated into a basic time-based salary. Second, individual unconsolidated bonuses often based on production targets. Third, unconsolidated bonuses which are group-derived and collectively paid. Although often assumed to be used as a direct motivator to improve individual employee performance, there are examples of performance-related compensation also playing a part in recruitment and retention of employees by enabling higher compensation levels which are more representative of market rates to be paid over and above collective compensation scales, and for various cultural and image-making purposes such as the pursuit of a non-union, individualistic culture with a reinforced line manager role. As such, performance-related compensation is typically inextricably linked with appraisal, although the potential corruptions of developmental appraisal systems by adding a compensation link, and the problems of maintaining objectivity in assessment criteria, have been well recognized.

Compensation management methods and techniques can significantly affect the relationship between an organization and its employees. Such methods and techniques should not create fixed cost patterns and operational constraints but should be managed as a variable linked to the strategy and success of the organization. Compensation should be managed in a way that reflects and is consistent with the culture of the organization. The rewards offered to employees, and the occasions for these rewards, are amongst the most visible and potent manifestations of the organization's culture.

The compensation system should be designed to drive, reinforce and sometimes alter the culture in such a way that the organization's goals and objectives will be supported. There are many different types of pay systems; - piecework with a wide variety of formulae; measured day-work and high-rate systems; plant-wide incentives and framework processes which affect pay. In its various ways all these systems all try to relate performance to pay, whether it is individually or through small or large groups. "Flexible compensation" or "cafeteria compensation" is another development in the compensation management arena. Flexible compensation is a relatively simple concept, which caters for the differing needs of employees. The total cost of employment is established for a particular position and from this the cost to the employer of providing certain compulsory benefits such as pension, group life and disability assurance and medical aid is deducted. The employees then select, from the range of benefits that the employer is prepared to provide, those that are relevant to their specific needs and requirements. The major advantages of this system are that there are no additional costs to the employer and the individual has the facility to structure a compensation package that meets their individual needs. The idea behind flexible benefits is simple; it reflects the belief that each individual should have the ability to choose the benefits that are most meaningful to them.

2.12 Definitions of Compensation Management

A few noteworthy definitions of Compensation Management are:

1. *"Compensation Management is a process of determining cost effective pay structure, designed to attract and retain, provide an incentive to work hard, and structured to ensure that pay levels are perceived as fair."*

   —Stephen P. Robbins, David A. DeCenzo, Robin Stuart-Kotze and Eileen B. Stewart

2. *"Compensation Systems are the financial reward structures organizations uses to compensate individuals for the work they perform for the organization."*

   —Linda K. Stroh, Gregory B. Northcraft and Margret AnnNeale

3. *"Compensation Management refers to payment systems which determine employee wages or salary, direct and indirect rewards".*

   —I. Kessler

2.13 Features of Compensation Management

The major features of compensation management are as follows:

1. It is an integration process of linking individual and team performance to organizational goals and strategy through reward motivation;
2. It provides extrinsic motivation to managers, employees and team to work effectively towards goal achievement;
3. It gives employees opportunities to employees to improve quality of their professional contributions and personal life quality;

4. It seeks to motivate employees through a rationale, transparent and ethical system of financial reward management;
5. It serves as a legally defensible premise for administration of financial rewards; and
6. It is a fundamental HR strategy to ensure individual, team and organizational success on ongoing basis.

2.14 Significance of Compensation Management

Compensation plays a pivotal role in effective management of human resources, which is crucial to the competitive advantage of organizations. The significance of compensation management is enlisted below:

1. It is essential for integrating employee efforts with organizational goals and objectives;
2. It is part of sound people management framework for recruiting, selecting, socializing, performing, developing and maintaining a capable and motivated workforce;
3. It has social implications as poorly paid employees are likely to indulge in social unrest and undesirable activities;
4. It is a management tool for controlling and directing employee's productive energies for improving organizational competence and performance;
5. It helps in generating a talent pool;
6. It helps in creating better brand equity through increased employee communications with customers, professionals and society at large;
7. It helps in maintaining compensation costs of an organizational efficiently;
8. The shareholders, business analysts and stakeholder, are satisfied with compensation levels, and see the organization as a good investment;
9. It helps in making compliance of government regulations on compensation;
10. It helps in improving work and organizational efficiency due to enhanced employee commitment; and
11. It helps in providing job satisfaction to employees.

2.15 Compensation Management Philosophy

Compensation management helps organizations in managing consistent performance in a manner which holds employees and managers accountable for supporting its objectives and strategy, successfully fulfilling assigned job responsibilities, and accomplishing individual performance goals. This would require the following pre-requisites:

(*a*) Business processes are as simple as possible;

(*b*) Lines of leadership and management are clear;

(*c*) Employees are empowered, which is an important driver of innovation;

(*d*) A distinct organizational culture;

(*e*) Workplace interactions are based on honesty, integrity and trust; and

(*f*) Openness to change.

Besides the above, effective compensation management requires a lot of clear communication, often face-to-face between managers and employees. If a manager does not interact frequently and effectively with his employees, then he has far fewer opportunities to steer them onto a path of greater productivity and optimized output. Successful organizations view compensation management as a process of instilling and maintaining excellence in performance, commitment and productivity on a long-term basis. However, compensation management often leaves behind winners and losers among the employees being linked to financial rewards (money!). Although money could be seen as a motivator, it is not the only or most powerful source of motivation. Motivated employees perform at levels that are higher than the acceptable standard. Individuals perceive compensation as a motivator or not depend on what they perceive as motivation. Herzberg's hygiene-motivator theory states that extrinsic rewards such as compensation do not motivate, it merely ensures that performance is at an acceptable level.

Therefore, compensation management is essentially based on human opportunities and achievements and its success is closely linked with how organizations create reward system to motivate employees towards successful attainment of organizational goals and objectives. In nutshell, the compensation management philosophy can be captured in the following six core strategies:

1. **Clarify** job responsibilities, agree upon performance expectations and clearly link rewards to achievement of performance expectations;
2. **Communicate** clearly the philosophy, rules, regulations, eligibility and all other pertinent details about compensation systems to the employees and managers;
3. **Counsel** to improve understanding of compensation systems and help to remove employee doubts or misunderstanding about it;
4. **Compare** performance to performance expectations agreed upon and then recommend appropriate financial reward;
5. **Cultivate** a culture where reward is the most powerful motivator of employee performance; and
6. **Celebrate** exemplary performance linked rewards.

Hence, compensation management shall require a proactive approach to management of human resources, a congenial work culture and value based management.

2.16 The Compensation Management Model

A model of compensation management is depicted in Fig. 2.2.

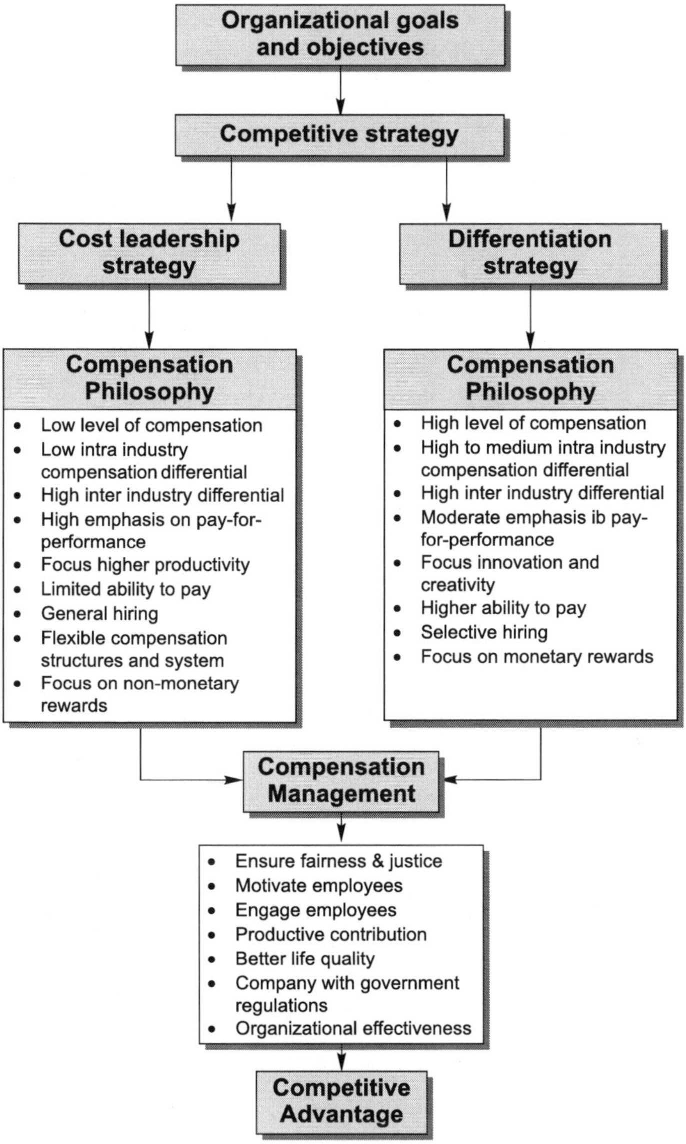

Fig. 2.2 The compensation management model.

It can be seen from the figure that compensation management starts from organizational goals and objectives. Every organization has its unique set of mission, vision, values and core competence. These sets of mission, vision, values and core competence broadly forms organizational goals and objectives. Goals and objectives constitute the foundation on which business plans are devised and strategies are formulated to achieve the stated business plans. It may be noted that business plans are short-term in nature usually lasting over 2 to 3 years whereas goals and objectives of the organization are long-term.

Once the business plans and strategic imperative are determined and defined, competitive strategy of the organization is established. Competitive strategy as per Michael Porter can be broadly classified into two groups viz. cost leadership strategy and differentiation strategy. If the organization intends to pursue a cost leadership strategy, then it focuses upon keeping cost of manufacturing products or rendering services at the lowest possible cost which other competitors cannot do. Their strategy is to keep operating cost under tight control. Since compensation paid to employees constitutes around 30% to 40% of the operating cost of an organization, therefore the compensation philosophies of the organization are built upon on cost considerations. Their compensation philosophies are marked with following distinctive characteristics:

(*a*) *Low level of compensation*: Compensation levels are generally kept at the lowest possible so that overall cost of manufacturing goods or rendering services can be kept at lowest cost to the organization. At the same time, the quality of goods manufactured or services rendered must be of high quality to withstand competition in the market.

(*b*) *Low intra industry compensation differential*: Since cost of operating cost through lower compensation cost is to be achieved and maintained therefore, compensation differential within the same industry is usually low.

(*c*) *High inter industry compensation differential*: Some industries like forging works on cost leadership while some industries like software work on differentiation strategy. Therefore, organization pursuing cost leadership strategy will have a relative higher compensation differential with respect to industries not pursuing cost leadership strategy.

(*d*) *High emphasis on pay-for-performance*: Organizations with cost leadership strategy tend to emphasize pay-for-performance programmes to gain maximum return on investment (*i.e.* employee compensation). By emphasizing performance, they seek to attain higher productivity which is essential for keeping cost low.

(*e*) *Focus higher productivity*: Cost leadership strategy entails maximum productivity to keep overall compensation cost low. Higher productivity of employees helps in being low cost producer of products.

(*f*) *Limited ability to pay*: Given cost is a major consideration; therefore organizations with cost leadership strategy have limited ability to pay.

(*g*) *General hiring*: Since compensation is on lower side therefore cost leadership strategy prone organizations cannot be selective in hiring.

(*h*) *Flexible compensation structures and systems*: Cost leadership firms emphasize variable components of compensation and have smaller fixed compensation structure. Also, they tend to concentrate on output based compensation systems.

(*i*) *Focus on non-monetary rewards*: These organizations given more focus on non-monetary rewards such as recognition programmes to keep financial costs under tight control.

If the organization intends to pursue a differentiation strategy, then it focuses upon innovation. Their strategy is to create innovative or creative products and services and attain competitive advantage over competitors through value for money propositions. Therefore, the compensation philosophies of the organization are built upon on fostering innovation. Their compensation philosophies are marked with following distinctive characteristics:

(*a*) *High level of compensation*: Compensation levels are generally kept at higher levels so that best talents can be attracted and retained in the organization. The idea is to give consumers 'something different' from what other competitors have to offer.

(*b*) *High to medium intra industry compensation differential*: Organizations with differentiation strategy tend to have high to medium compensation differential owing to their predominant focus on innovation through employees.

(*c*) *High inter industry compensation differential*: Owing to their differentiation strategy, inter industry compensation differentials are on higher side with respect to organizations pursuing cost leadership strategies.

(*d*) *Moderate emphasis on pay-for-performance*: Organizations with differentiation strategy tend to give moderate emphasis on pay-for-performance programmes to attract and retain best employees.

(*e*) *Focus on innovation and creativity*: Differentiation strategy entails maximizing product or service innovation to keep edge in the market.

(*f*) *Higher ability to pay*: Given innovation is a major consideration; therefore organizations with differentiation strategy have higher ability to pay to attracting and retaining talents.

(*e*) *Selective hiring*: Since compensation is on higher side therefore differentiation strategy prone organizations are selective in hiring.

(*f*) *Focus on monetary rewards*: These organizations given more focus on monetary rewards to motivate employees for better R&D, design, products and processes.

Compensation management is influenced by compensation philosophy of the organization. The level, structure and system of compensation are determined based on the chosen compensation philosophy. However, compensation management shall be effective only if the following attributes are present:

(*a*) *Ensure fairness and justice*: Compensation management must ensure that employees are paid according to their skills, competencies and contributions. Also, organizational justice in terms maintaining and upholding internal and external equity plays a pivotal role in making compensation as an effective tool of improving individual and organizational competence and performance.

(*b*) *Motivate employees*: The compensation level (lag, lead or match), structure and systems must be such so as to motivate employees to effectively achieve the goals and objectives of the organization.

(*c*) *Engage employees*: Compensation management must foster organizational commitment, job involvement and citizenship behaviours amongst employees so that they work efficiently towards business plans of the organization in a strategically agile manner.

(*d*) *Productive contributions*: Organizations must reward employees differentially for exhibiting differentiating performance and productivity.

(*e*) *Better quality of life*: Compensation management must be able to provide employees acceptable quality of life deemed necessary by the civil society.

(*f*) *Comply with government regulations*: Compensation management must satisfy the government regulations.

(*g*) *Organizational effectiveness*: Compensation must be managed in a way that ensures organizational effectiveness.

When compensation management is able to address all the above imperatives, organization is likely to gain and sustain its competitive advantage. This is because people help create sustainable competitive advantage for their organizations when employees are compensated according to their skills, competencies and contributions in a transparent, ethical and strategic manner.

2.17 Determination of Inter and Intra Industry Compensation Differential

Compensation is fundamental to any employment contract. It is a tool to compensate for rendering labour by the employees in order to provide an optimum return on investment to the employers. Moreover, compensation is increasingly used to motivate employees to improve their performance for effectively and efficiently achieving the goals and objectives of the organization. However, compensation is competitive business environment is not a linear proposition but is a multi-variate proposition. This is because a number of factors both internal and external to an organization affect compensation which results in differentials across employees within an organization and across employees of different organizations whether in the same industry or different industry. These factors operate simultaneously and tend to result in compensation differential. The factors which contribute to determination of inter and intra industry compensation differentials are as follows:

1. **Minimum wages**: The rate of minimum wages across different states of India is different due to socio-economic factors. Therefore, the minimum wages for similar or comparable skill categories are different in different states. Moreover, the rate of minimum wages for similar skill grades across different sectors of industry is also different. An example is agriculture which is one of the largest sources of employment yet minimum wages are much lower than what is applicable to industry. Thus, minimum wages results in inter and intra industry compensation differential.
2. **Demographic factors**: Compensation is influenced by going rate, that is, market rates. The going rates are different in different regions or parts of the country depending on the economic conditions. For instance, going rates in rural or backward areas could be lower than in urban or semi-urban areas thereby determining inter and intra compensation differentials.
3. **Premium for skill**: Skills can be categorized as general and specific. General skills such as basic mental, physical and literacy are required for entering employment. Thereupon, employees gain skills specific to an organization by virtue of working experience and training provided by the organization. Employees possessing specific skills are more valued and reflected in their differentiating compensation due to difficulty in obtaining or replacing such specific skills against general skills which are easily available in the labour market.
4. **Demand for employees**: The availability of unskilled employees are more than skilled employees at any given point of time. At the initial phase of industrialization of an economy, the demand for unskilled employees is more due to labour intensive processes employed by the organization. The major reason for employing labour intensive against technology intensive processes by organization is largely governed by the availability of vast pool of replaceable and cheap labour. Therefore, compensation differential between unskilled and skilled employees increases in the favour of skilled persons. However, as the economy grows and increasingly employee's newer technologies, the demand for unskilled employee's decreases while demand for skilled employee's increases till it reaches equilibrium. The compensation differential is virtually reduces to zero given most of the workforce is skilled as the demand for unskilled employees shrinks significantly.
5. **Collective bargaining**: Collective bargaining entails mutual discussions and negotiations between employers and trade unions for extending better compensation and other benefits to the employees. Collective bargaining takes place at plant, industry and national levels. For plant level bargaining and assuming negotiations to be effective, the compensation differential will be more for that plant as compared to those plants where collective bargaining is weak. Further, collective bargaining at industry or national level reduces the compensation

differentials between similar job groups within a particular industry in a given region or whole of India.

6. **Labour reserve**: Labour reserve can be both positive as well as negative. In a positive labour reserve scenario, labour markets are characterized by easy availability of trained and able manpower will be cheaper to hire and therefore compensation differentiation is likely to be on lower side. This because every able person will compete with each other to gain employment and will be willing to work for lower compensation. Thus, the compensation differential will be meager or negligible. On the other hand if the labour reserve is negative, that is restricted availability of trained and able manpower, then compensation differential will be more. However, this situation could be transitory as employees from positive labour reserve market will be attracted towards and flock to negative labour reserve market thereby gain increasing labour supply and thereby resulting in diminishing compensation differentials.
7. **Economic progress**: The level of economic progress of a region or part influences compensation differentials. Regions or parts characterized by high economic progress shall tend to employ skilled employees and outsource unskilled employees to reduce overall cost of compensation. Such organizations will pay their skilled employees more and pay minimum to the unskilled employees.
8. **Job experience**: Employees with longer experience or greater depth of skill shall be paid more than those employees who have lesser job experience. More experienced employees compensation differential against low or inexperienced employees shall be on higher side. More experienced employees have better search options as compared to inexperienced employees which tend to add premium to their experience.
9. **Short and long-run**: In the short-run, the compensation differential for a given skill category remain significant due to skill gaps and level of economic progress. However, in the long run the compensation differential gets reduced for a given skill level or labour due to skill upgradations.
10. **Level of profit**: Compensation and resultant differentials are largely influenced by the ability of an organization to pay. Organization's ability to pay regulated by its level of profitability. In other words, higher is the profitability of a given organization, more will be its ability to pay. Since profitability levels varies from one organization to another therefore compensation differential tends to exists across same or similar skill categories.
11. **Productivity**: Productivity is an index of output to input. This ratio impacts individual and consequently the organization's outcomes. Employees who are more productive tend to be rewarded with higher compensation than employees with lower productivity. This leads to increasing compensation differential between more productive and less productive employees. This is premise of pay-for-performance programmes.

Hence, we may conclude that a host of inter and intra industry factors determine compensation differential. These differentials seek to act as performance catalyst for the employees in their endeavour to effectively achieve goals and objectives of the organization.

India's Wage Differential Worrisome: ILO

India witnessed a mere 1% hike in wages against a 5% growth in productivity during the last two decades to employees, according to a recent study by International Labour Organization (ILO). The country ranked ninth in the list of countries offering highest disparity in wage and productivity growth between 1990 and 2007 amongst 32 countries surveyed by ILO.

Source: "HR News", Business Manager, Vol. 11, No. 6, December 2008, pp. 20-28.

2.18 Strategic Implications of Compensation Differential

Compensation differential is fundamental to employment relationships. These differentials are infact a testimony of industrial or individual differentiations. It tends to affect the bottom-line of the organizations in fast paced and dynamic competitive business environment where survival of the fittest can only be ensured. Since employees constitute competitive advantage of the organizations therefore compensation differentials has strategic implications for the organizations as enumerated below:

1. **Employer of choice**: Organizations with higher compensation differentials as compared to their competitors are better positioned to attract and retain talents to their organization. It is this very reason why certain organizations in every industrial sector are preferred by employees to gain and retain employment. Higher compensation enables employees to improve the quality of life which is reflected in their job satisfaction and engagement levels. Also, talented employees provide differentiating advantage to their organization thereby improving organization's competitiveness in the market place characterized by stiff competition.
2. **Effective outcomes**: Talents with higher compensation differentials tend to be more productive and help in effectively achieving the goals and objectives of the organization. Higher employee productivity leads to better organizational outcomes and consequently higher levels of competitiveness. In other words, such organizations are able to attain and sustain their competitive advantage for a longer period of time.
3. **Competitive priority**: Organizations are said to pursue either cost leadership or differentiation strategy. Organizations pursuing cost leadership strategy tend to pay as low as is possible and accordingly

the inter industry compensation differentiation are higher while the intra industry compensation differentiation are lower. On the other hand, organizations pursuing differentiation strategy values talents and are willing to compensate employees differentially in exchange for innovation and creativity. Therefore, different organizations pursuing different competitive priority will attach different value to compensation differential.

4. **Higher engagement levels**: Employees with higher compensation differential usually have higher levels of organizational commitment, job involvement, motivation and citizenship behaviours. This is because they understand that unless they contribute the very best to their organization it will be difficult for them to maintain organizational membership and that they will tend to lose high compensation differential being offered by their present organization.
5. **Skill upgradations**: Employees with higher compensation differentials will be highly motivated to upgrade their skill levels through training and skill certification process of their own volition. This will mean that skills of the employees will improve at a much lower cost to an organization given that employees want to maintain their competitive edge so that the organization finds it difficult to replace them. The organization will be benefited through increased skill levels and competence to perform jobs much efficiently and effectively. This will lead to organizational effectiveness in the long-run.
6. **Culture improvement**: Compensation differentials will help employees to forge a strong performance driven work culture within their organization. Increased emphasis on performance will help in raising the collective performance bar of the organization thereby improving organizational performance and competence on a long-term basis. Also, a strong performance oriented work culture entails better work practices and responses from the employees towards strategic business plans of the organization.

Hence, we may conclude that compensation differential helps in improving individual performance, skill and contributions which culminates into organizational success. Given this, many organizations are increasingly focusing upon pay-for-performance programmes with an objective of improving organizational performance and competitiveness in a dog-eat-dog business world.

CHAPTER REVIEW

- Reward means anything arising from employment relationship which employees perceives to have value for him.
- Reward management means the process of formulation, implementation, maintenance and communication of strategies and policies with the

purpose of rewarding people fairly, equitably and consistently in accordance with their relative contribution to the organization and to help the organization to achieve its goals and objectives.

- Reward management is based upon three basic premises of equity, achievement and camaraderie. Equity means that employees are treated justly in relation to the basic conditions of employment. Achievement refers to the employee's job related accomplishments. Camaraderie means that employees wish to have warm, interesting and cooperative relations with others in the workplace.
- Extrinsic reward means pay, promotions, and organization status that are provided to the employees by the organization. Feelings of achievement, accomplishment and self-satisfaction are intrinsic rewards.
- Designing a reward system is crucial for organizations in order to induce employees to perform well since every individual employee responds to different kinds of rewards depending on their life circumstances. Steps of designing a reward system include develop list, comprehend rewards, benchmark rewards, value proposition, different approaches, performance expectations, communications and periodic review.
- Individual reward system tends to reward individual accomplishments while team based rewards tends to reward entire group for task accomplishment.
- Compensation refers to all the ways in which an organization may reward employees for the services that they render.
- Compensation Management is a process of determining cost effective pay structure, designed to attract and retain, provide an incentive to work hard, and structured to ensure that pay levels are perceived as fair.
- Determination of inert and intra industry compensation differential arises due to a number of factors such as minimum wages, demographic factors, premium for skill, demand for employees, collective bargaining, labour reserve, economic progress, job experience, short and long run, level of profit, and productivity.

A. Conceptual Review Questions

1. What do you mean by reward? Explain the elements of rewards.
2. Discuss the theoretical framework underpinning reward management in the organizational context.
3. What are the objectives of reward management? Discuss the reward oriented performance management strategies.
4. Design a reward system for your organization. Illustrate with examples types of reward you would like to consider in reward system.
5. What are the different approaches to reward system? Which approach is better and why?

6. What is compensation management? Enlist its features and significance.
7. What is the philosophy behind compensation management?
8. Design the compensation management model for your organization.
9. Explain the determination of inter and intra industry compensation differentials.
10. Write short notes on:
    (*a*) Intrinsic and extrinsic rewards
    (*b*) Factors influencing compensation differentials
    (*c*) Strategic impact of compensation differentials

B. Analytical Questions

1. Does extrinsic rewards like compensation has profound impact in improving individual performance and productivity?
2. Is it appropriate to link rewards to performance? Why or why not?
3. "Overemphasizing rewards and compensation can ruin performance management system of an organization". Critically evaluate the statement.

CASE INCIDENT

Rewarding Talent or Liability

Mr. Pradeep Shukla, the CEO of a medium sized auto component manufacturer is looking for a new vice president of operations given the last incumbent left in a short span of time due to differences in management style with Mr. Shukla. The company has been in business for the last 10 years and has a modest turnover of 25 crores. It is mainly into manufacturing automotive steering and suspension components and supplies to leading passenger car manufacturers in India and certain overseas companies.

Mr. Shukla has retained Mr. PMS Khurana, a reputed management consultant of the region for head hunting for the position of vice president of operations. After some search Mr. Khurana zeroed on Mr. Anil Arora who is working as Chief Manager in a large and well known manufacturer of automotive pistons. Mr. Arora was a qualified engineer with master's degree in industrial engineering. He was taking care of quality control department in his company. Mr. Khurana impressed upon Mr. Shukla and personal meeting with Mr. Arora was fixed up.

Mr. Shukla was impressed with the perspectives of Mr. Arora and then he called upon Mr. Amresh Gupta his head of HR department to interact with Mr. Arora and give his feedback. Mr. Gupta interacted with Mr. Arora and gave emphasis on his present job profile, expertise and core competence. After his interactions of about an hour, he sat with Mr. Shukla who was accompanied by Mr. Khurana. Mr. Gupta emphatically pointed out that Mr. Arora does not have experience in manufacturing of steering and suspension components and he lacks exposure to operation functions being just limited to quality control work only. He insisted that some more candidates should be seen and Mr. Arora's case can be reviewed later.

Mr. Shukla had something else in his mind. He thought that Mr. Arora was a qualified engineer, had good perspectives and Mr. Khurana has strongly recommended him so he agreed to hire him. Mr. Arora was again called to discuss his compensation expectations. After negotiations, he was almost paid double of his present compensation as Mr. Shukla was very keen to hire an exceptional talent like Mr. Arora. Everything went all right and Mr. Arora has joined recently.

After two months, there was lot of dissatisfaction amongst the managers and staff. They thought Mr. Arora is a big mistake as he is neither technically competent has leadership capability. Mr. Shukla is now fed up with adverse remarks against Mr. Arora. He advised Mr. Gupta to seek feedback from his past company on a very confidential basis. It was later discovered that Mr. Arora has falsified his compensation and got an unethical 100% rise on it. Mr. Shukla called up Mr. Arora and it was discussed at length and Mr. Arora admitted that he has done his under advice of Mr. Khurana. Mr. Shukla instructed Mr. Gupta cancel Mr. Khurana's engagement as consultant to the company and also advised for 50% pay cut for Mr. Arora. Mr. Arora agreed for time being and started looking for job vehemently.

QUESTIONS

1. Was hiring of Mr. Anil Arora for VP-Operations correct and valid?
2. Why Mr. Pradeep Shukla did not pay heed to Mr. Amresh Gupta?
3. What was the role played by Mr. PMS Khurana?
4. What is your advice for Mr. Pradeep Shukla, Mr. PMS Khurana and Mr. Anil Arora as an expert of performance and reward man agement?

EXPERIENTIAL EXCERCISES

1. Working individually or in groups, interview five HR Managers at firms in your locality. Prepare a brief report for presentation to the class outlining the ways in which the HR department there handles the fixation and revision of compensation for the employees.
2. Prepare a brief report describing how organizations (any five) benchmark their reward and compensation practices with regard

to competitors especially in global meltdown and recession driven economic conditions. Discuss the effectiveness of the compensation benchmarking tools and techniques employed by these organizations.

3. Prepare a seminar presentation on one of the following themes:
   (*a*) Money is the greatest motivator of employee performance.
   (*b*) Non-financial rewards are more desirable than financial rewards.
   (*c*) Reward should be linked to organizational success rather than individual success.

❑❑❑

Learning Objectives

At the conclusion of this chapter, you should be able to :

- ❑ Discuss the process, strategic imperatives and components of compensation system
- ❑ Focusing on internal and external equity in compensation systems
- ❑ Understand the concept, philosophy, objectives, pre-requisites, types and criteria of pay structures
- ❑ Developing a pay structure
- ❑ Explain concepts of performance based pay and skills and competency based pay systems
- ❑ Describe the concept, features, significance, methods and limitations of incentive system
- ❑ Assess compensation and compa ratios
- ❑ Elucidate the impact of ethics in performance and reward management

3
Compensation System

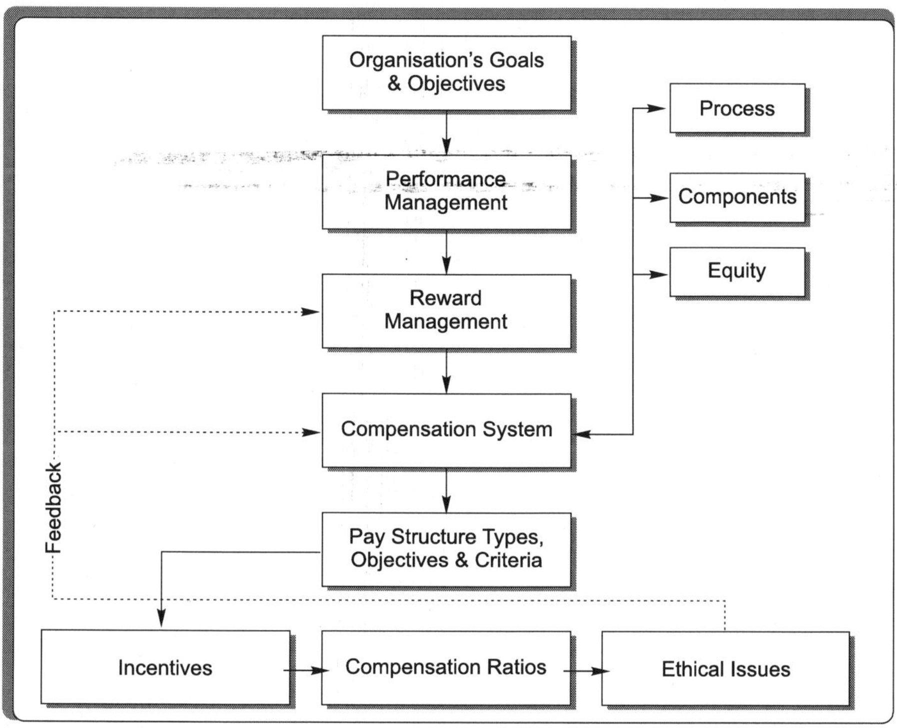

3.1 Compensation System: An Introduction

Compensation system is a strategic process of aligning pay, incentives and benefits (rewards) of employees with organizational goals and objectives. Compensation system is a formidable communicator and can be a powerful instrument for change and a major determinant of the culture of an organization.

The compensation system is depicted in Fig. 3.1.

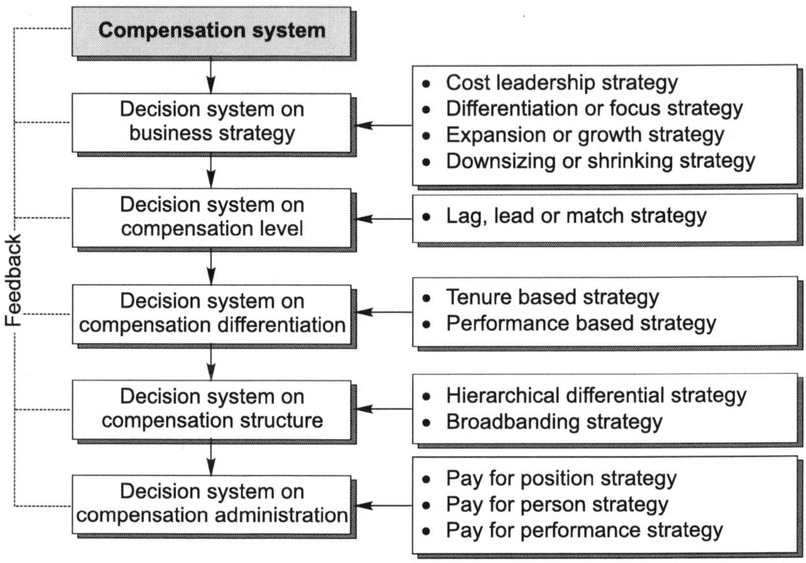

Fig. 3.1 Compensation System.

The details of each component of compensation system are as under:

1. **Decision System on Business Strategy :** The nature of an organization's strategy is the primary determinant of its compensation system. For example, an organization pursuing cost leadership strategy would keep overall compensation cost low while pursuing differentiation or focus strategy will involve paying well to attract and retain talents for unleashing innovation. An organization going into expansion will have a different organization strategy and consequently different compensation strategy than an organization, which is not getting into expansion mode. Greater expansion gives rise to a greater need of attracting and retaining high caliber employees in fastest possible time consistent with its goals and objectives. Such organizations shall offer higher compensation to meet its human resource needs than an organization not in expansion mode which shall require people mainly for replenishment. Thus, organization with no expansion plan shall use more objective criteria for compensation increases and bonuses are significantly greater proportion of total compensation than in organizations into downsizing or shrinking mode.

2. **Decision System on Compensation Level :** The compensation-level system determines whether an organization will have a lead, lag, or match policy. Compensation decisions made by organizations can significantly impact individual and group level consequences, including performance, skill development, work-related attitudes, and workforce composition. Compensation level and benefit policy can determine what types of employees are attracted to the organization by signaling job seekers to less visible organizational attributes. These policies will determine whether or not employees are willing to continue to work for the organization. If the compensation level or benefit level is not satisfactory, the desirability of movement will increase and it is more likely that withdrawal behaviours such as tardiness, absenteeism, and turnover will increase. Unsatisfactory compensation and benefit levels may also reduce the motivation of employees and eventually negatively affect individual, group, and organization performance.

3. **Decision System on Compensation Differentiation :** Individual level compensation differentiation may arise due to two decisions made by the organization. The first decision involves compensating employees based on seniority, which is, based on length of service. The length of service entails total years of experience of an employee both within the organization and outside. Compensating on seniority has been a traditional approach, which tends to reward individuals for possessing more experience. The other pertains to compensating employees based on merit. In this approach, employees who perform better are paid higher compensation irrespective of their length of service. Merit compensation is popular these days because it motivates employees to perform better in order to get higher compensation.

   Organization's compensating on seniority alone is less likely to attract high caliber employees especially the younger ones. On the other hand, if an organization relies solely on merit compensation, it will result in compensation dissatisfaction amongst more experienced employees and attrition rate amongst senior managers will increase. Therefore, organizations have to wisely choose amongst these two approaches so that the organization attains its goals and objectives effectively. However, it is always prudent to make an appropriate combination of the two approaches for best results.

4. **Decision System on Compensation Structure :** The compensation structure policy determines the compensation differences between levels of the organizational hierarchy. Compensation structure will also impact individual consequences. If there are significant compensation differences between hierarchical levels, employees may focus on being successful rather than effective. That is, they will try to engage in behaviours such as networking and ingratiation that allow movement to higher levels instead of focusing on behaviours important to effective job performance. If large compensation differentials exist and it is not likely that individuals will be able to move up in the organization and realize large compensation increases, decreased motivation to perform and increased turnover may result. However,

if the compensation differential is not large enough, individuals may not be motivated to pursue promotions and higher compensation.

5. **Decision System on Compensation Administration :** It refers to the organization's decision on means and measures to administer benefits to its employees. Organizations can compensate employees according to position, person and performance strategy. In position based compensation system, job positions are rewarded financially and not the job holders. Each job has a fixed compensation attached to it based on job evaluation technique. In the person based compensation system, job holders are financially rewarded for possessing requisite or higher skills and competencies. Therefore, different employees in same or similar jobs may be differentially compensated according to their level of education, training and skill. In pay performance compensation system, decisions are based on their job performance. It is believed that employees will be motivated to work harder to receive these rewards and potentially seek training or education to gain an advantage. If the decisions are based on subjective evaluations, ingratiation and networking behaviour may take precedence over job performance. If the decisions are based on tenure, higher performing employees may feel under-rewarded and seek jobs in organizations that will compensation them based on merit.

   These individual level outcomes can have implications for group and ultimately organizational outcomes. If the compensation decisions do not motivate strong job performance on an individual level, it is not likely an organization will perform well. The key to an effective compensation system is to make sure that the decisions made regarding the four dimensions fit the overall organizational strategy.

3.2 Strategic Implications of Compensation System

Performance management process is influenced by an organization's business strategy. Depending on the organization's business strategy, the pay level, pay structure, pay differentiation and pay systems will vary. Compensation or pay is used by organization to acquire, motivate, engage, and retain talents necessary for growth and success in a knowledge economy. An organization focusing on cost as a strategy will follow a pay level which is lower, pay differentiation amongst jobs and employees will be high and pay structure which is flexible. A differentiation strategy driven organization will follow a different strategy. Similarly, an organization intending to grow faster will have higher pay level to attract and retain talents and pay structure will be relatively smaller in structure.

Compensation system will also have significant impact on the organization's HR systems such as career management, succession planning, training and development and employer branding practices. Depending on the compensation management process, the pay level, pay differentiation, pay structures and pay systems will vary. Organizations emphasizing innovation will tend to put more emphasis on these HR systems to enable employees to perform better and produce differentiating outcomes.

3.3 Compensation and Its Components

Compensation means the set of rewards that organizations provide to individuals in return for their willingness to perform various jobs and tasks within the organization. Organizations all have different compensation policies with different content. It is what gives them their competitive advantage. These are grouped under the headings of fixed pay and variable pay as under:

1. Fixed Pay

It includes the following forms:

(*a*) *Base pay*: the guaranteed basic pay received each month by employees;

(*b*) *Competence: based pay*: a pay system where the organization has an express policy that recognizes competence and pays for it;

(*c*) *Fixed period employment contracts*: employment contracts that are for a fixed period of time, say two years, with performance goals attached;

(*d*) *Fringe benefits*: benefits received in addition to base pay (for example, company cars or thrift societies, housing, etc.);

(*e*) *International remuneration*: to any remuneration that is received overseas for example director's fees, bonuses, retirement, etc.;

(*f*) *Performance pay:* performance pay refers to paying for individual contributions usually measured by way of a performance management system. This pay is normally added to the guaranteed package by way of a salary increase and is therefore considered fixed pay;

(*g*) *Retirement funds*: provident funds, pension funds, deferred compensation; and

(*h*) *Total package*: the concept of all remuneration grossed up and monetized, and then employees have the choice of structuring their own package within organizational regulations.

2. Variable Pay

It includes the following forms:

(*a*) *Long term incentives*: incentive schemes where the measurement period or payout period is longer than one year, usually several years (e.g. Economic Value Add (EVA) schemes, phantom share schemes, deferred compensation, etc.);

(*b*) *Share schemes*: any type of share scheme, the most common being share options, performance shares, share purchase schemes;

(*c*) *Short-term incentives*: incentive schemes where the measurement period is around one year and payments are in cash (*e.g.* profit share, gain share, commission, bonus scheme, etc.);

(*d*) *Long term incentives*: incentive schemes where the measurement period is more than one year and payments are to be realized at a future date; and

(*e*) *Organization wide incentives*: incentive schemes devised for all the employees in collectivity.

3.4 Internal and External Equity in Compensation System

Pay structures are means and methods of administering an organization's pay philosophy and policies. However, pay being an important form of financial reward provided to employees for motivating higher job performance and organizational commitment, therefore are subject to employee perception on fairness and justice aspects. Pay structure is a strong determinant of employee's value in the organization. The perception employees have towards their own and other's pay constitute equity. Equity simply means fair treatment given to employees in matters of pay and benefits. Since we live in a relative world where everything is put into comparison or comparative framework, therefore employees also evaluate their own pay with respect to other employees within and outside their organizations.

Internal equity means pay according to relative value of their jobs within same organization. Comparison of pay by an employee A with another employee B who is performing same or similar kind of work is referred to as internal equity. Thus, internal equity involves the job position of an employee in the organizational hierarchy. The internal equity can be achieved by using job evaluation techniques.

Internal equity involves creating a series of grades or bands with wide ranges at the top of the pay structure and narrower ranges at the bottom. Each grade represents a different level within the organization. An organization should take a judicious decision on number of grades it needs to have, deciding on the spread, and creating a minimum and maximum range. The midpoint of one grade should be 15% higher than the midpoint of the grade below it.

External equity means comparison of pay for work performed by employees of similar jobs in other organization. Comparison of pay by an employee "A" in working in "X" organization with another employee 'B' working "Y" organization who is performing same or similar kind of work is referred to as external equity. External equity arises primarily due to differences in how each organization formulates its pay structures by assessing internal factors and market pricing analysis.

One of the best ways of ensuring external equity involves collecting market data through pay surveys. However, market data may not be available for all the jobs. Such jobs are often slotted into comparable grades for the organization according to the scope of the job, the responsibilities, the size of the budget the job handles, etc. It may be noted that in the market pricing system is that the midpoint of a job is to be compared with midpoint of that job in the market and not the internal grade. Over time, the employee's pay should move closer to market as performance moves closer to expectations for that job.

Hence, we may conclude that internal and external equity in compensation is crucial for long-term performance, productivity and commitment of employees. In the absence of such equity considerations, employees will either become unproductive or redundant or leave for better paying organizations.

3.5 Basic Concept of Pay Structure

Pay structure is a mechanism for determining different levels of pay for various jobs based on their relative worth to the organization and market rates. Pay structures establishes pay differentials across different jobs or groups of jobs in the organization. For example, a carpenter's job will carry a pay of Rs. 3,000/- while a supervisor will get Rs. 5,000/-. These differentials arise due to internal factors such as the skill, education, experience and value of the job performance for organization's effective functioning and effectiveness. Job evaluation programmes are established and carried out for determining pay rates for different types of jobs in an organization. External factors are determined through various pay surveys, government notifications (like minimum wages) and compensation benchmarking with competitors. It is crucial for an organization to pay in accordance with its ability and market rates. In the absence of external competitiveness of pay, the organization will not be able to attract or retain talents which are necessary for gaining and/or sustaining competitiveness.

A few noteworthy definitions of pay structure are as follows:

1. *"A pay structure provides a framework within which an organization defines the different levels of pay for jobs, on the basis of assessments of their relative internal value and of external relativities (market rate)."*

   —Armstrong and Murlis

2. *"Pay structure is the hierarchy of pay rates or levels among jobs in an organization."*

   —Heneman and Schwab

3.6 Philosophy Behind Pay Structure

Pay structure essentially follows either one of two philosophies, outcome-based or behaviour-based. In an outcome-based pay structure, pay differentials to be paid to individuals within each job class are driven by the performance of the individual. Outcome includes both outputs and the behaviour that is associated with it. In this system, emphasis is being made on higher individual outputs with citizenship behaviours. The output is equally important as the conduct of the employee on the job. In other words, outcome based pay structures rewards employees for their higher skills and competencies as exhibited by them through increased output as well as good citizenship behaviours. The philosophy is to motivate higher performance with better accountability in order to meet the economic, social and psychological needs of the employees. Accordingly, result based pay structures are designed to reward employees for higher productivity and increased accountability.

In behaviour based pay structures, pay differentials are based upon behavioural traits of the employee such as initiative, analytical thinking, attitude, perseverance, loyalty, commitment, motivation, team spirit and so on and so forth. The philosophy underpinning this system is that employees with positive traits are more likely to perform better given their strong behavioural traits. It is assumed that individuals with higher intellect are better performers than individuals with lower intellect. Skills and competencies are assumed to be the result of better behavioural attributes. Accordingly, pay structures are designed to reward differentially employees with better behaviours rather than skills.

Pay structure has traditionally focused on determining the effect of outcome-based versus behaviour-based control on employee's motivation and performance. However, no general consensus concerning the impact of control system type has been reached. Both systems have advantages and disadvantages. No single control system is superior but either system may be preferable depending on the circumstances.

3.7 Objectives of Pay Structure

The major objectives of pay structure are as follows:

(*a*) **Rationale basis**: It provides a rationale basis for motivating and rewarding employees for better performance;

(*b*) **Talent management**: It helps in attracting and retaining talented employees for sustaining competitive advantage of the organization;

(*c*) **Equity**: It provides a framework upon which transparent and equitable pay policy can be effectively implemented;

(*d*) **Coherent**: It ensures that the pay policy, system and practices are internally coherent and externally competitive; and

(*e*) **Legal defense**: It provides a legal defense against lawsuits on pay discrimination brought out against the organization by the employees.

3.8 Pre-Requisites of Pay Structure

An effective pay structure is based on the following pre-requisites

1. It should be in consonance with organization's strategy and business plans. For example, cost leadership strategy will call for a different pay structure as compared to another organization which is pursuing a differentiation strategy;
2. It must be flexible and should be able to adjust to changing internal and external factors. For example, if the organization is now facing increased competition, it will have to restructure pay systems and similarly if the organization is facing skill shortages or labour market is booming, then pay structures must be responsive to adapt to these dynamic changes;
3. It must be able to reward differentially high performing and average performing employees so as to motivate all employees to perform better;
4. It must ensure objectivity in terms of skill and competency and contributions of the employees working on different jobs and at different hierarchical levels of the organization;
5. It should meet needs and aspirations of the employees so that they can be productive on their jobs and maintain quality life styles;
6. It must be communicated to employees clearly for greater employee acceptance and organizational justice perceptions; and
7. Budgets must be devised to control, monitor and effectively implement pay structure for achieving organizational goals and objectives.

3.9 Types of Pay Structures

The most common types of pay structures are as follows:

1. **Graded pay structures**: A graded pay structure consists of sequence of job grades to each of which is attached a pay range. A pay range defines the minimum and maximum rate payable to any job in a given grade and indicates the scope provided for job-holders to progress through the range.

   Pay range provides scope for differentiating employees in terms of skills, competency and performance. Since different employees perform at different levels of efficiency, therefore pay ranges provides for different rates of progressive rewards. The major advantage of graded pay structure is that it provides internal equity and communicates opportunities for career progression based on contributions. However, the major limitation is that it is very complex and creates pay rigidities.
2. **Broadbanding**: It is the compression of a hierarchy of pay grades into a small number of wide bands. Each of the bands spans the pay opportunities previously covered by several separate pay ranges. It is increasingly getting attention of compensation specialists for its flexibility

in formulating and implementing pay structures. Approaches to broadbanding vary given strategic, HR and reward strategies influence the design of pay structures which meets the needs of flexi-organizations of today.

3. **Job family modeling**: Job family is a group of jobs. Job family modeling is an approach for developing and defining pay structures and career maps. It involves the following steps:
   (*a*) Identifying groups in which the type of work is similar but where it is carried out at different levels;
   (*b*) Analyzing the essential nature of each of these groups or job families;
   (*c*) Establishing the levels of work carried out within each family;
   (*d*) Defining the differentiating factors between each level in the family in terms of role size;
   (*e*) Producing functional or generic role specifications.

The major advantage of this approach includes a systematic way of defining job roles and managing career growth, provides flexible reward programmes, and promotes higher performance through increased ownership of the employees.

3.10 Criteria for Determining Pay Structure

The criteria for fixation of pay structure are as follows:

1. **The Organization's Ability to Pay:** Organization decisions on job and pay structure are determined to a large extent by its ability to pay. Ability to pay is further influenced by various factors such as its financials (*e.g.* profitability), pay policies for different categories of employees and pressures from trade unions.

   Organizations made up largely of members of craft unions have pay structure almost completely determined by the union. Organizations whose members come largely from a well organized and competitive labour market but are not unionized have a market oriented pay structure. Organizations have only limited choice because jobs are easily identified and are quite uniform throughout the market. Organizations having many specialized jobs dealing in labour markets too disorganized to provide adequate grading and pricing and lacking unionization have primarily internally determined pay structure. Product markets may influence such pay structure if labour cost is high relative to total cost. Internally determined pay structure result from management decisions and may range from highly rational structures flowing from job evaluation to a system of personal rates. Technology provides some uniformity in job structures in organizations engaged in common lines of production. Unions through their insistence on traditional relationships establish some key jobs and job clusters and provide an upward thrust to the entire structure.

Key jobs acquire their status from labour markets, product markets and comparison with other organizations often fostered by unions. Job clusters come from technologies and employee skill groupings. Pay increases should be given by organizations which can afford them. Organizations that have good sales and therefore high profits tend to pay higher pay than those which are running at loss or earning low profits because of the high cost of production or low sales.

In short-run, the economic influence on the ability to pay is practically nil. All organizations irrespective of their profits or losses must pay no less than their competitors and need pay no more if they wish to attract and keep employees. In the long- run, the ability to pay is very important. During economic boom, organizations pay high pay to carry on profitable business operations and because of their increased ability to pay. During economic recession, pay is cut because funds are not available. Marginal firms and non-profit organizations pay relatively low pay because of low or no profits.

2. **Supply and Demand of Labour:** The labour market conditions or supply and demand forces operate at the national, regional and local levels and determine organizational pay structure. If the demand for certain skills is high and the supply is low the result is a rise in the price to be paid for these skills. When prolonged and acute, these labour market pressures probably force most organizations to reclassify hard to fill jobs at a higher level than that suggested by the job evaluation. The other alternative is to pay higher pay if the labour supply is scarce and lower pay when it is excessive. Similarly, if there is great demand for labour expertise, pay rise but if the demand for manpower skill is minimal the pay will be relatively low.

   Most organizations replace the external labour market with an internal labour market that makes decisions by administrative means rather than according to supply and demand. These organizations have restricted ports of entry, which are highly sensitive to the labour market but rely on the organization's internal labour supply to fill most job openings. The exception occurs when there is an internal and external shortage of people to fill vacancies for specific skills. In fact, any job for which qualified people are in short supply becomes a market sensitive job. Shortages in the labour market provide those who are qualified to fill the jobs an opportunity to negotiate better terms of employment. Another part of the negotiations is for a better job. Employees in jobs where there is a shortage of qualified employees will demand changes in job content that will increase the job's value to the organization and in the eyes of other employees.

3. **Prevailing Market Rate:** An organization's pay policies and structures are influenced by the rates payable by the industry and the community. This is done for several reasons:

(*a*) Competition demands that competitors adhere to the same pay level;

(*b*) Various government laws and judicial pronouncements make the adoption of uniform pay rates an attractive proposition;

(*c*) Trade unions encourage this practice so that their members can have equal pay, equal work and geographical differences may be eliminated;

(*d*) Functionally related firms in the same industry require essentially the same quality of employees, with the same skills and experience. This results in a considerable uniformity in pay rates; and

(*e*) If the same or about the same general rates of pay are not paid to the employees as are paid by the organization's competitors, it will not be able to attract and maintain a sufficient quantity and quality of manpower.

Some organizations pay on the higher side of the market in order to obtain goodwill or to ensure an adequate supply of labour, while other organizations have lower pay to offer because economically they have to or because by lowering hiring requirements they can keep jobs adequately manned.

4. **Cost of Living:** The cost of living pay criterion is usually regarded as an auto minimum equity pay criterion. This criterion calls for pay adjustments based on increases or decreases in an acceptable cost of living index. When the cost of living increases, employees and trade unions demand adjusted pay to offset the erosion of real pay. However, when living costs are stable or decline the management does not resort to this argument as a reason for pay reductions.

5. **Living Wage:** This criterion states that pay should be adequate to enable an employee to maintain himself and his family at a reasonable level of existence. However, employers do not generally favour using the concept of a living wage to guide pay determination because they prefer to base the pay of an employee on his contribution rather than on his need.

6. **Productivity:** Productivity is a ratio of out to input. It measures the contribution of all the resource factors such as men, machines, methods, materials and management. No productivity index can be devised which will measure only the productivity of a specific factor of production. Another problem is that productivity can be measured at several levels – job, plant, industry, or national, economic level. Thus, although theoretically it is a sound pay criterion, operationally many problems and complications arise because of definitional measurement and conceptual issues.

7. **Trade Union's Bargaining Power:** The stronger and more powerful the trade union, the higher will be the pay. A trade union's bargaining power is often measured in terms of its membership, its financial strength and nature of its leadership. Trade unions affect pay structure but the differential effects of craft and industrial unionism and the type of bargaining relationship are considerable. Craft unions tend to determine craft rates as well as the design

of craft jobs for all organizations employing members of the craft. Industrial unions may attempt to impose pay structure on organizations, even if the pay structure clashes with product-market realities.

Union strategy with respect to general increases can also affect pay structure. Flat increases in terms of specified amount maintain absolute differentials but compress the structure in relative terms whereas flat percentage increases maintain relative differentials and increase absolute differentials.

8. **Job Requirements:** Generally, the more difficult a job, the higher is the pay. Measures of job difficulty are frequently used when the relative value of one job to another in an organization is to be ascertained. Jobs are graded according to the relative skill, effort, responsibility, and job conditions required.
9. **Managerial Attitudes:** Top managers exercise decisive influence on the pay structures and therefore their desire to maintain or enhance the organization's prestige has been a major factor in the pay policy and structure of a number of organizations. Desires to improve or maintain morale, to attract high caliber employees, to reduce turnover, and to provide a high living standard for employees as possible also appear to be factors in management's pay policy decisions.
10. **Skill Levels Available in the Market:** With the rapid growth of industries, business, trade, there is a shortage of skilled resources. The technological development, automation has been affecting the skill levels at faster rates. Thus, the pay levels of skilled employees are constantly changing and an organization has to keep its pay level and pay structure to suit the market needs.

3.11 Developing Pay Structure

According to Armstrong and Murlis, process of developing pay structure involves the following steps:

1. An analysis of organization's vision, mission, values and core competence is the starting point. Mapping of employees in terms of various parameters such as age, qualification, experience, skills, competence, performance, etc. and reviewing reward policies and programmes of the organization provides understanding of the organizational needs and actual situation;
2. Since analysis and understanding requires professional expertise, therefore a decision whether an external management consultant will be engaged or it will be done internally is to be taken;
3. The cost, time and other support resource needs to be identified and estimation made for arriving at some consensus or agreement;

4. The stakeholders of pay structure development must be decided especially the employees. The nature and extent of employee's involvement in the process should be clearly determined and communicated to them;
5. After reviewing existing pay structure, a framework of what should be the pay structure should be established which meets organization's and employee's needs;
6. It is crucial to obtain pay rates from the market through pay surveys which will provide a kind of benchmark for setting the pay structure in the organization;
7. A final decision on the type of structure required and main design and operational features needs to be taken; and
8. A detailed design for the structure and how it will be managed and maintained should be documented.

3.12 Performance Based Pay

In a performance based pay (PBP) system, some portion of an employee's earnings is tied to specific behaviours or results which are considered desirable by the organization and in a true performance based pay employees are rewarded for meeting and exceeding performance expectations. The objective of performance pay is to develop a productive, efficient, effective organization that enhances employee motivation and performance. It include assumptions about how people are motivated, what makes them work harder and how they wish to be treated or viewed as well as how they view themselves. PBP systems have been shown to increase performance in both basic and applied research studies when compared to hourly wages. Some research has shown as much as 200% to 300% improvement in performance with incentive system (Frisch & Dickenson, 1990).

Performance based pay serves the following purposes:

1. Since individual wages and salary is tied with work unit and organizational performance, therefore employees are highly motivated to achieve organizational goals and objectives so that they get more monetary benefits. Thus, strategic attainment of organizational goals and objectives get facilitated;
2. Linking pay to performance helps in reinforcing desired behaviours and eliminating undesirable behaviours in employees. Thus, it serves as a control lever of employee behaviour;
3. It motivates enhanced performance at individual as well as team level because unless the organizational goals and objectives are effectively achieved, no one gets anything worthwhile; and
4. It helps in recognizing and rewarding employee contributions.

Performance based pay ties an employee's pay to their performance on the job. In performance based pay model the employees are expected to be performing well and are rewarded based on the outcome of their work. In this model the 'carrot' is in front of the employee and receives after the performance. Pay will vary with some measure of individual, team, or organizational performance. It is believed that performance based pay will attract and retain better employees and offer incentives to motivate and reward improved performance. This is because uniform employee pay schedules are ineffective in attracting and retaining sufficient numbers of effective employees and as out of touch with pay practices in other industries that tie salary to employee performance.

Performance based pay systems generally deliver rewards in the extrinsic form of money. If employees are not only interested in the pay they earn but also are motivated by other components of their job *e.g.* satisfaction from job completion or challenging work, then increasingly pay may either have a smaller positive, zero or even a negative effect on performance.

Three human needs co-exit simultaneously *viz.* supportive of work, good management and well-designed organizations are required for employees to have successful group or team experiences (for relatedness) and for continuous lifelong (for growth) as well as a feeling of accomplishment. Thus, performance based pay puts a great emphasis on the material needs of the employees and should not therefore ignore other needs like social relationships or learning.

Performance based pay can even decrease performance if it undercuts employee's intrinsic motivation. Rewards have been found to undermine intrinsic motivation if they are perceived to be controlling. If employees are intrinsically motivated, they will try to meet their obligations even when they cannot be contractually required to do so, and indeed even when their performance cannot be verified.

From the Fig. 3.2, we may conclude that pay being an extrinsic reward helps in motivating employees to perform better. However, it may be noted that the relationship between pay and performance is not absolute but relative to the needs motivation of the employees. If the employees has physiological and safety needs, his primarily focus shall be on pay and increase in pay will result in higher performance. That is the reason of junior level employees is primarily motivated to perform with higher value of reward. But as the individual satisfies his physiological and safety needs, his performance remains relatively stable with increases in pay. Increased financial rewards like pay is no more a strong motivator for him but given his large increases, he continues to perform at a performance bar (shown by straight line) which continues for some time till his social needs becomes stronger. The employee needs love, support and a sense of belonginess from the organizational members particularly his manager and peer group. If his love needs are met then his next need of esteem need appears. At this stage, if the employees recognition needs are not duly accompanied with increased pay, his motivation to perform even better vaporizes and his actual performance deteriorates gradually over time. It is crucial for the organization to provide various rewards like promotion, public appreciation, re-assignments, etc. to motivate the employee to perform better as pay has lost performance pulling effect. However, if the situation is not changed and his recognition or esteem needs remains unfulfilled, then his performance comes down sharply. This is an alarming stage for the organization. But, his final need of self-actualization appears on the scene. It may be worthwhile to mention that only a small number of employees actually experience self-actualization need. At this stage, the individual employee looks for reasons for which he was born and tends to get closer to the spirituality. He reviews his professional achievements, the rewards and recognition he has received and he has been able to successfully serve the purpose which he feels is his destiny. If this need is not fulfilled then the employee actually performs poorly and soon become a dead wood for the organization.

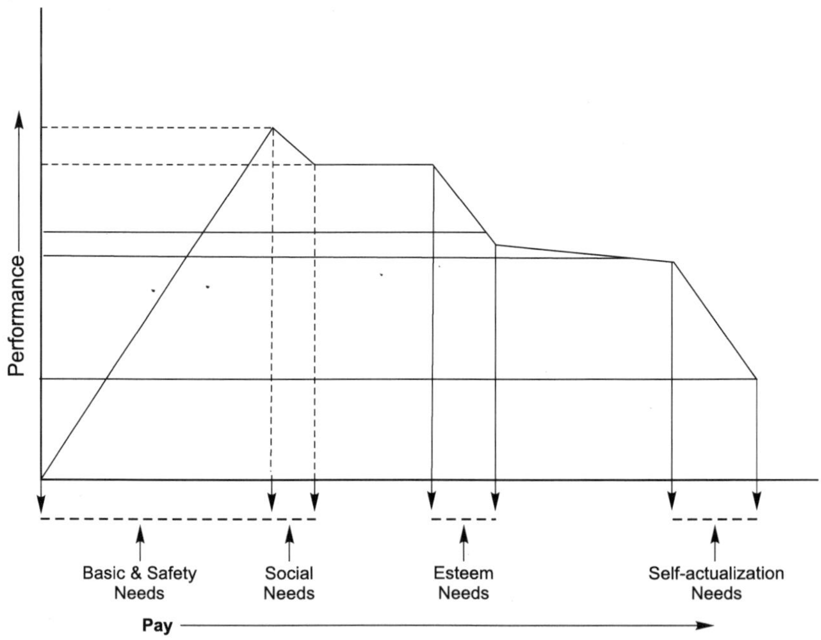

Fig. 3.2 Performance and Pay Matrix.

Hence, we may conclude that performance based pay has its own limitations but overall it can work well upto certain level and circumstances. It is pertinent to note that theoretically needs operate individually but in reality these needs operate severally thereby making implementation of performance based pay even more complex.

3.13 A Performance Linked Reward Policy

This may be called the "Performance Linked Reward Policy" of Swagata Seafood Ltd., New Delhi.

Objectives:

1. The policy shall apply to personnel of corporate office of the Company, except Grades M–1 and M–2.
2. Increment shall be granted based on performance and shall comprise of two components:
   (i) General Rise
   (ii) Performance Linked Incentive (to be called as Performance Reward)

Broadly Increments (general rise + incentive) to be granted shall be in the following range:

S.No.	Performance Ranking	Score	Increment Range	Remarks
1.	special Contribution	---	---	As per discretion of management
2.	Outstanding	91 & above	20%-25%	
3.	Very Good	71 to 90	15%-20	
4.	Good	51 TO 70	10%-15%	
5.	Improvement	41 to 50	5%-10%	Conditional sunject to review after 3 months
6.	Unsatisfactory	0 to 40	0%	

(i) General Rise Scheme

General rise shall be computed by the following formulae:

General Rise = % Increase in Gross Salary + Matrix Value × Performance Rating

(Gross Salary means and includes Basic Pay, all Allowances, Co. PF & Bonus)

Matrix Value shall be as under:

S.No.	Grade Classification	Matrix Value
1.	M – 3 to M – 4	Rs. 700.00
2.	M – 5 to M – 6	Rs. 500.00
3.	OS – 1 to OS – 2	Rs. 400.00
4.	OS – 3 to OS – 4	Rs. 300.00
5.	OS – 5 to OS – 6	Rs. 200.00
6.	W – 1 to W – 3	Rs. 50.00

Percentage Increase in Gross Salary shall be as under:

S.NO.	Performance Ranking Salary	% Increase in Gross	Matrix Value	Performance Factor
1.	Special Contribution	At the sole discretion of the management	—	—
2.	Outstanding	15% Value	Relevant	4
3.	Very Good	12% Value	Relevant	3
4.	Good	10% Value	Relevant	2
5.	Improvement Required	8%	Relevant Value	1
6.	Unsatisfactory	0%	Nil	0

For example, an employee Ms. Tandra Deb designated as Senior Manager (M–5) and drawing Rs. 50, 000 p.m. CTC having rated as Very Good performer shall get general rise = Rs. 50000 × 12% + Rs. 500 × 3 = Rs. 6000.00 + Rs. 1500 = Rs. 7500.00 (*i.e.* 15% rise w.r.t. Gross Salary)

(ii) Performance Linked Incentive Scheme

General Outlines

1. Incentive at the prescribed rate shall be payable to an employee whose annual revision is due based on performance for employees in levels of Asstt. Manager (M-6 grade) and above only.
2. Incentive cycle shall be from April to March *i.e.* financial year. Employees, whose increments / revisions fall due in between, shall be paid on prorata basis.
3. Amount of incentive once earned by an employee on one performance /incentive cycle come to 'zero' level on reaching next due date of increment / revision. In other words, incentive amount cannot be carried forward from one performance / incentive cycle to another. Employee has to earn incentive based on performance each year / performance cycle.
4. Incentive shall be paid on monthly basis through payroll under the pay head "Performance Reward" for all employees not within the purview of ESI scheme.
5. The incentive payment can be paid based on % system or value system as mentioned below underneath:

Grade Classification	Grade	% Of Gross Salary as Incentive
Managerial	M-6 to M-5	6%
Managerial	M-4 to M-3	5%

Thus, Ms. Tandra Deb's total increment shall be:

Total Increment = General Rise + Performance Reward

Rs. 7500.00 + 50,000 × 5% = Rs. 7500 + Rs. 2500 = Rs. 10,000/- (20% w.r.t. Gross Salary)

6. All taxes, as applicable, on performance linked incentive amount shall be borne by the concerned employee.
7. It may be noted that the grant of incentives is not a matter of right of employees. Management reserves all right to take appropriate decision in respect of release, withholding or stoppage of incentive payment as it may deem fit and proper after due consideration of performance and conduct of the employee.
8. The criteria for payment of incentive amount shall be defined at the beginning of each performance cycle. For example, consistent achievement of KRAs, very good overall performance, behaviour, etc.
9. For qualitative functions like HR, Administration, Accounts, etc., KRAs shall be set in the pattern of key performance areas.
10. It is important to differentiate between increment and Salary Re–fixation/ Restructuring. Therefore, whenever Salary Re–fixation/Restructuring is made it should be specifically mentioned in his/her revision letter that such and such amount is on account of Salary Re–fixation/Restructuring and such and such amount is on account of increment so that nobody expects that hefty raises shall take place in future also as a past trend.

3.14 Skills and Competency Based Pay

Skills and competency-based systems has gained increased prominence in recent years due to the following reasons such as to (i) raise the performance bar, (ii) help align individual behaviour with business strategies, (iii) provide a new employer-employee contract, (iv) change the measure of success from ladder based approaches, and (v) provide a spark for creating a culture of learning. Six strategies for a successful competency based programme are: (i) change from complex to simple, that is, keep the programme simple and understandable; (ii) obtain more data without drowning in the details; (iii) provide practical models for effective coaching of employees and managers; (iv) cut the length of review periods making reviews more frequent; (v) separate performance discussion from pay increases; and (vi) measure progress and make changes, that is, define a metric for a successful programme and use it.

Skills and competency based pay compensates employees on the basis of the job-related skills, competencies and knowledge they possess. Competencies refer to the set of knowledge, skills, abilities and behaviours that contribute to successful job performance. Competencies are not traditional performance standards and objectives, personality traits, work activities, diplomas and certificates. Competencies are observable and measurable. They are critical to success and drive organizational as well as individual performance. They are performance factors that contribute to success, behaviours that reflect motivation and attitude, and demonstrations of knowledge and skills. Behaviours are the observable actions one uses to achieve results. Thus, competency based pay reward individual employees; the reward is based on demonstrating their competency with relatively detailed information about performance standards. These standards both guide appraiser judgments and make known to the employee that they need to demonstrate their competency to receive pay.

The skill and competency based pay is based on the premise that pay should be linked to the knowledge, skills, abilities and behaviours in the job or acquisition or application of additional skills by the employees. The employees are expected to be motivated by their high skills as it results in higher pay. Paying for skills and competencies means that one pays for the person's skills more than for his performance. The pay is based on what the employee the employee is capable of doing, instead of what he performs.

Employees with high growth need strength will be more attracted to a skill and competency based compensation system than those with lower growth need strength. The characteristic of self-efficacy also appears relevant to individual's attraction to skills and competency based pay systems. Perceived self-efficacy is concerned with judgments of how well one can execute courses of action. Employees working under skill and competency based compensation systems are rewarded only for skills they are capable of using, and compensation raises follow new additions of skills. Skills and competency based pay places significance on continuous personal improvement and maintained proficiency. These environmental characteristics appear more suitable for individuals who have high belief in their abilities. This pay plans are generally thought to create more challenging work environment for individuals and those with a strong sense of efficacy exert greater effort to master challenges. Employees with low ability levels will be less satisfied with skill based pay than those with higher ability levels.

Finally, to successfully implement competency-based pay, a number of things have to be in place first: a budget to pay for the increase, an assessment tool that is perceived as fair, trained management and staff, a high level of trust in the evaluators, and patience for developing competencies over time.

3.15 Basic Concept of Incentive System

As financial concerns become increasingly important for organizations, consumers, and governments, managing employee performance is becoming more important than ever. Organizations can choose to rely on traditional management techniques by emphasizing managers to oversee and direct employee actions, or they can choose to supplement management with some form of product-based contingent reward to align employee interests more closely with that of the organization. Over time, an organization's success or failure may be determined by its ability to produce, manage and maintain improvements in performance. One way in which organizations are trying to boost employee productivity is implementing incentive systems.

Incentive is a tool of motivation and inducement offered to employees to perform work, or to work upto or beyond acceptable standards. Incentive system often consists of financial, psychological and social rewards. Examples of financial incentives are compensation increases, bonuses and other incentives that include monetary factors. Examples of psychological and social incentives are promotions, increased responsibility and recognition. These incentives have more to do with employee's self-esteem than with their monetary needs. Incentive system is usually built on financial rewards but may also include non-financial rewards. It acts as an inducement to employees for achieving higher productivity and profitability for the organization. Incentives also encourage the commitment of employees and reinforce existing cultures and values where these foster high levels of performance, innovation and teamwork. An efficient incentive system must provide for minimum guaranteed compensation based on time based system and extra remuneration for increased output. In other words, an incentive system contains the characteristics of time based and output based forms of compensation payment.

3.16 Definitions of Incentive System

A few noteworthy definitions of incentive are as follows:

1. *"An incentive is something that influences people to act in certain ways. An incentive system is a collection of incentives and a set of procedures for using them. Organizations use incentive systems to motivate their employees."*

   —Kemmerer & Thiagarajan

2. *"An incentive scheme is a plan or programmes to motivate individual for good performance. An incentive is most frequently built on monetary rewards, but may also include a variety of non monetary rewards or prizes."*

   —Burrack & Smith

3. *"An incentive is an important mechanism that encourages and motivates managers to achieve organizational objectives."*

   —Anthony and Govindarajan

3.17 Features of Incentive System

A good incentive system must possess the following features:

(*a*) The performers should track their performance daily. The payout can be monthly, but feedback should be available daily;

(*b*) Separate incentive pay system should be installed which is apart from regular pay;

(*c*) Consider non-cash incentives should be considered. These are not confused with ordinary pay and actually have advantages over cash;

(*d*) Individual incentives are more effective than group incentives. An incentive for group accomplishments can be added, but the plan should differentiate between individual contributions and accomplishments;

(*e*) It should be ensured that day-to-day management is positive. No matter how much money is put into rewards, there will be waste of both money and time if negative reinforcement is being used as management style. There's no substitute for daily contact with employees—asking how they're doing, asking if help with any problems is required and, most importantly, recognizing even small improvements; and

(*f*) Effectiveness of plan on performance, cost and employee satisfaction should be evaluated systematically.

3.18 Significance of Incentive System

The major significance of incentive system is as follows:

(*a*) Incentives tend to induce employees for better performance and higher productivity;

(*b*) It seeks to emphasize to the employees those goals or performance expectations which are critical for organizational success;

(*c*) It helps in supervision of those jobs were individual monitoring of work activities are difficult;

(*d*) It builds commitment of the employees to the organization due to financial rewards given to the employees;

(*e*) It facilitates improvement of quality of life of the employees due to enhanced earnings; and

(*f*) It promotes a culture of performance in the organization whereby collective performance bar is significantly raised.

3.19 Types of Incentive System

Incentives may be classified into three broad categories as follows:

I. Individual Incentive Plans

Under this plan, earnings are directly related to the performance of the individual employee. Individual incentives may be based on time or output.

In time-based plans, a standard time is determined and incentive is paid if an employee completes the job in less than standard time. In output-based plans, a standard of output is determined and an employee producing more than standard output is given incentive. Output linked incentives are of the following types:

(i) Earnings varying in proportion to output.

(ii) Earnings varying proportionately less than output.

(iii) Earnings varying proportionately more than output.

(iv) Earnings varying differently at different levels of output.

Various types of individual incentive plans are given below:

1. **Halsey Premium Plan:** Under this plan, the average time required for every activity is calculated on the basis of average efficiency of average worker, known as standard time. Workers completing their work within standard time are paid incentive at a standard rate. The workers completing their works in less than standard time are paid the incentive according to the standard rate and bonus on the basis of time saved by them. The rate of bonus may be 33.33% or 50%.

   For example, an employer shares with the employee 50% of the wages saved on account of time saved by the worker, Earning is calculated as under:

   Earnings = Hours worked × Rate per hour + (50% of time saved × rate per hour)

   Here time saved = standard time – time worked

   In Halsey-Weir Premium Plan, the employer shares with the employee 33.33% of the wages saved on account of time saved y the worker, Earning is calculated as under:

   Earnings = Hours worked × Rate per hour + (33.33% of time saved × rate per hour)

   Here time saved = standard time – time worked

2. **Rowan Premium Plan:** Under this plan, workers are paid over and above the wages for the hours they put in, an extra payment for hours worked in proportion to time saved and standard time. Standard time is determined in the same manner as in Halsey Plan.

   Earnings = Hours worked × Rate per hour + (Time saved/Standard time × Hours worked × Rate per hour)

3. **Taylor Differential Piece Rate System:** Under this plan, standard time for every work is determined on the basis of time and motion study. Two rates of payment are determined – high rate and low rate. Workers completing their work within or before standard time are paid according to the high rate and workers completing work in more than standard time are paid at low rate.

Here the inefficient worker is penalized and the efficient worker is rewarded. For example,

Considering that if the output is below standard, the worker shall be paid 80% of the rate per piece. If the output is above standard, the worker shall be paid 120% of the rate per piece.

Standard rate per piece is Rs. 5 (say)

Standard output is 80 units in a day.

Output of A = 75 units and Output of B = 90 units

Earnings of A = 75 units × 80% of Rs. 5 = Rs. 75 × 4 = Rs. 300

Earnings of B = 90 units × 120% of Rs. 5 = 90 × 6 = Rs. 540

4. **Gantt Task Bonus Plan:** This is a combination of time rate and piece rate methods. Under this plan, minimum payment to be given to the workers is determined. Workers completing work within or before standard time are paid a Bonus (20%, 25% or 33.33%). Considering Bonus @20%, earnings are:

Output	Payment
Below Standard	Guaranteed time rate
At Standard	120% of time rate
Above Standard	120% of time rate

5. **Emerson Efficiency Plan:** Under this plan, standard time for the job is determined scientifically and a minimum time wage is guaranteed to all the workers. The efficiency of the worker is determined in the ration of actual time taken by the worker with the standard time of the work. Emerson believed that generally worker produces only 67% of the standard output; therefore Bonus is paid at an increasing percentage beyond the prescribed level of efficiency *i.e.* 67%.

   Earnings = Time taken × Rate per hour + % of Bonus × Time taken × Rate per hour

6. **Merrick Differential Piece Rate System:** Under this plan, three rate of payment are determined as mentioned below:

Efficiency	Payment
Upto 83.33%	Ordinary piece rate
83.33% to 100%	110% of ordinary piece rate
Above 100%	130% of ordinary piece rate

7. **Bedeaux Point Premium:** Under this plan, standard time for every work is detrmined scientifically. Standard performance is expressed in terms of points. Every point is equal to standard rate per minute. Minimum time rate is guaranteed to all the workers. Workers completing work within or before standard time are paid Bonus @ 25%.

   Earnings = Standard time × Rate per hour + 75% of Rate per hour (standard time – actual time taken)

II. Team Incentive Plans

Under this plan, earnings of a team (group) are directly related to the performance of the team as a whole. Such incentives are often deferred through stock-option arrangements, pension top-up or other long-term pay out contract. Several types of teams variously named: Parallel, Process, Project, Hybrid, and Virtual.

Creating incentive plans within a team environment has several key benefits. Making goals contingent on the efforts of a team discourages "free riders" and capitalizes on the cohesion and perceived pressure from a group.

There are several factors that catalyze success in implementing a team incentive plan. First, incentive plan should be worthwhile and team members are to be empowered to meet attainable goals. Evaluation and rewards must consider the difficulty of the assignment and the probability of failure. People will not take risks if they are penalized for taking on difficult assignments.

It is also important to reward early and often, linking rewards to different phases of projects. This reinforces short-term accomplishments without losing sight of long-term goals. The hierarchies that create status and power differentials should be reduced.

Lastly, organizations should consider rewarding teams through lump sum payments for landmark accomplishments. However, it important to recognize individual excellence by identifying and rewarding key contributors through group nomination, using cross functional groups for the evaluation of nominees.

Effective team incentives plans should be based on evidence of:

(*a*) Team meeting target achievements.

(*b*) Team meeting and exceeding customer (internal and external) expectations.

(*c*) The individual employee improves the team.

(*d*) The team enhances the individual contribution.

(*e*) The team and the individual demand a lot of themselves.

Various types of team incentive plans are given below:

1. **Gainsharing:** Gainsharing is a philosophy of incorporating employee participation, recognition, problem identification, and accountability while improving personal and organizational performance. It is a group incentive bonus plan that requires employee involvement in determining how to improve the performance of the group or organization by better utilizing resources. Any gains in productivity and/or cost reductions during a given time period are shared between the organization and the workers.

An effective gainsharing formula must meet the following criteria:

(*a*) It must be fair to the organization by being a true measure of performance over time and working towards achieving the strategic objectives of the organization;

(*b*) It must benefit the organization when gains are made and protect the organization during a down period;

(*c*) It must be fair to the employees and they should be able to make a difference by modifying their behaviour;

(*d*) The employees must be able to understand how the formula works and how their behaviours will affect the outcome of the gains;

(*e*) The calculations must be easily made and based on information that is available on a timely basis;

(*d*) It must be flexible to accommodate changes in organization goals, objectives, and priorities; and

(*e*) It should help direct the attention of the employees to problem areas.

While implementing a gainsharing programme, following critical success factors need to be considered:

(*a*) It must be part of the overall goals and objectives of the organization and not implemented because "everybody else is doing it";

(*b*) It should be custom tailored to support the overall objectives of the organization and to ensure that the measurement system is designed to create alignment in achieving the desired culture;

(*c*) In order to create a customized plan the organization must under stand their culture, business strategy, and desired behaviours;

(*d*) It must ensure that employees are involved into system. This includes having the employees involved in defining the plan and also having a formal involvement system once the plan has been imple mented; and

(*e*) Defining the team and relating the reward to the appropriate level of team. In order to form teams successfully they must receive proper training, share a vision and common values, a sense of faith in the employees must be present by management, and the culture needs to be supportive of risk taking and the failures that may coincide with it.

2. **Scanlon Plan:** Under this plan, all employees are encouraged to give their suggestions on cost saving and improving work methods. A committee consisting of representatives of workers and management screens suggestions received. If the suggestions are implemented resulting into cost saving, all employees are paid on the basis of cost saved. The incentive is linked to cost saving emerging out of a suggestion scheme.

   A typical Scanlon plan will measure labour costs as a percentage of the sales value of production. However, other organizations have made modifications to the measurements in the typical Scanlon plan. Some organizations will also include the cost of tools and materials. Any gains that are seen are split between the employees and the organization at some agreed upon percentage. A percentage of the employees share is set-aside in a reserve fund to cover months where actual costs exceeded expected costs. Any money left over in the reserve fund at the end of the year is paid out to the employees. Bonuses of 10% to 15% are not uncommon and it is recommended that all employees, including managers, take part in the same bonus plan.

Even though there are various types of Scanlon plans, all are based on a participative management philosophy, worker involvement, and a group reward system. The basic principles of the Scanlon plan are closely linked to the management philosophy of Douglas McGregor's Theory Y, which are:

(*a*) The expenditure of physical and mental effort in work is as natural as play or rest;

(*b*) External control and the threat of punishment are not the only means for bringing about effort toward organizational objectives. People will exercise self-direction and self-control in the service of objectives to which they are committed;

(*c*) Commitment to objectives is a function of the rewards, tangible and intangible, associated with their achievement;

(*d*) The average human being learns under proper conditions, not only to accept responsibility but also to seek it; and

(*e*) The capacity to exercise a relatively high degree of imagination, ingenuity, and creativity in the solution of organizational problems is widely, not narrowly, distributed in a population.

3. **Employee Stock Option Plan**: Employee stock option plan has entered in India in 1990s and is becoming popular especially for managerial personnel. Under this plan, employees are allotted the shares of the company below the market price in such way that they enjoy long-term benefits, either due to appreciation in share prices or options are convertible at different time periods ranging between one to five years.

Broadly employee stock option plans are of the following types:

(*a*) A *"Phantom Stock Plan"* is a long-term incentive plan and acts like a stock option arrangement in an organization where dilution of share value is a concern. An accounting formula is developed to create value for a share.

(*b*) Targets are developed which support the enhancement of the value of the organization to the ultimate business stakeholders.

(*c*) A *"Golden Hand-Cuff Plans"* is also long-term incentive plans designed to keep specific employees, with key talents, close to the organization for the future. These plans are made up of cash, ownership, incentives and tax and benefit perquisites. These same plans can also play a role in developing a "poison pill" to resist unwanted attempts to merge with or sell ownership to a third-party organization.

(*d*) In *Stock Appreciation Rights*, an employee is entitled to receive cash payment based on the increase in the value of the stock from the time of the award until a specified future date.

(*e*) In *Performance Shares*, an employee is awarded a specified number of shares when long-term objectives of the organization have been met. Usually the goal is to achieve a specified increase in the earning per share over a period of 3 to 5 years. The main advantage of this type of incentive is that the award is based on performance measures that can be at least partially controlled by the employee concerned. The major limitation is that the bonus is based on performance measured by accounting measures which may not always bring out the true economic worth of the organization.

(*f*) In *Performance Unit*, a cash bonus is paid on achieving specific long term targets. This plan is a combination of stock appreciation rights and performance shares. This type of incentive plans is used by oranizations which are either no listed on stock exchanges or if the listed trading is very thin. The success of this type of plan is depends largely on how well the long-term targets have been established.

4. **Goal Sharing Plan**: Goal Sharing rewards employees for meeting specific goals. These goals are not necessarily based on the bottom line and may include quality, service and job performance. Goal Sharing is developed at a team level.

According to *Ross and Ross* (1991), the following factors are necessary for success of gain sharing programmes:

(*a*) Management commitment;

(*b*) Strong need to change or a strong commitment to continuous improvement;

(*c*) Management acceptance and encouragement of employee input;

(*d*) High levels of cooperation and interaction;

(*e*) Employment security;

(*f*) Information sharing on productivity and costs;

(*g*) Goal setting;

(*h*) Commitment of all involved parties to the process of change and improvement; and

(*i*) Agreement on a performance standard and calculation that is understandable, seen as fair, and closely related to managerial objectives.

5. **Collective Wage Bonus System:** Under this plan, rather than paying bonus or incentive wage to any individual employee, all employees are paid an agreed upon bonus irrespective of differences in individual efficiency or output. The standard or measure of efficiency is determined and bonus at the agreed rate is granted once the results are over the standard performance.

This plan is suitable where it is costly or difficult to measure the output of employees. This plan results in increased harmony among employees but it does not distinguish an efficient employee from an inefficient employee which results in demoralization of competent employees. Generally, collective wage bonus system takes place in unionized organizations.

III. Organization Wide Incentive Plans

Under this method, performance of the whole organization is used as the basis for calculating earnings of employees.

Various types of organization wide incentive plans are given below:

1. **Bonus:** Bonus is the most controversial method of payment to employees by the organizations because it has been treated as incentive by some, rights of employees by others and deferred wage by still some more.

   In India, Government of India set up Bonus Commission in 1961. Based on the recommendation of the Bonus Commission, government enacted The Payment of Bonus Act, 1965.

   Main features of the act are:

   Applicable to all employees drawing wages (Basic + DA) upto and including 10,000.00 per month.

   Minimum Bonus @ 8.33% of wages (maximum 20%) is payable to all eligible employees.

   However, its payment being compulsory doesn't work as an incentive.

2. **Profit Sharing:** Profit sharing is an arrangement whereby a certain percentage of the profits are distributed at fixed intervals usually annually or semi-annually in some definite ratio to all employees who have been the employees of the organization for a stated period.

   Under this scheme, employers agree to pay a certain part of the profits of their organization to their employees over and above the wages and salaries. Traditionally profits have been considered to be an exclusive right of the employers. With the change of time, this concept has changed as now the employees are regarded as the partners of the industry and accordingly the profits must be shared with the employees to keep them motivated.

   There are three types of profit sharing:

   (*a*) *Current or cash profit sharing system:* It involves payment of profits directly to the employees in cash, cheque or stock just after determination of profits;

   (*b*) *Deferred profit sharing system:* Profits are credited to accounts of employees to be paid at retirement or other stated situations like disability; and

   (*c*) *Combination profit sharing system:* Part of the profit is paid out currently in cash and other part of it is deferred.

Profit sharing system forms part of progressive HR policies embodying incentive characteristics and providing results not obtained from other systems. Effective profit sharing increases profits, enhances efficiency and creates a climate for improved employee relations. The effectiveness of this plan is highly dependent on desire of the employees involved and the commitment of the top management.

Profit-sharing had lost its motivational power for two reasons. First, employees will not be motivated today for a payment that may be months away. Second, there is no connection between effort and reward making it difficult for an employee to see how their performance can affect the overall profit of an organization.

3. **Co-Partnership**: Co-partnership implies both profit sharing and control sharing. Under this plan, employees are allotted shares of the organization either on cash payment basis or in lieu of various incentives payable and they become shareholders of the organization. They participate in capital, profits and control of the organization.

   However, in free economy, co-partnership has very limited influence.

4. **Cafeteria Plan**: Cafeteria Plan is a system under which each employee has some choice as to the form and timing of all or a portion of his total compensation. It is like 'choose your own reward plan'. Each human being is unique in his own ways and hence the motivational value of different incentives plans has varying degrees of relevance/influence on each employee. Under this plan, employees can choose the most suitable plan being available from a pool of such plans, which may go upto 1800 individual compensation plans.

   However, such large number of plans can cause confusion and difficulty in administration.

Incentive plans are complex processes and therefore incentive plans should be self-funding. Stakeholder interest dictates that incentive pool generation needs to be aligned to corporate performance in the context of how the competition is doing. A 30% profit growth is of limited value if the key competitor is generating 50% profit growth.

Incentive focus should for gaining higher stakeholder value. It is noted that the lower the salary for an individual the less stock options support corporate performance. Best practice seems to indicate it is smart to recognize a team or unit as a mini-business within the organization and link team portions of incentive to performance changes at the team or unit levels. Typical changes that need to be tracked are:

- Changes to operating cash flow for the unit or team.
- Changes in time to market.
- Changes in employee turnover.
- Changes in customer retention.

3.20 Limitations of Incentive System

The introduction and implementation of incentive systems have not been without controversy. While there appears to be consensus over the use of incentive packages to align employees and manager's interest with owners, there is disagreement on:

(*a*) **The size of the compensation packages:** Often employers and employees have differing views on the size of compensation which leads to difficulty in implementing incentive schemes.

(*b*) **Particular elements of the packages:** Employers propose a number and type of elements for the purpose of incentive wage payment whereas employees want different number and another type of elements.

(*c*) **The performance standards on which they are based:** Incentives are tied to individual, team and organizational performance. Hence, many times controversies do arise on account of manner or rationale of the standards of performance determined or established on which incentives have been based.

(*d*) **The process of determining reward especially for the top most executives of organizations:** Trade unions and governance consultants critically examine the incentive plans of the executive particularly that of CEOs. Moreover, often the gap between incentive amount of employees and top executive are much wider which causes heartburns and frustrations in the employees.

3.21 Compensation Ratios

Compensation constitutes 30% to 40% of the operating cost of an organization. Since cost of compensation is a significant part of overall operation cost, therefore it is prudent for the organizations to benchmark their compensation to different parameters to analyze whether it is on lower, average or higher side. Compensation ratio is obtained by dividing total compensation in a given period by the variable under study (*e.g.* sales turnover or profit). It also provides crucial information on internal equity and external equity as well. Compensation ratio can be calculated on the following variables:

(*a*) **Based on sales turnover:** Total compensation cost of all employees for a given period are computed and divided by the sales turnover for that period. Generally, it is believed that the ratio upto 5% is average, ratio ranging from 5% to 10% is high while ratio in excess of 10% is abnormal. Higher compensation ratio indicates that cost of compensation is higher and organizations intending to compete on cost leadership will have difficulties in the marketplace since product cost will be raised.

(*b*) **Based on profit:** Total compensation cost of all employees for a given period are computed and divided by the profit for that period. This indicates the profit left for undertaking future expansion or growth plans. A higher ratio will mean lower cash reserve for expansion or growth plans of the organization and vice versa.

(*c*) **Based on gender**: Compensation of all male employees is divided by total compensation cost for a given period and ratio is computed. Again, compensation of all female employees is divided by total compensation cost for a given period and ratio is computed. A comparison of these two ratios indicates whether the organization is an equal opportunity employer for both the gender or biased towards female employees. Generally, compensation ratio of male employees are favourable as there is a wide spread social and economic bias against women employees. Such women employees are often paid less than their male counterparts for doing same or similar nature of work. In India, government has taken a legislative measure via The Equal Remuneration Act, 1976 for preventing biases against female employees in matters of compensation.

(*d*) **Based on hierarchy**: Compensation of all managerial employees is divided by total compensation cost for a given period and ratio is computed. Again, Compensation of all workers is divided by total compensation cost for a given period and ratio is computed. A comparison of these two ratios indicates whether managerial personnel are paid abnormal sums or not. Usually compensation of CEOs and workers are compared and the ratio ranges from 130 to 150. In India, Boothlingam and Sachar Committee were constituted to look into this kind of ratios. While Boothlingam committee suggested for a capping for CEO compensation but Sachar committee suggested that government should keep out of any ceiling or prescription on CEO compensation. However, section 129 of the companies act, 1965 provides for an upper ceiling of CEO compensation @ 11% of gross profits of the company.

(*e*) **Based on location**: Many multinational enterprises compares the compensation ratios of their different units across the world to analyze which country or region is cost effective in terms of compensation. It helps them to concentrate cost leadership based products to the country or region with lowest ratio. Generally, total compensation of each location is divided by the sales turnover (or profit) to arrive at the ratio.

(*f*) **Based on job rate**: Total compensation paid to an employee is divided by the amount that would be paid to a fully competent performer in the job. This ratio is expressed as a percentage. A detailed discussion appears in next section.

(*g*) **Based on market rate**: Compensation ratio of an organization is calculated and compared with compensation ratios of other competitors to analyze whether organization's pay policy follows a lead, match or lag approach.

(*h*) **Based on nature of employment**: Generally workers are both directly and indirectly (through an agency or contractor) are engaged for performing various work activities in the organization. The total compensation of direct workers is divided by total compensation and this process is repeated for indirect workers. These two ratios are compared for further strategizing the methods of payment.

Hence, we may conclude that compensation ratios help in benchmarking compensation for attaining higher individual productivity and organizational performance.

3.22 Compa Ratio

A compa ratio (or comparison ratio) provides an organization with a benchmark to determine how close actual pay rates compare to the organization's defined midpoint (or job rate) of a pay range. It is the average of employee's actual compensation paid divided by the midpoint. Mathematically it is as under:

Compa Ratio = (Actual compensation / Midpoint) × 100%

The compa ratio gives a measure of how an employee is paid relative to a competent performer in a given job. If the compa ratio is 100% then it means that the employee is being paid in line with a competent performer. If the compa ratio is greater than 100% then the employee is being paid more than what a competent performer in the job would normally get. If the compa ratio is less than 100% then the employee is being paid lower than the competent performer. This implies that in the first case, the employee is competent performer, in the second case an outstanding performer and in the third case an average performer. This analysis can be used to align an employee's pay with his performance and therefore is a valuable tool for implementing performance based pay programmes in the organization.

A commonly accepted range for compa ratio is 80% to 120%, which in turn can be divided into five zones as follows:

Compa Ratio	Definition
80% – 87%	New, inexperienced or below average performing employees
88% – 95%	Employees gaining experience but not yet fully competent on the job.
96% – 103%	Employee is fully competent performer as is performing on the job as per performance expectations
104% – 111%	Employee performing the job at a higher level than performance expectations
112% – 120%	Employees who are recognized as outstanding performers.

Compa ratios are a valuable tool for obtaining a benchmark on employee compensation against pre-determined standards. However, while using compa ratios lock-step with pay raises may hinder an organization's flexibility, the figure can be helpful in ensuring that top performers receive the compensation commensurate with their contributions.

Let us consider an example to under the concept of compa ratio. In a pharmaceutical manufacturing organization, there are five production executives viz. A, B, C, D, and E whose market rate varies from Rs. 20,000/- per month to Rs. 24,000/- per month, with a midpoint of those two at Rs. 24,000. if executive A, B, C, D, and E draws Rs. 21,000/-, Rs. 23,000/-, Rs. 24, 000/-, Rs. 26,000/- and Rs. 28,000/- per month, the compa ratio would be as under:

Production Executive A = (Rs. 21,000 / Rs. 24,000) × 100% = 87.5%

Production Executive B = (Rs. 23,000 / Rs. 24,000) × 100% = 95.8%

Production Executive C = (Rs. 24,000 / Rs. 24,000) × 100% = 100%

Production Executive D = (Rs. 26,000 / Rs. 24,000) × 100% = 108.3%

Production Executive E = (Rs. 28,000 / Rs. 24,000) × 100% = 116.7%

From the above we may conclude that Production Executive A and Production Executive B are just average performers, Production Executive C is a competent performer and Production Executive D and Production Executive E are outstanding performers. In other words, A and B are below performance bar, C at performance bar and D and E are above performance bar.

Hence, we may conclude that compa ratio helps management in setting pay for performance programmes, analyze performance levels of the employees and initiate measures to review internal and external equity in compensation.

3.23 Ethics in Performance and Reward Management

Ethics in business is difficult to define and to handle; irrespective of the name attributed to it—business ethics, corporate social responsibility, corporate citizenship, sustainability, or good corporate governance. Nevertheless, no organization can afford to neglect the ethical level and the impact of values on their business and their employees. Ethics issues emerge in an organization both externally and internally *e.g.* in regard to organizational culture, business principles, communication, leadership, performance or reward. Thus, it can be said that ethics are prevalent in every organization, and that the business can only profit from them if they are aligned through formal measures to form coherent organizational ethics. Many organizations have understood the need to actively establish ethics management systems but very few actually adhere to it. One of the current major problems of ethics in organizational context remains the linkage between performance and reward.

Performance and reward management are foundations of human behaviour and conduct. Performance and reward are the two sides of the same coin. This is because performance determines the level, value and nature of reward to be given. Performance refers to behaviour that drives result and reward means those things which motivate an employee to continue with excellence or to improve performance. In other words, performance is the cause and reward is the effect (see figure 3.3). Individual performance is responsible to a large extent behind the success of an organization. Performing employees pave the way for organization's competitive advantage that is both sustainable and sustained over a longer period of time.

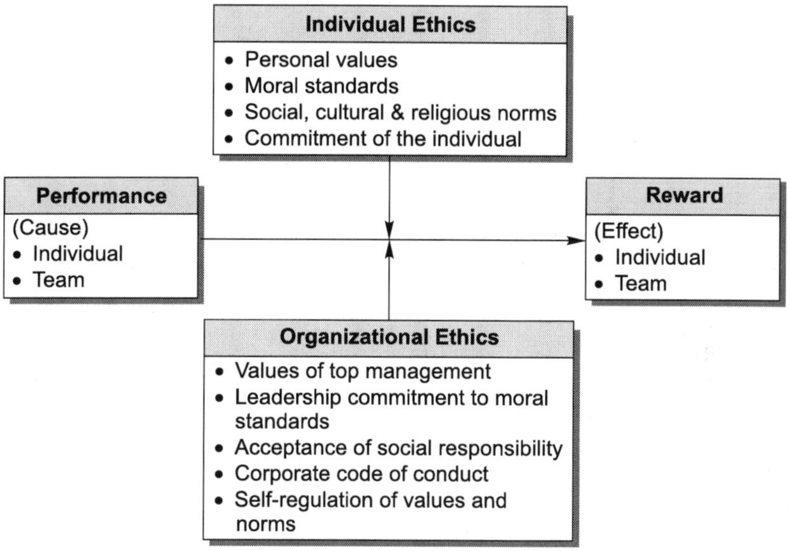

Fig. 3.3 Performance, Reward & Ethics

Since performance originates from behaviour which propels results and results are induced through rewards, therefore human integrity and moral values assumes paramount importance. This is because an individual's behaviour is driven by his attitude, beliefs and values which influences his conduct and ultimately results. Since rewards are intricately linked to performance, therefore individuals are often tempted to manipulate or act in a manner which is unethical in order to seek rewards. The cravings could be for financial rewards or non-financial rewards or both depending on the circumstances and need level of the individual. It may be noted that unethical behaviour for seeking rewards are not just limited to typical employees or managers but even to CEOs. The recent fiasco of Satyam Computer Services is a pointer to the case. On 07th January 2009 Mr. Ramalinga Raju, the Chairman of Satyam Computer Services admitted to have committed financial misrepresentation and fraud to the tune of Rs. 7,800 crores. This is India's biggest corporate fraud. While Mr. Raju resigned as Chairman followed by CFO on the next day leaving its 53,000 employees in the lurch. Satyam has so far been known for its excellent business performance, people policies and won many awards and accolades. This only reiterates the ethical problem associated with performance–reward linkages. Satyam is not the only case, there are many such reported cases all over the world. Thus, this case again implies that ethics needs to be inbuilt component of performance and reward management systems when a Chairman can commit such frauds.

Ethical behaviour cannot be just ensured by pronouncing code of conduct for the employees and management or by stating ethics policy of the organization. Ethical performance and reward management emanates from leadership (top management) and it percolates down to the lowest level employee. Organization's leadership must be truly committed to ethical values and institutionalize systems to ensure their, managers, employees and shareholders ethical thinking and conduct. With a leadership that is truly committed to ethics, employees will only behave and deal with internal and external customers in ethical ways and manner. Performance and reward management policies, systems and processes must clearly communicate to the managers and employees that ethical performance will only lead to ethical rewards. Performance planning, monitoring, appraisal and development must ensure that performance expectations set are ethical both in terms of their intent and achievement options and reward systems should be able to clearly differentiate ethical performance from unethical performance. The traditional mindset which is more focused on financial or quantitative figures should be prevented against. Otherwise individual and corporate misrepresentations, misreporting and frauds would continue to waste crores of rupees of the investors and spell doom on the economy.

The Satyam fiasco has only telling impact on the employees only who will have to bear the brunt. But a few of the employees were hand in glove with the Chairman otherwise a fraud of this magnitude could have not been ever committed. This implies that employees and managers must stay vigilant to not only their but organization's unethical behaviour and conduct. Whether there is a whistle blowing policy laid down or not, employees must always stand against unethical corporate behaviours. It is when employees view themselves more as stakeholders and less as job holders, will they be able to stay vigilant and uphold ethics in individual and corporate performance and reward management.

CHAPTER REVIEW

- Compensation system involves decisions system on business strategy (Cost leadership strategy, differentiation or focus strategy, expansion or growth strategy, and downsizing or shrinking strategy), compensation level (lag, lead or match pay with competitors), compensation differential (tenure based or performance based strategy), compensation structure (traditional or broadbanding strategy), and compensation administration (pay for position, person and performance strategy).
- Components of compensation include both fixed pay (base pay, competence pay, performance pay, fringe benefits, etc.) and variable pay Incentives, ESOPs, etc.).

- Internal equity means pay according to relative value of their jobs within same organization while External equity means comparison of pay for work performed by employees of similar jobs in other organization.
- Pay structure is the hierarchy of pay rates or levels among jobs in an organization.
- Pay structure essentially follows either one of two philosophies, outcome-based or behaviour-based. In an outcome based pay structure, pay differentials to be paid to individuals within each job class are driven by the performance of the individual. In behaviour based pay structures, pay differentials are based upon behavioural traits of the employee such as initiative, analytical thinking, attitude, perseverance, loyalty, commitment, motivation, team spirit and so on and so forth.
- There are three types of pay structures viz. (i) A graded pay structure consists of sequence of job grades to each of which is attached a pay range, (ii) Broadbanding is the compression of a hierarchy of pay grades into a small number of wide bands, and (iii) Job family is a group of jobs. Job family modeling is an approach for developing and defining pay structures and career maps.
- Performance based pay (PBP) involves some portion of an employee's earnings is tied to specific behaviours or results which are considered desirable by the organization.
- Skills and competency based pay compensates employees on the basis of the job-related skills, competencies and knowledge they possess.
- An incentive is a financial inducement given to employees for improving performance so as to effectively achieve goals and objectives of the organization.
- In Halsey Premium Plan, incentive is calculated by Earnings = Hours worked × Rate per hour + (50% of time saved × rate per hour).
- In Rowan Premium Plan, Earnings = Hours worked × Rate per hour + (Time saved/Standard time × Hours worked × Rate per hour).
- In Taylor Differential Piece Rate System, that if the output is below standard, the worker shall be paid 80% of the rate per piece. If the output is above standard, the worker shall be paid 120% of the rate per piece.
- In Gantt Task Bonus System, payment to be given to the workers is determined. By completion of work within or before standard time with a Bonus (20%, 25%or 33.33%).
- In Emerson Efficiency Plan, Earnings = Time taken × Rate per hour + % of Bonus × Time taken × Rate per hour.
- In Merrick Differential Piece Rate System, Upto 83.33% for ordinary piece rate, 83.33% to 100% for 110% of ordinary piece rate and above for 100%, 130% of ordinary piece rate.

- In Bedeaux Point Premium, Earnings = Standard time × Rate per hour + 75% of Rate per hour (standard time – actual time taken).
- In Gainsharing, half of the savings in labour cost as a result of output in excess of the standard is distributed among workers and bonus is paid half yearly.
- In Scanlon Plan, the incentive of an employee is linked to cost saving emerging out of a suggestion scheme.
- In Stock Option, employees are given various stock schemes for inducing future performance and retaining key persons.
- A compa ratio (or comparison ratio) provides an organization with a benchmark to determine how close actual pat rates compare to the organization's defined midpoint (or job rate) of a pay range.

A. Conceptual Review Questions

1. Discuss compensation system with appropriate illustration.
2. Enlist the strategic implications of compensation system.
3. Explain the components of compensation.
4. Define and explain pay structure. What are the approaches to pay structures?
5. What do you understand by internal and external equity in compensation? Give few examples.
6. What is incentive? Enlist its features and significance.
7. Explain the different types of incentive systems in operation in industrial organizations.
8. Elucidate the significance of ethics in performance and reward management.
9. Write short notes on:

   (*a*) Performance based pay

   (*b*) Competency based pay

   (*c*) Compensation ratio

   (*d*) Pitfalls of incentive system

B. Analytical Questions

1. Does organizational strategy influence pay structures?
2. "Incentive system is an attempt of the management to overcome inadequate supervision and guidance by managers". Do you agree?
3. "Incentives instigate greed in people rather than performance". Criti cally evaluate the statement.

CASE INCIDENT

The Competent HR Consultancy Services, Bangalore

P.N. Chakravarty and Ajit Deb founded The Competent HR Consultancy Services two years ago in Bangalore to provide three types of HR services to organizations in Bangalore region.

Their first and most profitable market is small businesses. Instead of hiring a full-time person to develop job descriptions, job specifications, performance appraisal forms, compensation plans, structures and systems, etc., it is more cost effective for many small firms to contract with The Competent HR Consultancy Services to do so.

The second service is the provision of payroll outsourcing for participating firms for a reasonable fee.

The third service involves extensive management consulting activities including outplacement, executive recruitment, training and development, and coaching/counseling services.

Chakravarty and Deb are quite informal in their own management style. Chakravarty is a trained psychologist and wants to have a solid working team. Deb, although telling everyone outwardly that this is what he wants, is from another school of thought. He doesn't like or trust Hindi speaking people and believes in hierarchical management. He expects employees to be creative in their work groups but to 'do as they are told or else!' The implication is that if employees do not have their noses to the grindstone – or they disagree with his approach they should pack up their belongings and go.

Chakravarty and Deb occupy the positions of Vice President and President respectively. The company comprises of around 30 employees and several temporary contractors. The programme managers are all male. The newest hires have been females in both professional and secretarial positions who are paid well below the prevailing compensation rates.

Chakravarty and Deb hold Friday-afternoon staff meetings every week that includes booze, dirty jokes and racist comments against of Hindi origin. Some of the female in this relatively new and growing firm have indicated to Chakravarty that they feel rather uncomfortable in the staff meetings and would prefer not to attend. Deb has made it clear that attendance is mandatory.

The manager incharge of outsourced payroll processing is a former maintenance foreman who has little background or experience in the field. His performance in securing new clients is poor and he does not appear to have an appreciation for professional confidentiality.

There are interpersonal problems between the various work groups and the firm is rife with remours. The employees are becoming increasingly concerned about the future success and sustenance of the firm in Bangalore area. Several of the professionals on staff are very angry that the owners do not practice the very management styles and performance emphasis that they are teaching and selling to clients. Staff members are also afraid that the firm might be experiencing financial problems since cheques have been delayed and two employee's salary cheques have bounced recently. This is of grave concern to several of the employees who are the sole support of their families.

QUESTIONS

1. Describe the work culture at The Competent HR Consultancy Services.
2. What are the major causes of concern for the staff members? How can the performance of the firm be improved?
3. How, you as a Performance Management Expert can get things back on track. Explain your key strategies.

EXPERIENTIAL EXCERCISES

1. Working individually or in groups, interview five management consultancy firms specializing in compensation management in your locality. Prepare a brief report for presentation to the class outlining the ways in which the organizations today are handling incentive systems.
2. Prepare a seminar presentation on one of the following themes:

   (*a*) Compensation management as tool of performance improvement during periods of economic boom.

   (*b*) Compensation management as a tool of cost reduction during economic downturn.

   (*c*) Compensation management during corporate restructuring: key issues and strategies.

❑❑❑

Learning Objectives

At the conclusion of this chapter, you should be able to :

- Understand the legal framework of reward management.
- Discuss institutions regulating compensation in private and public sector.
- Understand the pay commission set up from time to time

4
Wage Laws

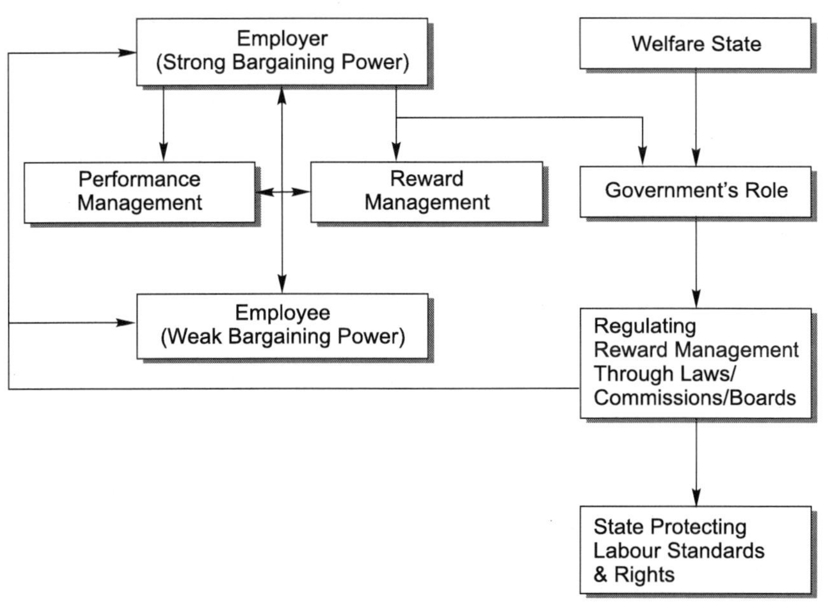

4.1 Statutory Provisions Governing Different Components of Reward System

Reward particularly financial reward like wage is governed by various statutory legislation framed by the government to secure betterment and well-being of the employees in organizations. The very objective of these wage related legislation is based upon the principles enshrined in our constitution. In the absence of such legislative framework, employees particularly the lower level employees are susceptible to exploitation by employers. These legislative measures seek to ensure that minimum labour standards in matters of wages and benefits are adhered to by organizations including payment of minimum wages.

The major legislations governing compensation are given below:

The Payment of Wages Act, 1936

1. Preamble

An act to regulate the payment of wages to certain classes of employed Persons. Where as it is expedient to regulate the payment of wages to certain classes of persons (employed persons);

It is hereby enacted as follows:

1. Short title extent commencement and application.
2. (*i*) This Act may be called the Payment of Wages Act 1936.

   (*ii*) It extends to the whole of India.

   (*iii*) It shall come into force on such date as the Central Government may by notification in the Official Gazette appoint.

   (*iv*) It applies in the first instance to the payment of wages to persons employed in any factory to persons employed (otherwise than in a factory) upon any railway by a railway administration or either directly or through a sub-contractor by a person fulfilling a contract with a railway administration and to persons employed in an industrial or other establishment specified in sub-clauses (a) to (g) of clause (ii) of section 2.

   (*v*) The State Government may after giving three months' notice of its intention of so doing by notification in the Official Gazette extend the provisions of this Act or any of them to the payment of wages to any class of persons employed in any establishment of class of establishments specified by the Central Government or a State Government under sub-clause (h) of clause (ii) of section 2:

   Provided that in relation to any such establishment owned by the Central Government no such notification shall be issued except with the concurrence of that government.

(*vi*) Nothing in this Act shall apply to wages payable in respect of a wage-period which over such wage-period average one thousand six hundred rupees a month or more.

2. Definitions

In this Act unless there is anything repugnant in the subject or context:

(*i*) "employed person" includes the legal representative of a deceased employed person;

(*ia*) "employer" includes the legal representative of a deceased employer;

(*ib*) "factory" means a factory as defined in clause (m) of section 2 of the Factories Act 1948 (63 of 1948) and includes any place to which the provisions of that Act have been applied under sub-section (1) of section 85 thereof;

(*ii*) "industrial or other establishment" means any –

(*a*) tramway service or motor transport service engaged in carrying passengers or goods or both by road for hire or reward;

(*aa*) air transport service other than such service belonging to or exclusively employed in the military naval or air forces of the Union or the Civil Aviation Department of the Government of India;

(*b*) dock wharf or jetty;

(*c*) inland vessel mechanically propelled;

(*d*) mine quarry or oil-field;

(*e*) plantation;

(*f*) workshop or other establishment in which articles are produced adapted or manufactured with a view to their use transport or sale;

(*g*) establishment in which any work relating to the construction development or maintenance of buildings roads bridges or canals or relating to operations connected with navigation irrigation or to the supply of water or relating to the generation transmission and distribution of electricity or any other form of power is being carried on;

(*h*) any other establishment or class of establishments which the Central Government or a State Government may having regard to the nature thereof the need for protection of persons employed therein and other relevant circumstances specify by notification in the Official Gazette.

(iia) "mine" has the meaning assigned to it in clause (j) of sub-section

(1) of section 2 of the Mines Act 1952 (35 of 1952);

(*iii*) "plantation" has the meaning assigned to it in clause (f) of section 2 of the Plantations Labour Act 1951 (69 of 1951);

(*iv*) "prescribed" means prescribed by rules made under this Act;

(*v*) "railway administration" has the meaning assigned to it in clause (6) of section 3 of the Indian Railways Act 1890 (9 of 1890); and

(*vi*) "wages" means all remuneration (whether by way of salary allowances or otherwise) expressed in terms of money or capable of being so expressed which would if the terms of employment express or implied were fulfilled by payable to a person employed in respect of his employment or of work done in such employment and includes:

(*a*) any remuneration payable under any award or settlement between the parties or order of a court;

(*b*) any remuneration to which the person employed is entitled in respect of overtime work or holidays or any leave period;

(*c*) any additional remuneration payable under the terms of employment (whether called a bonus or by any other name);

(*d*) any sum which by reason of the termination of employment of the person employed is payable under any law contract or instrument which provides for the payment of such sum whether with or without deductions but does not provide for the time within which the payment is to be made;

(*e*) any sum to which the person employed is entitled under any scheme framed under any law for the time being in force, but does not include:

(1) any bonus (whether under a scheme of profit sharing or otherwise) which does not form part of the remuneration payable under the terms of employment or which is not payable under any award or settlement between the parties or order of a court;

(2) the value of any house-accommodation or of the supply of light water medical attendance or other amenity or of any service excluded from the computation of wages by a general or special order of the State Government;

(3) any contribution paid by the employer to any pension or provident fund and the interest which may have accrued thereon;

(4) any travelling allowance or the value of any travelling concession;

(5) any sum paid to the employed person to defray special expenses entailed on him by the nature of his employment; or

(6) any gratuity payable on the termination of employment in cases other than those specified in sub-clause (d).

3. Responsibility for payment of wages:

Every employer shall be responsible for the payment to persons employed by him of all wages required to be paid under this Act:

Provided that in the case of persons employed (otherwise than by a contractor):

(*a*) in factories if a person has been named as the manager of the factory under clause (f) of sub-section (1) of section 7 of the Factories Act 1948 (63 of 1948);

(*b*) in industrial or other establishments if there is a person responsible to the employer for the supervision and control of the industrial or other establishments;

(*c*) upon railways (otherwise than in factories) if the employer is the railway administration and the railway administration has nominated a person in this behalf for the local area concerned.

The person so named the person so responsible to the employer or the person so nominated as the case may be shall also be responsible for such payment.

4. Fixation of wage-periods:

(1) Every person responsible for the payment of wages under section 3 shall fix periods (in this Act referred to as wage-periods) in respect of which such wages shall be payable.

(2) No wage-period shall exceed one month.

5. Time of payment of wages:

(1) The wages of every person employed upon or in:

(*a*) any railway factory or industrial or other establishment upon or in which less than one thousand persons are employed, shall be paid before the expiry of the seventh day,

(*b*) any other railway factory or industrial or other establishment shall be paid before the expiry of the tenth day, after the last day of the wage-period in respect of which the wages are payable:

Provided that in the case of persons employed on a dock wharf or jetty or in a mine the balance of wages found due on completion of the final tonnage account of the ship or wagons loaded or unloaded as the case may be shall be paid before the expiry of the seventh day from the day of such completion.

(2) Where the employment of any person is terminated by or on behalf of the employer the wages earned by him shall be paid before the expiry of the second working day from the day on which his employment is terminated:

Provided that where the employment of any person in an establishment is terminated due to the closure of the establishment for any reason other than a weekly or other recognised holiday the wages earned by him shall be paid before the expiry of the second day from the day on which his employment is so terminated.

(3) The State Government may by general or special order exempt to such extent and subject to such conditions as may be specified in the order the person responsible for the payment of wages to persons employed upon any railway (otherwise than in a factory) or to persons employed as daily-rated workers in the Public Works Department of the Central Government or the State Government from the operation of this section in respect of wages of any such persons or class of such persons :

Provided that in the case of persons employed as daily-rated workers as aforesaid no such order shall be except in consultation with the Central Government.

(4) Save as otherwise provided in sub-section (2) all payments of wages shall be made on a working day.

6. Wages to be paid in current coin or currency notes:

All wages shall be in current coin or currency notes or in both :

Provided that the employer may after obtaining the written authorisation of the employed person pay him the wages either by cheque or by crediting the wages in his bank account.

7. Deductions which may be made from wages:

(1) Notwithstanding the provisions of sub-section (2) of section 47 of the Indian Railways Act 1890 (9 of 1890) the wages of an employed person shall be paid to him without deductions of any kind except those authorised by or under this Act.

Explanation I: Every payment made by the employed person to the employer or his agent shall for the purposes of this Act be deemed to be a deduction from wages.

Explanation II: Any loss of wages resulting from the imposition, for good and sufficient cause upon a person employed of any of the following penalties namely :-

(*i*) the withholding of increment or promotion (including the stoppage of increment at an efficiency bar);

(*ii*) the reduction to a lower post or time scale or to a lower stage in a time scale; or

(*iii*) suspension;

shall not be deemed to be a deduction from wages in any case where the rules framed by the employer for the imposition of any such penalty are in conformity with the requirements if any which may be specified in this behalf by the State Government by notification in the Official Gazette.

(2) Deductions from the wages of an employed person shall be made only in accordance with the provisions of this Act and may be of the following kinds only namely :

(*a*) fines;

(*b*) deductions for absence from duty;

(*c*) deductions for damage to or loss of goods expressly entrusted to the employed person for custody or for loss of money for which he is required to account where such damage or loss is directly attributable to his neglect or default;

(*d*) deductions for house-accommodation supplied by the employer or by government or any housing board set up under any law for the time being in force (whether the government or the board is the employer or not) or any other authority engaged in the business of subsidising house-accommodation which may be specified in this behalf by the State Government by notification in the Official Gazette;

(*e*) deductions for such amenities services supplied by the employer as the State Government or any officer specified by it in this behalf may by general or special order authorise.

Explanation: The word "services" in this clause does not include the supply of tools and raw materials required for the purposes of employment;

(*f*) deductions for recovery of advances of whatever nature (including advances for travelling allowance or conveyance allowance) and the interest due in respect thereof or for adjustment of over-payments of wages;

(*ff*) deductions for recovery of loans made from any fund constituted for the welfare of labour in accordance with the rules approved by the State Government and the interest due in respect thereof;

(*fff*) deductions for recovery of loans granted for house-building or other purposes approved by the State Government and the interest due in respect thereof;

(*g*) deductions of income-tax payable by the employed person;

(*h*) deductions required to be made by order of a court or other authority competent to make such order;

(*i*) deductions for subscriptions to and for repayment of advances from any provident fund to which the Provident Funds Act 1952 (19 of 1952) applies or any recognised provident funds as defined in section 58A of the Indian Income Tax Act 1922 (11 of 1922) or any provident fund approved in this behalf by the State Government during the continuance of such approval;

(*j*) deductions for payments to co-operative societies approved by the State Government or any officer specified by it in this behalf or to a scheme of insurance maintained by the Indian Post Office;

(*k*) deductions made with the written authorisation of the person employed for payment of any premium on his life insurance policy to the Life Insurance Corporation Act of India established under the Life Insurance Corporation 1956 (31 of 1956) or for the purchase of securities of the Government of India or of any State Government or for being deposited in any Post Office Saving Bank in furtherance of any savings scheme of any such government.

(*kk*) deductions made with the written authorisation of the employed person for the payment of his contribution to any fund constituted by the employer or a trade union registered under the Trade Union Act 1926 (16 of 1926) for the welfare of the employed persons or the members of their families or both and approved by the State Government or any officer specified by it in this behalf during the continuance of such approval;

(*kkk*) deductions made with the written authorisation of the employed person for payment of the fees payable by him for the membership of any trade union registered under the Trade Union Act 1926 (16 of 1926);

(*l*) deductions for payment of insurance premia on Fidelity Guarantee Bonds;

(*m*) deductions for recovery of losses sustained by a railway administration on account of acceptance by the employed person of counterfeit or base coins or mutilated or forged currency notes;

(*n*) deductions for recovery of losses sustained by a railway administration on account of the failure of the employed person to invoice to bill to collect or to account for the appropriate charges due to that administration whether in respect of fares freight demurrage wharfage and cranage or in respect of sale of food in catering establishments or in respect of sale of commodities in grain shops or otherwise;

(*o*) deductions for recovery of losses sustained by a railway administration on account of any rebates or refunds incorrectly granted by the employed person where such loss is directly attributable to his neglect or default;

(*p*) deductions made with the written authorisation of the employed person for contribution to the Prime Minister's National Relief Fund or to such other Fund as the Central Government may by notification in the Official Gazette specify;

(*q*) deductions for contributions to any insurance scheme framed by the Central Government for the benefit of its employees.

(3) Notwithstanding anything contained in this Act the total amount of deductions which may be made under sub-section (2) in any wage-period from the wages of any employed person shall not exceed:

(*i*) in cases where such deductions are wholly or partly made for payments to co-operative societies under clause (j) of sub-section (2) seventy-five per cent of such wages and

(*ii*) in any other case fifty per cent of such wages:

Provided that where the total deductions authorised under sub-section (2) exceed seventy five per cent or as the case may be, fifty per cent of the wages the excess may be recovered in such manner as may be prescribed.

(4) Nothing contained in this section shall be construed as precluding the employer from recovering from the wages of the employed person or otherwise any amount payable by such person under any law for the time being in force other than the Indian Railways Act 1890 (9 of 1890).

8. Fines:

(1) No fine shall be imposed on any employed person save in respect of such acts and omissions on his part as the employer with the previous approval of the State Government or of the prescribed authority may have specified by notice under sub-section (2).

(2) A notice specifying such acts and omissions shall be exhibited in the prescribed manner on the premises in which the employment carried on or in the case of persons employed upon a railway (otherwise than in a factory) at the prescribed place or places.

(3) No fine shall be imposed on any employed person until he has been given an opportunity of showing cause against the fine or otherwise than in accordance with such procedure as may be prescribed for the imposition of fines.

(4) The total amount of fine which may be imposed in any one wage-period on any employed person shall not exceed an amount equal to three per cent of the wages payable to him in respect of that wage-period.

(5) No fine shall be imposed on any employed person who is under the age of fifteen years.

(6) No fine imposed on any employed person shall be recovered from him by installments or after the expiry of sixty days from the day on which it was imposed.

(7) Every fine shall be deemed to have been imposed on the day of the act or omission in respect of which it was imposed.

(8) All fines and all realisations thereof shall be recorded in a register to be kept by the person responsible for the payment of wages under section 3 in such form as may be prescribed; and all such realisations shall be applied only to such purposes beneficial to the persons employed in the factory or establishment as are approved by the prescribed authority.

Explanation: When the persons employed upon or in any railway, factory or industrial or other establishment are part only of a staff employed under the same management all such realisations may be credited to a common fund maintained for the staff as a whole provided that the fund shall be applied only to such purposes as are approved by the prescribed authority.

9. Deductions for absence from duty:

(1) Deductions may be made under clause (b) of sub-section (2) of section 7 only on account of the absence of an employed person from the place or places where by the terms of his employment, he is required to work such absence being for the whole or any part of the period during which he is so required to work.

(2) The amount of such deduction shall in no case bear to the wages payable to the employed person in respect of the wage-period for which the deduction is made in a larger proportion than the period for which he was absent bears to the total period within such wage-period during which by the terms of his employments he was required to work :

Provided that subject to any rules made in this behalf by the State Government if ten or more employed persons acting in concert absent themselves without due notice (that is to say without giving the notice which is required under the terms of their contracts of employment) and without reasonable cause such deduction from any such person may include such amount not exceeding his wages for eight days as may by any such terms be due to the employer in lieu of due notice.

Explanation: For the purposes of this section an employed person shall be deemed to be absent from the place where he is required to work if although present in such place he refuses in pursuance of a stay-in strike or for any other cause which is not reasonable in the circumstances to carry out his work.

10. Deductions for damage or loss:

(1) A deduction under clause (*c*) or clause (*o*) of sub-section (*2*) of section 7 shall not exceed the amount of the damage or loss caused to the employer by the neglect or default of the employed person.

(1A) A deduction shall not be made under clause (*c*) or clause (*m*) or clause (*n*) or clause (*o*) of sub-section (2) of section 7 until the employed person has been given an opportunity of showing cause against the deduction or otherwise than in accordance with such procedure as may be prescribed for the making of such deductions.

(2) All such deductions and all realisations thereof shall be recorded in a register to be kept by the person responsible for the payment of wages under section 3 in such form as may be prescribed.

11. Deductions for services rendered:

A deduction under clause (*d*) or clause (*e*) of sub-section (2) of section 7 shall not be made from the wages of an employed person, unless the house-accommodation amenity or service has been accepted by him as a term of employment or otherwise and such deduction shall not exceed an amount equivalent to the value of the house-accommodation amenity or service supplied and in the case of deduction under the said clause (*e*) shall be subject to such conditions as the State Government may impose.

12. Deductions for recovery of advances:

Deductions under clause (*f*) of sub-section (2) of section 7 shall be subject to the following conditions namely :

(*a*) recovery of an advance of money given before employment began shall be made from the first payment of wages in respect of a complete wage-period but no recovery shall be made of such advances given for traveling-expenses;

(*aa*) recovery of an advance of money given after employment began shall be subject to such conditions as the State Government may impose;

(*b*) recovery of advances of wages not already earned shall be subject to any rules made by the State Government regulating the extent to which such advances may be given and the installments by which they may be recovered.

12A. Deductions for recovery of loans:

Deductions for recovery of loans granted under clause (fff) of sub-section (2) of section 7 shall be subject to any rules made by the State Government regulating the extent to which such loans may be granted and the rate of interest payable thereon.

13. Deductions for payments to co-operative societies and insurance schemes:

Deductions under clause (*j*) and clause (*k*) of sub-section (2) of section 7 shall be subject to such conditions as the State Government may impose.

13A. Maintenance of registers and records:

(1) Every employer shall maintain such registers and records giving such particulars of persons employed by him the work performed by them the wages paid to them the deductions made from their wages the receipts given by them and such other particulars and in such form as may be prescribed.

(2) Every register and record required to be maintained under this section shall for the purposes of this Act be preserved for a period of three years after the date of the last entry made therein.

14. Inspectors:

(1) An Inspector of Factories appointed under sub-section (1) of section 8 of the Factories Act 1948 (63 of 1948) shall be an Inspector for the purposes of this Act in respect of all factories within the local limits assigned to him.

(2) The State Government may appoint Inspectors for the purposes of this Act in respect of all persons employed upon a railway (otherwise than in a factory) to whom this Act applies.

(3) The State Government may by notification in the Official Gazette appoint such other persons as it thinks fit to be Inspectors for the purposes of this Act and may define the local limits within which and the class of factories and industrial or other establishments in respect of which they shall exercise their functions.

(4) An Inspector may,

(*a*) make such examination and inquiry as he thinks fit in order to ascertain whether the provisions of this Act or rules made there under are being observed;

(*b*) with such assistance if any as he thinks fit enter inspect and search any premises of any railway factory or industrial or other establishment at any reasonable time for the purpose of carrying out the objects of this Act;

(*c*) supervise the payment of wages to persons employed upon any railway or in any factory or industrial or other establishment;

(*d*) require by a written order the production at such place as may be prescribed of any register maintained in pursuance of this Act and taken on the spot or otherwise statements of any persons which he may consider necessary for carrying out the purposes of this Act;

(*e*) seize or take copies of such registers or documents or portions thereof as he may consider relevant in respect of an offence under this Act which he has reason to believe has been committed by an employer;

(*f*) exercise such other powers as may be prescribed :

Provided that no person shall be compelled under this sub-section to answer any question or make any statement tending to incriminate himself.

(4A) The provisions of the Code of Criminal Procedure 1973 (2 of 1974) shall so far as may be apply to any search or seizure under this sub-section as they apply to any search or seizure made under the authority of a warrant issued under section 94 of the said Code.

(5) Every Inspector shall be deemed to be a public servant within the meaning of the Indian Penal Code (45 of 1860).

14A. Facilities to be afforded to Inspectors:

Every employer shall afford an Inspector all reasonable facilities for making any entry inspection supervision examination or inquiry under this Act.

15. Claims arising out of deductions from wages or delay in payment of wages and penalty for malicious or vexatious claims;

(1) The State Government may by notification in the Official Gazette appoint a presiding officer of any Labour Court or Industrial Tribunal constituted under the Industrial Disputes Act 1947 (14 of 1947) or under any corresponding law relating to the investigation and settlement of industrial disputes in force in the State or any Commissioner for Workmen's Compensation or other officer with experience as a Judge of a Civil Court or as a Stipendiary Magistrate to be the authority to hear and decide for any specified area all claims arising out of deductions from the wages or delay in payment of the wages of persons employed or paid in that area including all matters incidental to such claims:

Provided that where the State Government considers it necessary so to do it may appoint more than one authority for any specified area and may by general or special order provide for the distribution or allocation of work to be performed by them under this Act.

(2) Where contrary to the provisions of this Act any deduction has been made from the wages of an employed person or any payment of wages has been delayed such person himself or any legal practitioner or any official of a registered trade union authorised in writing to act on his behalf or any Inspector under this Act or any other person acting with the permission of the authority appointed under sub-section (1) may apply to such authority for a direction under sub-section (3) :

Provided that every such application shall be presented within twelve months from the date on which the deduction from the wages was made or from the date on which the payment of the wages was due to be made as the case may be:

Provided Further that any application may be admitted after the said period of twelve months when the applicant satisfies the authority that he had sufficient cause for not making the application within such period.

(3) When any application under sub-section (2) is entertained the authority shall hear the applicant and the employer or other person responsible for the payment of wages under section 3 or give them an opportunity of being heard and after such further inquiry (if any) as may be necessary may without prejudice to any other penalty to which such employer or other person is liable under this Act direct the refund to the employed person of the amount deducted or the payment of the delayed wages together with the payment of such compensation as the authority may think fit not exceeding ten times the amount deducted in the former case and not exceeding twenty-five rupees in the latter and even if the amount deducted or the delayed wages are paid before the disposal of the application direct the payment of such compensation as the authority may think fit not exceeding twenty-five rupees :

Provided that no direction for the payment of compensation shall be made in the case of delayed wages if the authority is satisfied that the delay was due to:

(*a*) a bona fide error or bona fide dispute as to the amount payable to the employed person or

(*b*) the occurrence of an emergency or the existence of exceptional circumstances such that the person responsible for the payment of the wages was unable though exercising reasonable diligence to make prompt payment, or

(c) the failure of the employed person to apply for or accept payment.

(4) If the authority hearing an application under this section is satisfied:

(*a*) that the application was either malicious or vexatious the authority may direct that a penalty not exceeding fifty rupees be paid to the employer or other person responsible for the payment of wages by the person presenting the application; or

(*b*) that in any case in which compensation is directed to be paid under sub-section (3) the applicant ought not to have been compelled to seek redress under this section the authority may direct that a penalty not exceeding fifty rupees be paid to the State Government by the employer or other person responsible for the payment of wages.

(4A) Where there is any dispute as to the person or persons being the legal representative or representatives of the employer or of the employed person the decision of the authority on such dispute shall be final.

(4B) Any inquiry under this section shall be deemed to be a judicial proceeding within the meaning of sections 193 219 and 228 of the Indian Penal Code (45 of 1860).

(5) Any amount directed to be paid under this section may be recovered:

(*a*) if the authority is a Magistrate by the authority as if it were a fine imposed by him as Magistrate, and

(*b*) if the authority is not a Magistrate by any Magistrate to whom the authority makes application in this behalf as if it were a fine imposed by such Magistrate.

16. Single application in respect of claims from unpaid group:

(1) Employed persons are said to belong to the same unpaid group if they are borne on the same establishment and if deductions have been made from their wages in contravention of this Act for the same cause and during the same wage-period or periods or if their wages for the same wage-period or periods have remained unpaid after the day fixed by section 5.

(2) A single application may be presented under section 15 on behalf or in respect of any number of employed persons belonging to the same unpaid group and in such case every person on whose behalf such application is presented may be awarded maximum compensation to the extent specified in sub-section (3) of section 15.

(3) The authority may deal with any number of separate pending applications presented under section 15 in respect of persons belonging to the same unpaid group as a single application presented under sub-section (2) of this section and the provisions of that sub-section shall apply accordingly.

17. Appeal:

(1) An appeal against an order dismissing either wholly or in part an application made under sub-section (2) of section 15 or against a direction made under sub-section (3) or sub-section (4) of that section may be preferred within thirty days of the date on which the order or direction was made in a Presidency-town before the Court of Small Causes and elsewhere before the District Court:

(*a*) by the employer or other person responsible for the payment of wages under section 3 if the total sum directed to be paid by way of wages and compensation exceeds three hundred rupees or such direction has the effect of imposing on the employer or the other person a financial liability exceeding one thousand rupees, or

(*b*) by an employed person or any legal practitioner or any official of a registered trade union authorised in writing to act on his behalf or any Inspector under this Act or any other person permitted by the authority to make an application under sub-section (2) of section 15 if the total amount of wages claimed to have been with held from the employed person exceeds twenty rupees or from the unpaid group to which the employed person belongs or belonged exceeds fifty rupees, or

(*c*) by any person directed to pay a penalty under sub-section (4) of section 15.

(1A) No appeal under clause (a) of sub-section (1) shall lie unless the memorandum of appeal is accompanied by a certificate by the authority to the effect that the appellant has deposited the amount payable under the direction appealed against.

(2) Save as provided in sub-section (1) any order dismissing either wholly or in part an application made under sub-section (2) of section 15 or a direction made under sub-section (3) or sub-section (4) of that section shall be final.

(3) Where an employer prefers an appeal under this section the authority against whose decision the appeal has been preferred may and if so directed by the court referred to in sub-section (1) shall pending the decision of the appeal withhold payment of any sum in deposit with it.

(4) The court referred to in sub-section (1) may if it thinks fit submit any question of law for the decision of the High Court and if it so does shall decide the question in conformity with such decision.

17A. Conditional attachment of property of employer or other person responsible for payment of wages:

(1) Where at any time after an application has been made under sub-section (2) of section 15 the authority or where at any time after an appeal has been filed under section 17 by an employed person or any legal practitioner or any official of a registered trade union authorised in writing to act on his behalf or any Inspector under this Act or any other person permitted by the authority to make an application under sub-section (2) of section 15 the Court referred to in that section is satisfied that the employer or other person responsible for the payment of wages under section 3 is likely to evade payment of any amount that may be directed to be paid under section 15 or section 17 the authority or the court as the case may be except in cases where the authority or court is of opinion that the ends of justice would be defeated by the delay after giving the employer or other person an opportunity of being heard may direct the attachment of so much of the property of the employer or other person responsible for the payment of wages as is in the opinion of the authority or court sufficient to satisfy the amount which may be payable under the direction.

(2) The provisions of the Code of Civil Procedure 1908 (5 of 1908) relating to attachment before judgment under that Code shall so far as may be apply to any order for attachment under sub-section (1).

18. Powers of authorities appointed under section 15:

Every authority appointed under sub-section (1) of section 15 shall have all the powers of a civil court under the Code of Civil Procedure 1908 (5 of 1908) for the purpose of taking evidence and of enforcing the attendance of witnesses and compelling the production of documents and every such authority shall be deemed to be a civil court for all the purposes of section 195 and of Chapter XXVI of the Code of Criminal Procedure 1973 (2 of 1974).

20. Penalty for offences under the Act:

(1) Whoever being responsible for the payment of wages to an employed person contravenes any of the provisions of any of the following sections namely section 5 except sub-section (4) thereof section 7 section 8 except sub-section (8) thereof , section 9 section 10 except sub-section (2) thereof and section 11 to 13 both inclusive shall be punishable with fine which shall not be less than two hundred rupees but which may extend to one thousand rupees.

(2) Whoever contravenes the provisions of section 4 sub-section (4) of section 5 section 6 sub-section (8) of section 8 sub-section (2) of section 10 or section 25 shall be punishable with fine which may extend to five hundred rupees.

(3) Whoever being required under this Act to maintain any records or registers or to furnish any information or return –

- (*a*) fails to maintain such register or record; or
- (*b*) willfully refuses or without lawful excuse neglects to furnish such information or return; or
- (*c*) willfully furnishes or causes to be furnished any information or return which he knows to be false; or
- (*d*) refuses to answer or willfully gives a false answer to any question necessary for obtaining any information required to be furnished under this Act shall for each such offence be punishable with fine which shall not be less than two hundred rupees but which may extend to one thousand rupees.

(4) Whoever:

- (*a*) willfully obstructs an Inspector in the discharge of his duties under this Act; or
- (*b*) refuse or willfully neglects to afford an Inspector any reasonable facility for making any entry inspection examination supervision or inquiry authorised by or under this Act in relation to any railway factory or industrial or other establishment; or
- (*c*) willfully refuses to produce on the demand of an Inspector any register or other document kept in pursuance of this Act; or

(*d*) prevents or attempts to prevent or does anything which he has any reason to believe is likely to prevent any person from appearing before or being examined by an Inspector acting in pursuance of his duties under this Act;

shall be punishable with fine which shall not be less than two hundred rupees but which may extend to one thousand rupees.

(5) If any person who has been convicted of any office punishable under this Act is again guilty of an offence involving contravention of the same provision he shall be punishable on a subsequent conviction with imprisonment for a term which shall not be less than one month but which may extend to six months and with fine which shall not be less than five hundred rupees but which may extend to three thousand rupees.

Provided that for the purpose of this sub-section no cognizance shall be taken of any conviction made more than two years before the date on which the commission of the offence which is being punished came to the knowledge of the Inspector.

(6) If any person fails or willfully neglects to pay the wages of any employed person by the date fixed by the authority in this behalf he shall without prejudice to any other action that may be taken against him be punishable with an additional fine which may extend to one hundred rupees for each day for which such failure or neglect continues.

21. Procedure in trial of offences:

(1) No court shall take cognizance of a complaint against any person for an offence under sub-section (1) of section 20 unless an application in respect of the facts constituting the offence has been presented under section 15 and has been granted wholly or in part and the authority empowered under the latter section or the appellate Court granting such application has sanctioned the making of the complaint.

(2) Before sanctioning the making of a complaint against any person for an offence under sub-section (1) of section 20 the authority empowered under section 15 or the appellate Court as the case may be shall give such person an opportunity of showing cause against the granting of such sanction and the sanction shall not be granted if such person satisfies the authority or Court that his default was due to:

(*a*) a bona fide error or bona fide dispute as to the amount payable to the employed person, or

(*b*) the occurrence of an emergency or the existence of exceptional circumstances such that the person responsible for the payment of the wages was unable though exercising reasonable diligence to make prompt payment, or

(*c*) the failure of the employed person to apply for or accept payment.

(3) No Court shall take cognizance of a contravention of section 4 or of section 6 or of a contravention of any rule made under section 26 except on a complaint made by or with the sanction of an Inspector under this Act.

(3A) No Court shall take cognizance of any offence punishable under sub-section (3) or sub-section (4) of section 20 except on a complaint made by or with the sanction of an Inspector under this Act.

(4) In imposing any fine for an affiance under sub-section (1) of section 20 the court shall take into consideration the amount of any compensation already awarded against the accused in any proceedings taken under section 15.

22. Bar of suits:

No Court shall entertain any suit for the recovery of wages or of any deduction from wages in so far as the sum so claimed:

(*a*) forms the subject of an application under section 15 which has been presented by the plaintiff and which is pending before the authority appointed under that section or of an appeal under section 17; or

(*b*) has formed the subject of a direction under section 15 in favour of the plaintiff; or

(*c*) has been adjudged in any proceeding under section 15 not to be owned to the plaintiff; or

(*d*) could have been recovered by an application under section 15.

22A. Protection of action taken in good faith:

No suit prosecution or other legal proceeding shall lie against the government or any officer of the government for anything which is in good faith done or intended to be done under this Act.

23. Contracting out:

Any contract or agreement whether made before or after the commencement of this Act whereby an employed person relinquishes any right conferred by this Act shall be null and void in so far as it purports to deprive him of such right.

24. Application of Act to railways air transport services mines and oilfields:

The powers by this Act conferred upon the State Government shall, in relation to railways air transport services mines and oilfields be powers of the Central Government.

25. Display by notice of abstracts of the Act:

The person responsible for the payment of wages of persons employed in a factory or an industrial or other establishment shall cause to be displayed in such factory or industrial or other establishment a notice containing such abstracts of this Act and of the rules made there under in English and in the language of the majority of the persons employed in the factory, or industrial or other establishment as may be prescribed.

25A. Payment of undisbursed wages in case of death of employed person:

(1) Subject to the other provisions of the Act all amounts payable to an employed person as wages shall if such amounts could not or cannot be paid on account of his death before payment or on account of his whereabouts not being known:

(*a*) be paid to the person nominated by him in this behalf in accordance with the rules made under this Act; or

(*b*) where no such nomination has been made or where for any reasons such amounts cannot be paid to the person so nominated be deposited with the prescribed authority who shall deal with the amounts so deposited in such manner as may be prescribed.

(2) Where in accordance with the provisions of sub-section (1) all amounts payable to an employed person as wages –

(*a*) are paid by the employer to the person nominated by the employer person; or

(*b*) are deposited by the employer with the prescribed authority, the employer shall be discharged of his liability to pay those wages.

26. Rule-making power:

(1) The State Government may make rules to regulate the procedure to be followed by the authorities and courts referred to in sections 15 and 17.

(2) The State Government may by notification in the Official Gazette make rules for the purpose of carrying into effect the provisions of this Act.

(3) In particular and without prejudice to the generality of the foregoing power rules made under sub-section (2) may:

(*a*) require the maintenance of such records registers returns and notice as are necessary for the enforcement of the Act prescribe the form thereof and the particulars to be entered in such registers or records;

(*b*) require the display in a conspicuous place on premises where employment is carried on of notices specifying rates of wages payable to persons employed on such premises;

(*c*) provide for the regulate inspection of the weights measures and weighing machines used by employers in checking or ascertaining the wages of persons employed by them;

(*d*) prescribe the manner of giving notice of the days on which wages will be paid;

(*e*) prescribe the authority competent to approve under sub-section (1) of section 8 acts and omissions in respect of which fines may be imposed;

(*f*) prescribe the procedure for the imposition of fines under section 8 and for making of the deductions referred to in section 10;

(*g*) prescribe the conditions subject to which deductions may be made under the proviso the sub-section (2) of section 9;

(*h*) prescribe the authority competent to approve the purposes on which the proceeds of fines shall be expended;

(*i*) prescribe the extent to which advances may be made and the installments by which they may be recovered with reference to clause (b) of section 12;

(*ia*) prescribe the extent to which loans may be granted and the rate of interest payable thereon with reference to section 12A;

(*ib*) prescribe the powers of Inspectors for the purposes of this Act;

(*j*) regulate the scales of costs which may allowed in proceedings under this Act;

(*k*) prescribe the amount of court-fees payable in respect of any proceedings under this Act

(*l*) prescribe the abstracts to be contained in the notices required by section 25;

(*la*) prescribe the form and manner in which nominations may be made for the purposes of sub-section (1) of section 25A the cancellation or variation of any such nomination or the making of any fresh nomination in the event of the nominee predeceasing the person making nomination and other matters connected with such nominations;

(*lb*) specify the authority with whom amounts required to be deposited under clause (b) of sub-section (1) of section 25A shall be deposited and the manner in which such authority shall deal with the amounts deposited with it under that clause;

(m) provide for any other matter which is to be or may be prescribed.

(4) In making any rule under this section the State Government may provide that a contravention of the rule shall be punishable with fine which may extend to two hundred rupees.

(5) All rules made under this section shall be subject to the condition of previous publication and the date to be specified under clause (3) of

section 23 of the General Clauses Act 1897 (10 of 1897) shall not be less than three months from the date on which the draft of the proposed rules was published.

(*6*) Every rule made by the Central Government under this section shall be laid as soon as may be after it is made before each House of Parliament while it is in session for a total period of thirty days which may be comprised in one session or in two or more successive sessions and if before the expiry of the session immediately following the session or the successive sessions aforesaid both Houses agree in making any modification in the rule or both Houses agree that the rule should not be made the rule shall thereafter have effect only in such modified form or be of no effect as the case may be; so however that any such modification or annulment shall be without prejudice to the validity of anything previously done under that rule.

The Minimum Wages Act, 1948

1. Preamble

An act to provide for fixing minimum rate of wages in certain employments.

Where it is expedient to provide for fixing minimum rates of wages in certain employments:

It is hereby enacted as follows:

"The justification for statutory fixation of minimum wages is obvious. Such provisions which exists in more advanced countries are even more necessary in India, where workers organisations are yet poorly developed and worker's bargaining power is consequently poor." (Gazette of India).

Short title and extent

(1) This Act may be called the Minimum Wages Act 1948.

(2) It extends to the whole of India.

2. Interpretation:

In this Act unless there is anything repugnant in the subject or context:

(*a*) "adolescent" means a person who has completed his fourteenth year of age but has not completed his eighteenth year;

(*aa*) "adult" means a person who has completed his eighteenth year of age;

(*b*) "appropriate government" means:

(*i*) in relation to any scheduled employment carried on by or under the authority of the Central Government or a railway administration or in relation to a mine oilfield or major port or any corporation established by a Central Act the Central Government and

(*ii*) in relation to any other scheduled employment the State Government;

(*bb*) "child" means a person who has not completed his fourteenth year of age;

(*c*) "competent authority" means the authority appointed by the appropriate government by notification in its Official Gazette to ascertain from time-to-time the cost of living index number applicable to the employees employed in the scheduled employments specified in such notification;

(*d*) "cost of living index number" in relation to employees in any scheduled employment in respect of which minimum rates of wages have been fixed means the index number ascertained and declared by the competent authority by notification in the Official Gazette to be the cost of living index number applicable to employee in such employment;

(*e*) "employer" means any person who employs whether directly or through another person or whether on behalf of himself or any other person one or more employees in any scheduled employment in respect of which minimum rates of wages have been fixed under this Act and includes except in sub-section (3) of section 26:

(*i*) in a factory where there is carried on any scheduled employment in respect of which minimum rates of wages have been fixed under this Act any person named under clause (f) of sub-section (1) of section 7 of the Factories Act 1948 (63 of 1948) as manager of the factory;

(*ii*) in any scheduled employment under the control of any government in India in respect of which minimum rates of wages have been fixed under this Act the person or authority appointed by such government for the supervision and control of employees or where no person or authority is so appointed the head of the department;

(*iii*) in any scheduled employment under any local authority in respect of which minimum rates of wages have been fixed under this Act the persons appointed by such authority for the supervision and control of employees or where no person is so appointed the chief executive officer of the local authority;

(*iv*) in any other case where there is carried on any scheduled employment in respect of which minimum rates of wages have been fixed under this Act any person responsible to the owner for the supervision and control of the employees or for the payment of wages;

(*f*) "prescribed" means prescribed by rules made under this Act;

(*g*) "schedule employment" means an employment specified in the Schedule or any process or branch of work forming part of such employment;

(*h*) "wages" means all remuneration capable of being expressed in terms of money which would if the terms of the contract of employment express or implied were fulfilled be payable to a person employed in respect of his employment or of work done in such employment and includes house rent allowance but does not include:

(*i*) the value of

(*a*) any house accommodation supply of light water medical attendance; or

(*b*) any other amenity or any service excluded by general or special order of the appropriate government;

(*ii*) any contribution paid by the employer to any person fund or provident fund or under any scheme of social insurance;

(*iii*) any traveling allowance or the value of any traveling concession;

(*iv*) any sum paid to the person employed to defray special expenses entailed on him by the nature of his employment; or

(*v*) any gratuity payable on discharge;

(*i*) "employee" means any person who is employed for hire or reward to do any work skilled or unskilled manual or clerical in a scheduled employment in respect of which minimum rates of wages have been fixed; and includes an out-worker to whom any articles or materials are given out by another person to be made up cleaned washed altered ornamented finished repaired adapted or otherwise processed for sale for the purposes of the trade or business of that other person where the process is to be carried out either in the home of the out-worker or in some other premises not being premises under the control and management of that other person; and also includes an employee declared to be an employee by the appropriate government; but does not include any member of the Armed Forces of the Union.

3. Fixing of minimum rates of wages:

(1) The appropriate government shall in the manner hereinafter provided:

(*a*) fix the minimum rates of wages payable to employees employed in an employment specified in Part I or Part II of the Schedule and in an employment added to either Party by notification under section 27:

Provided that the appropriate government may in respect of employees employed in an employment specified in Part II of the Schedule instead of fixing minimum rates of wages under this clause for the whole State fix such rates for a part of the State or for any specified class or classes of such employment in the whole State or part thereof;

(*b*) review at such intervals as it may think fit such intervals not exceeding five years the minimum rates of wages so fixed and revise the minimum rates if necessary:

Provided that where for any reason the appropriate government has not reviewed the minimum rates of wages fixed by it in respect of any scheduled employment within any interval of five years nothing contained in this clause shall be deemed to prevent it from reviewing the minimum rates after the expiry of the said period of five years and revising them if necessary and until they are so revised the minimum rates in force immediately before the expiry of the said period of five years shall continue in force.

(1A) Notwithstanding anything contained in sub-section (1) the appropriate government may refrain from fixing minimum rates of wages in respect of any scheduled employment in which there are in the whole State less than one thousand employees engaged in such employment but if at any time the appropriate government comes to a finding after such inquiry as it may make or cause to be made in this behalf that the number of employees in any scheduled employment in respect of which it has refrained from fixing minimum rates of wages has risen to one thousand or more it shall fix minimum rates of wages payable to employees in such employment as soon as may be after such finding.

(2) The appropriate government may fix:

(*a*) a minimum rate of wages for time work (hereinafter referred to as "a minimum time rate");

(*b*) a minimum rates of wages for piece work (hereinafter referred to as "a minimum piece rate");

(*c*) a minimum rate of remuneration to apply in the case of employees employed on piece work for the purpose of securing to such employees a minimum rate of wages on a time work basis (hereinafter referred to as "a guaranteed time rate");

(*d*) a minimum rate (whether a time rate or a piece rate) to apply in substitution for the minimum rate which would otherwise be applicable in respect of overtime work done by employees (hereinafter referred to as "overtime rate").

(2A) Where in respect of an industrial dispute relating to the rates of wages payable to any of the employees employed in a scheduled employment any proceeding is pending before a Tribunal or National Tribunal under the Industrial Disputes Act 1947 (14 of 1947) or before any like authority under any other law for the time being in force or an award made by any Tribunal National Tribunal or such authority is in operation and a notification fixing or revising the minimum rates of wages in respect of the scheduled employment is issued during the pendency of such proceeding or the operation of the award then notwithstanding anything contained in this Act the minimum rates of wages so fixed or so revised shall not apply to those employees during the period in which the proceeding is pending and the award made therein is in operation or as the case may be where the notification is issued during the period of operation of an award during that period; and where such proceeding or award relates to the rates of wages payable to all the employees in the scheduled employment no minimum rates of wages shall be fixed or revised in respect of that employment during the said period.

4. In fixing or revising minimum rates of wages under this section:

(*a*) different minimum rates of wages may be fixed for:

(*i*) different scheduled employments;

(*ii*) different classes of work in the same scheduled employment;

(*iii*) adults adolescents children and apprentices;

(*iv*) different localities;

(*b*) minimum rates of wages may be fixed by any one or more of the following wage periods; namely :

(*i*) by the hour

(*ii*) by the day

(*iii*) by the month or

(*iv*) by such other larger wage-period as may be prescribed;

and where such rates are fixed by the day or by the month the manner of calculating wages for a month or for a day as the case may be may be indicated: Provided that where any wage-periods have been fixed under section 4 of the Payment of Wages Act 1936 (4 of 1936) minimum wages shall be fixed in accordance therewith.

5. Minimum rate of wages:

(1) Any minimum rate of wages fixed or revised by the appropriate government in respect of scheduled employments under section 3 may consist of:

(*i*) a basic rate of wages and a special allowance at a rate to be adjusted at such intervals and in such manner as the appropriate government may direct to accord as nearly as practicable with the variation in the cost of living index number applicable to such workers (hereinafter referred to as the "cost of living allowance"); or

(*ii*) a basic rate of wages with or without the cost of living allowance and the cash value of the concessions in respect of suppliers of essential commodities at concession rates where so authorised; or

(*iii*) an all-inclusive rate allowing for the basic rate the cost of living allowance and the cash value of the concessions if any.

(2) The cost of living allowance and the cash value of the concessions in respect of supplied of essential commodities at concession rate shall

be computed by the competent authority at such intervals and in accordance with such directions as may be specified or given by the appropriate government.

6. Procedure for fixing and revising minimum wages:

(1) In fixing minimum rates of wages in respect of any scheduled employment for the first time under this Act or in revising minimum rates of wages so fixed the appropriate government shall either:

(*a*) appoint as many committees and sub-committees as it considers necessary to hold enquiries and advise it in respect of such fixation or revision as the case may be, or

(*b*) by notification in the Official Gazette publish its proposals for the information of persons likely to be affected thereby and specify a date not less than two months from the date of the notification on which the proposals will be taken into consideration.

(2) After considering the advice of the committee or committee appointed under clause (a) of sub-section (1) or as the case may be all representations received by it before the date specified in the notification under clause (b) of that sub-section the appropriate government shall by notification in the Official Gazette fix or as the case may be revise the minimum rates of wages in respect of each scheduled employment and unless such notification otherwise provides it shall come into force on the expiry of three months from the date of its issue :

Provided that where the appropriate government proposes to revise the minimum rates of wages by the mode specified in clause (b) of sub-section (1) the appropriate government shall consult the Advisory Board also.

7. Advisory Board:

For the purpose of co-ordinating work of committees and sub-committees appointed under section 5 and advising the appropriate government generally in the matter of fixing and revising minimum rates of wages the appropriate government shall appoint an Advisory Board.

8. Central Advisory Board:

(1) For the purpose of advising the Central and State Governments in the matters of the fixation and revision of minimum rates of wages and other matters under this Act and for co-ordinating the work of the Advisory Boards the Central Government shall appoint a Central Advisory Board.

(2) The Central Advisory Board shall consist of persons to be nominated by the Central Government representing employers and employees in the scheduled employments who shall be equal in number and independent persons not exceeding one-third of its total number of

members; one of such independent persons shall be appointed the Chairman of the Board by the Central Government.

9. Composition of committees etc.:

Each of the committees sub-committees and the Advisory Board shall consist of persons to be nominated by the appropriate government representing employers and employees in the scheduled employments who shall be equal in number and independent persons not exceeding one-third of its total number of members; one of such independent persons shall be appointed the Chairman by the appropriate government.

10. Correction of errors:

(1) The appropriate government may at any time by notification in the Official Gazette correct clerical or arithmetical mistakes in any order fixing or revising minimum rates of wages under this Act or errors arising therein from any accidental slip or omission.

(2) Every such notification shall as soon as may be after it is issued be placed before the Advisory Board for information.

11. Wages in kind:

(1) Minimum wages payable under this Act shall be paid in cash.

(2) Where it has been the custom to pay wages wholly or partly in kind the appropriate government being of the opinion that it is necessary in the circumstances of the case may by notification in the Official Gazette authorise the payment of minimum wages either wholly or partly in kind.

(3) If appropriate government is of the opinion that provision should be made for the supply of essential commodities at concession rates the appropriate government may by notification in the Official Gazette authorise the provision of such supplies at concessional rates.

(4) The cash value of wages in kind and of concessions in respect of supplies of essential commodities at concession rates authorised under sub-sections (2) and (3) shall be estimated in the prescribed manner.

12. Payment of minimum rate of wages:

(1) Where in respect of any scheduled employment a notification under section 5 is in force the employer shall pay to every employee engaged in a scheduled employment under him wages at a rate not less than the minimum rate of wages fixed by such notification for that class of employees in that employment without any deductions except as may be authorised within such time and subject to such conditions as may be prescribed.

(2) Nothing contained in this section shall affect the provisions of the Payment of Wages Act 1936 (4 of 1936).

13. Fixing hours for normal working day etc.:

(1) In regard to any scheduled employment minimum rates of wages in respect of which have been fixed under this Act the appropriate government may:

(*a*) fix the number of hours of work which shall constitute a normal working day inclusive of one or more specified intervals;

(*b*) provide for a day of rest in every period of seven days which shall be allowed to all employees or to any specified class of employees and for the payment of remuneration in respect of such days of rest;

(*c*) provide for payment for work on a day of rest at a rate not less than the overtime rate.

(2) The provisions of sub-section (1) shall in relation to the following classes of employees apply only to such extent and subject to such conditions as may be prescribed:

(*a*) employees engaged on urgent work or in any emergency which could not have been foreseen or prevented;

(*b*) employees engaged in work in the nature of preparatory or complementary work which must necessarily be carried on outside the limits laid down for the general working in the employment concerned;

(*c*) employees whose employment is essentially intermittent;

(*d*) employees engaged in any work which for technical reasons has to be completed before the duty is over;

(*e*) employees engaged in a work which could not be carried on except at times dependent on the irregular action of natural forces.

(3) For the purposes of clause (c) of sub-section (2) employment of an employee is essentially intermittent when it is declared to be so by the appropriate government on the ground that the daily hours of duty of the employee or if there be no daily hours of duty as such for the employee the hours of duty normally include periods of inaction during which the employee may be on duty but is not called upon to display either physical activity or sustained attention.

14. Overtime:

(1) Where an employee whose minimum rate of wages is fixed under this Act by the hour by the day or by such a longer wage-period as may be prescribed works on any day in excess of the number of hours constituting a normal working day the employer shall pay him for every hour or for part of an hour so worked in excess at the overtime rate fixed under this Act or under any law of the appropriate government for the time being in force whichever is higher.

(2) Nothing in this Act shall prejudice the operation of the provisions of section 59 of the Factories Act 1948 (63 of 1948) in any case where those provisions are applicable.

15. Wages of worker who works for less than normal working day:

If an employee whose minimum rate of wages has been fixed under this Act by the day works on any day on which he was employed for a period less than the requisite number of hours constituting a normal working day he shall save as otherwise hereinafter provided be entitled to receive wages in respect of work done by him on that day as if he had worked for a full normal working day :

Provided however that he shall not be entitled to receive wages for a full normal working day:

(*i*) in any case where his failure to work is caused by his unwillingness to work and not by the omission of the employer to provide him with work and

(*ii*) in such other cases and circumstances as may be prescribed.

16. Wages for two or more classes of work:

Where an employee does two or more classes of work to each of which a different minimum rate of wages is applicable the employer shall pay to such employee in respect of the time respectively occupied in each such class of work wages at not less than the minimum rate in force in respect of each such class.

17. Minimum time rate wages for piece work:

Where an employee is employed on piece work for which minimum time rate and not a minimum piece rate has been fixed under this Act the employer shall pay to such employee wages at not less than the minimum time rate.

18. Maintenance of registers and records:

(1) Every employer shall maintain such registers and records giving such particulars of employees employed by him the work performed by them the wages paid to them the receipts given by them and such other particulars and in such form as may be prescribed.

(2) Every employer shall keep exhibited in such manner as may be prescribed in the factory workshop or place where the employees in the scheduled employment may be employed or in the case of out-workers in such factory workshop or place as may be used for giving out work to them notices in the prescribed form containing prescribed particulars.

(3) The appropriate government may by rules made under this Act provide for the issue of wage books or wage slips to employees employed in

any scheduled employment in respect of which minimum rates of wages have been fixed and prescribed to manner in which entries shall be made and authenticated in such wage books or wage slips by the employer or his agent.

19. Inspectors:

(1) The appropriate government may by notification in the Official Gazette appoint such persons as it thinks fit to be Inspectors for the purposes of this Act and define the local limits within which they shall exercise their functions.

(2) Subject to any rules made in this behalf an Inspector may within the local limits for which he is appointed:

(*a*) enter at all reasonable hours with such assistants (if any) being persons in the service of the government or any local or other public authority as he thinks fit any premises or place where employees are employed or work is given out to out-workers in any scheduled employment in respect of which minimum rates of wages have been fixed under this Act for the purpose of examining any register record of wages or notices required to be kept or exhibited by or under this Act or rules made thereunder and require the production thereof for inspection;

(*b*) examine any person whom he finds in any such premises or place and who he has reasonable cause to believe is an employee employed therein or an employee to whom work is given out therein;

(*c*) require any person giving out-work and any out-workers to give any information which is in his power to give with respect to the names and addresses of the persons to for and from whom the work is given out or received and with respect to the payments to be made for the work;

(*d*) seize or take copies of such register record or wages or notices or portions thereof as he may consider relevant in respect of an offence under this Act which he has reason to believe has been committed by an employer; and

(*e*) exercise such other powers as may be prescribed.

(3) Every Inspector shall be deemed to be a public servant within the meaning of the Indian Penal Code (45 of 1860).

(4) Any person required to produce any document or thing or to give any information by an Inspector under sub-section (2) shall be deemed to be legally bound to do so within the meaning of section 175 and section 176 of the Indian Penal Code (45 of 1860).

20. Claim:

(1) The appropriate government may by notification in the Official Gazette appoint any Commissioner for Workmen's Compensation or any officer of the Central Government exercising functions as a Labour Commissioner for any region or any officer of the State Government not below the rank of Labour Commissioner or any other officer with experience as a judge for a civil court or as a Stipendiary Magistrate to be the authority to hear and decide for any specified area all claims arising out of payment of less than the minimum rates of wages or in respect of the payment of remuneration for days of rest or for work done on such days under clause (b) or clause (c) of sub-section (1) of section 13 or of wages at the overtime rate under section 14 to employees employed or paid in that area.

(2) Where an employee has any claim of the nature referred to in sub-section (1) the employee himself or any legal practitioner or any official of a registered trade union authorised in writing to act on his behalf or any Inspector or any person acting with the permission of the authority appointed under sub-section (1) may apply to such authority for a direction under sub-section (3):

Provided that every such application shall be presented within six months from the date on which the minimum wages or other amount became payable :

Provided Further that any application may be admitted after the said period of six months when the applicant satisfies the authority that he had sufficient cause for not making the application within such period.

(3) When any application under sub-section (2) is entertained the authority shall hear the applicant and the employer or give them an opportunity of being heard and after such further inquiry if any as it may consider necessary may without prejudice to any other penalty to which the employer may be liable under this Act direct:

(*i*) in the case of a claim arising out of payment of less than the minimum rates of wages the payment to the employee of the amount by which the minimum wages payable to him exceed the amount actually paid together with the payment of such compensation as the authority may think fit not exceeding ten times the amount of such excess;

(*ii*) in any other case the payment of the amount due to the employee together with the payment of such compensation as the authority may think fit not exceeding ten rupees;

and the authority may direct payment of such compensation in cases where the excess or the amount due is paid by the employer to the employee before the disposal of the application.

(4) If the authority hearing any application under this section is satisfied that it was either malicious or vexatious it may direct that a penalty not exceeding fifty rupees be paid to be employer by the person presenting the application.

(5) Any amount directed to be paid under this section may be recovered:

(*a*) if the authority is a Magistrate by the authority as if it were a fine imposed by the authority as a Magistrate or

(*b*) if the authority is not a Magistrate by any Magistrate to whom the authority makes application in this behalf as if it were a fine imposed by such Magistrate.

(6) Every direction of the authority under this section shall be final.

(7) Every authority appointed under sub-section (1) shall have all the powers of a civil court under the Code of Civil Procedure 1908 (5 of 1908) for the purpose of taking evidence and of enforcing the attendance of witnesses and compelling the production of documents and every such authority shall be deemed to be a civil court for all the purposes of section 195 and Chapter XXXV of the Code of Criminal Procedure 1898 (5 of 1898).

21. Single application in respect of a number of employees:

(1) Subject to such rules as may be prescribed a single application may be presented under section 20 on behalf or in respect of any number of employees employed in the scheduled employment in respect of which minimum rates of wages have been fixed and in such cases the maximum compensation which may be awarded under sub-section (3) of section 20 shall not exceed ten times the aggregate amount of such excess or ten rupees per head as the case may be.

(2) The authority may deal with any number of separate pending applications presented under section 20 in respect of employees in the scheduled employments in respect of which minimum rates of wages have been fixed as a single application presented under sub-section (1) of this section and the provisions of that sub-section shall apply accordingly.

22. Penalties for certain offences any employer who:

(*a*) pays to any employee less than the minimum rates of wages fixed for that employee's class of work or less than the amount due to him under the provisions of this Act or

(*b*) contravenes any rule or order made under section 13; shall be punishable with imprisonment for a term which may extend to six months or with fine which may extend to five hundred rupees or with both:

Provided that in imposing any fine for an offence under this section the court shall take into consideration the amount of any compensation already awarded against the accused in any proceedings taken under section 20.

22A. General provision for punishment of other offences:

Any employer who contravenes any provision of this Act or of any rule or order made thereunder shall if no other penalty is provided for such contravention by this Act be punishable with fine which may extend to five hundred rupees.

22B. Cognizance of offences:

(1) No court shall take cognizance of a complaint against any person for an offence:

(*a*) under clause (a) of section 22 unless an application in respect of the facts constituting such offence has been presented under section 20 and has been granted wholly or in part and the appropriate government or an officer authorised by it is this behalf has sanctioned the making of the complaint;

(*b*) under clause (b) of section 22 or under section 22A except on a complaint made by or with the sanction of an Inspector.

(2) No court shall take cognizance of an offence

(*a*) under clause (a) or clause (b) of section 22 unless complaint thereof is made within one month of the grant of sanction under this section;

(*b*) under section 22A unless complaint thereof is made within six months of the date on which the offence is alleged to have been committed.

22C. Offences by companies

(1) If the person committing any offence under this Act is a company every person who at the time the offence was committed was in charge of and was responsible to the company for the conduct of the business of the company as well as the company shall be deemed to be guilty of the offence and shall be liable to be proceeded against and punished accordingly :

Provided that nothing contained in this sub-section shall render any such person liable to any punishment provided in this Act if he proves that the offence was committed without his knowledge or that he exercised all due diligence to prevent the commission of such offence.

(2) Notwithstanding anything contained in sub-section (1) where any offence under this Act has been committed by a company and it is proved that the offence has been committed with the consent or connivance of or is attributable to any neglect on the part of any director manager secretary or other officer of the company such

director manager secretary or other officer of the company shall also be deemed to be guilty of that offence and shall be liable to be proceeded against and punished accordingly.

Explanation: For the purposes of this section:

(*a*) "company" means any body corporate and includes a firm or other association of individuals and

(*b*) "director" in relation to a firm means a partner in the firm.

22D. Payment of undisbursed amounts due to employees:

All amounts payable by an employer to an employee as the amount of minimum wages of the employee under this Act or otherwise due to the employee under this Act or any rule or order made thereunder shall if such amounts could not or cannot be paid to the employee on account of his death before payment or on account of his whereabouts not being known be deposited with the prescribed authority who shall deal with the money so deposited in such manner as may be prescribed.

22E. Protection against attachment of assets of employer with government:

Any amount deposited with the appropriate government by an employer to secure the due performance of a contract with that government and any other amount due to such employer from that government in respect of such contract shall not be liable to attachment under any decree or order of any court in respect of any debt or liability incurred by the employer other than any debt or liability incurred by the employer towards any employee employed in connection with the contract aforesaid.

22F. Application of Payment of Wages Act 1936 to scheduled employments:

(1) Notwithstanding anything contained in the Payment of Wages Act 1936 (4 of 1936) the appropriate government may by notification in the Official Gazette direct that subject to the provisions of sub-section (2) all or any of the provisions of the said Act shall with such modifications if any as may be specified in the notification apply to wages payable to employees in such scheduled employments as may be specified in the notification.

(2) Where all or any of the provisions of the said Act are applied to wages payable to employees in any scheduled employment under sub-section (1) the Inspector appointed under this Act shall be deemed to be the Inspector for the purpose of enforcement of the provisions so applied within the local limits of his jurisdiction.

23. Exemption of employer from liability in certain cases:

Where an employer is charged with an offence against this Act he shall be entitled upon complaint duly made by him to have any other person whom he charges as the actual offender brought before the court at the time appointed for hearing the charge; and if after the commission of the offence has been proved the employer proves to the satisfaction of the court:

(*a*) that he has used due deligence to enforce the execution of this Act; and

(*b*) that the said other person committed the offence in question without his knowledge consent or connivance.

that other person shall be convicted of the offence and shall be liable to the like punishment as if he were the employer and the employer shall be discharged:

Provided that in seeking to prove as aforesaid the employer may be examined on oath and the evidence of the employer or his witness if any shall be subject to cross-examination by or on behalf of the person whom the employer charges as the actual offender and by the prosecution.

24. Bar of suits:

No court shall entertain any suit for the recovery of wages in so far as the sum so claimed:

(*a*) forms the subject of an application under section 20 which has been presented by or on behalf of the plaintiff or

(*b*) has formed the subject of a direction under that section in favour of the plaintiff or

(*c*) has been adjudged in any proceeding under that section not to be due to the plaintiff or

(*d*) could have been recovered by an application under that section.

25. Contracting out:

Any contract or agreement whether made before or after the commencement of this Act whereby an employee either relinquishes or reduces his right to a minimum rate of wages or any privilege or concession accruing to him under this Act shall be null and void in so far as it purports to reduce the minimum rate of wages fixed under this Act.

26. Exemption and exceptions:

(1) The appropriate government may subject to such conditions if any as it may think fit to impose direct that the provisions of this Act shall not apply in relation to the wages payable to disabled employees.

(2) The appropriate government if for special reasons it thinks so fit by notification in the Official Gazette direct that subject to such conditions and for such period as it may specify the provisions of this Act or any of them shall not apply to all or any class of employees employed in any scheduled employment or to any locality where there is carried on a scheduled employment.

(2A) The appropriate government may if it is of opinion that having regard to the terms and conditions of service applicable to any class of employees in a scheduled employment generally or in a scheduled employment in a local area or to any establishment or a part of any establishment in a scheduled employment it is not necessary to fix minimum wages in respect of such employees of that class or in respect of employees in such establishment or such part of any establishment as are in receipt of wages exceeding such limit as may be prescribed in this behalf direct by notification in the Official Gazette and subject to such conditions if any as it may think fit to impose that the provisions of this Act or any of them shall not apply in relation to such employees.

(3) Nothing in this Act shall apply to the wages payable by an employer to a member of his family who is living with him and is dependent on him.

Explanation: In this sub-section a member of the employer's family shall be deemed to include his or her spouse or child or parent or brother or sister.

27. Power of State Government to add to Schedule:

The appropriate government after giving by notification in the Official Gazette not less than three months' notice of its intention so to do may by like notification add to either Part of the Schedule any employment in respect of which it is of opinion that minimum rates of wages should be fixed under this Act and thereupon the Schedule shall in its application to the State be deemed to be amended accordingly.

28. Power of Central Government to give directions:

The Central Government may give directions to a State Government as to the carrying into execution of this Act in the State.

29. Power of Central Government to make rules:

The Central Government may subject to the condition of previous publication by notification in the Official Gazette make rules prescribing the term of office of the members the procedure to be followed in the conduct of business the method of voting the manner of filling up casual vacancies in membership and the quorum necessary for the transaction of business of the Central Advisory Board.

30. Power of appropriate government to make rules:

(1) The appropriate government may subject to the condition of previous publication by notification in the Official Gazette make rules for carrying out the purposes of this Act.

(2) Without prejudice to the generality of the foregoing power such rules may:

(*a*) prescribe the term of office of the members the procedure to be followed in the conduct of business the method of voting the manner of filling up casual vacancies in membership and the quorum necessary for the transaction of business of the committees sub-committees and the Advisory Board;

(*b*) prescribe the method of summoning witnesses production of documents relevant to the subject-matter of the enquiry before the committees sub-committees and the Advisory Board;

(*c*) prescribe the mode of computation of the cash value of wages in kind and of concessions in respect of supplies of essential commodities at concession rates;

(*d*) prescribe the time and conditions of payment of and the deductions permissible from wages;

(*e*) provide for giving adequate publicity to the minimum rates of wages fixed under this Act;

(*f*) provide for a day of rest in every period of seven days and for the particulars to be entered in such registers and records;

(*g*) prescribe the number of hours of work which shall constitute a normal working day;

(*h*) prescribe the cases and circumstance in which an employee employed for a period of less than the requisite number of hours constituting a normal working day shall not be entitled to receive wages for a full normal working day;

(*i*) prescribe the form of registers and records to be maintained and the particulars to be entered in such registers and records;

(*j*) provide for the issue of wage book and wage slips and prescribe the manner of making and authenticating entries in wage books and wage slips;

(*k*) prescribe the powers of Inspectors for purposes of this Act;

(*l*) regulate the scale of costs that may be allowed in proceedings under section 20;

(*m*) prescribe the amount of court-fees payable in respect of proceedings under section 20; and

(*n*) provide for any other matter which is to be or may be prescribed.

30A. Rules made by Central Government to be laid before Parliament:

Every rule made by the Central Government under this Act shall be laid as soon as may be after it is made before each House of Parliament while it is in session for a total period of thirty days which may be comprised in one session or two successive sessions and if before the expiry of the session in which it is so laid or the session immediately following both Houses agree in making any modification in the rule or both Houses agree that the rule should not be made the rule shall thereafter have effect only in such modified form or be of no effect as the case may be so however that any such modification or annulment shall be without prejudice to the validity of anything previously done under that rule.

31. Validation of fixation of certain minimum rates of wages:

Where during the period:

(*a*) commencing on the 1st day of April 1952 and ending with the date of the commencement of the Minimum Wages (Amendment) Act 1954 (26 of 1954); or

(*b*) commencing on the 31st day of December 1954 and ending with the date of the commencement of the Minimum Wages (Amendment) Act 1957 (30 of 1957); or

(*c*) commencing on the 31st day of December 1959 and ending with the date of the commencement of the Minimum Wages (Amendment) Act 1961 (31 of 1961) minimum rate of wages have been fixed by an appropriate government as being payable to employees employed in any employment specified in the schedule in the belief or purported belief that such rates were being fixed under clause (a) of sub-section (1) of section 3 as in force immediately before the commencement of the Minimum Wages (Amendment) Act 1954 (26 of 1954) or the Minimum Wages (Amendment) Act 1957 (30 of 1957) or the Minimum Wages (Amendment) Act 1961 (31 of 1961) as the case may be such rates shall be deemed to have been fixed in accordance with law and shall not be called in question in any court on the ground merely that the relevant date specified for the purpose in that clause had expired at the time the rates were fixed :

Provided that nothing contained in this section shall extend or be construed to extend to affect any person with any punishment or penalty whatsoever by reason of the payment by him by way of wages to any of his employees during any period specified in this section of an amount which is less than the minimum rates of wages referred to in this section or by reason of non-compliance during the period aforesaid with any order or the rule issued under section 13.

SCHEDULE PART I

- Employment in any wollen carpet making or shawl weaving establishment.
- Employment in any rice mill flour mill or dal mill.
- Employment in any tobacco (including bidi making) manufactory.
- Employment in any plantation that is to say any estate which is maintained for the purpose of growing cinchona rubber tea or coffee.
- Employment in any oil mill.

- Employment under any local authority.
- Employment on the construction or maintenance of roads or in building operations.
- Employment in stone breaking or stone crushing.
- Employment in any lac manufactory.
- Employment in any mica works.
- Employment in public motor transport.
- Employment in tanneries and leather manufactory.
- Employment in gypsum mines.
- Employment in barytes mines.
- Employment in bauxite mines.
- Employment in manganese mines.
- Employment in the maintenance of buildings and employment in the construction and maintenance of runways.
- Employment in china clay mines.
- Employment in kyantite mines.
- Employment in copper mines.
- Employment in clay mines covered under the Mines Act 1952 (35 of 1952).
- Employment in magnesite mines covered under the Mines Act 1952 (35 of 1952).
- Employment in white clay mines.
- Employment in stone mines.

SCHEDULE PART II

(1) Employment in agriculture that is to say in any form of farming including the cultivation and tillage of the soil dairy farming the production cultivation growing and harvesting of any agricultural or horticultural commodity the raising of live-stock bees or poultry and any practice performed by a farmer or on a farm as incidental to or in conjunction with farm operation (including any forestry or timbering operations and the preparation for market and delivery to storage or to market or to carriage for transportation to market of farm produce).

Equal Remuneration Act, 1976

Preamble

An Act to provide for the payment of equal remuneration to men and women workers and for the prevention of discrimination, on the ground of sex, against women in the matter of employment and for matters connected therewith or incidental thereto. BE it enacted by Parliament in the Twenty-seventh Year of the Republic of India as follows:

1. ***Short title, extent and commencement*:** (1) This Act may be called the Equal Remuneration Act, 1976.

   (2) It extends to the whole of India.

   (3) It shall come into force on such date, not being later than three years from the passing of this Act, as the Central Government may, by notification, appoint and different dates may be appointed for different establishments or employments.

2. ***Definitions*:** In this Act, unless the context otherwise requires,-
   (a) "appropriate Government" means:

   (*i*) in relation to any employment carried on by or under the authority of the Central Government or a railway administration, or in relation to a banking company, a mine, oilfield or major port or any corporation established by or under a Central Act, the Central Government, and

   (*ii*) in relation to any other employment, the State Government;

   (*b*) "commencement of this Act" means, in relation to an establishment or employment, the date on which this Act comes into force in respect of that establishment or employment;

   (*c*) "employer" has the meaning assigned to it in clause (f) of section 2 of the Payment of Gratuity Act, 1972 (39 of 1972);

   (*d*) "man" and "woman" mean male and female human beings, respectively, of any age;

   (*e*) "notification" means a notification published in the Official Gazette;

   (*f*) "prescribed" means prescribed by rules made under this Act;

   (*g*) "remuneration" means the basic wage or salary, and any additional emoluments whatsoever payable, either in cash or in kind, to a person employed in respect of employment or work done in such employment, if the terms of the contract of employment, express or implied, were fulfilled;

   (*h*) "same work or work of a similar nature" means work in respect of which the skill, effort and responsibility required are the same, when performed under similar working conditions, by a man or a woman and the differences, if any, between the skill, effort and responsibility required of a man and those required of woman are not of practical importance in relation to the terms and conditions of employment :

   (*i*) "worker" means a worker in any establishment or employment in respect of which this Act has come into force;

   (*j*) words and expressions used in this Act and not defined but defined in the Industrial Disputes Act, 1947 (14 of 1947), shall have the meanings respectively assigned to them in that Act.

3. ***Act to have overriding effect:*** The provisions of this act shall have effect notwithstanding anything inconsistent therewith contained in any other law or in the terms of any award, agreement or contract of service, whether made before or after the commencement of this Act, or in any instrument having effect under any law for the time being in force.

4. ***Duty of employer to pay equal remuneration to men and women workers for same work or work of similar:*** (1) No employer shall pay to any worker, employed by him in an establishment or employment, remuneration, whether payable in cash or in kind, at rates less favourable than those at which remuneration is paid by him to the workers of the opposite sex in such establishment or employment for performing the same work or work of a similar nature.

   (2) No employer shall, for the purpose of complying with the provisions of sub-section (1), reduce the rate of remuneration of any worker.

   (3) Where, in an establishment or employment, the rates of remuneration payable before the commencement of this Act for men and women workers for the same work or work of a similar nature are different only on the ground of sex, then the higher (in cases where there are only two rates), or, as the case may be, the highest (in cases where there are more than two rates), of such rates shall be the rate at which remuneration shall be payable, on and from such commencement, to such men and women workers:

Provided that nothing in this sub-section shall be deemed to entitle a worker to the revision of the rate of remuneration payable to him or her with reference to the service rendered by him or her before the commencement of this Act.

5. ***No discrimination to be made while recruiting men and women workers:*** On and from the commencement of this Act, no employer shall, while making recruitment for the same work or work of a similar nature, or in any condition of service subsequent to recruitment such as promotions, training or transfer, make any discrimination against women except where the employment of women in such work is prohibited or restricted by or under any law for the time being in force:

   Provided that the provisions of this section shall not affect any priority or reservation for Scheduled Castes or Scheduled Tribes, ex-servicemen, retrenched employees or any other class or category of persons in the matter of recruitment to the posts in an establishment or employment.

6. ***Advisory committee:*** (1) For the purpose of providing increasing employment opportunities for women, the appropriate Government shall constitute one or more Advisory Committees to advise it with regard to the extent to which women may be employed in such establishments or employments as the Central Government may, by notification, specify in this behalf.

   (2) Every Advisory Committee shall consist of not less than ten persons, to be nominated by the appropriate Government, of which one-half shall be women.

(3) In tendering its advice, the Advisory Committee shall have regard to the number of women employed in the concerned establishment or employment, the nature of work, hours of work, suitability of women for employment, as the case may be, the need for providing increasing employment opportunities for women, including part-time employment and such relevant factors as the Committee may think fit.

(4) The Advisory Committee shall regulate its own procedure.

(5) The appropriate Government may, after considering the advice tendered to it by the Advisory Committee and after giving to the persons concerned in the establishment or employment an opportunity to make representations, issue such directions in respect of employment of women workers, as the appropriate Government may think fit.

7. ***Power of appropriate government to appoint authorities for hearing and deciding claims and complaints:*** (1) The appropriate Government may, by notification, appoint such officers, not below the rank of a Labour officer, as it thinks fit to be the authorities for the purpose of hearing and deciding :

(*a*) complaints with regard to the contravention of any provision of this Act;

(*b*) claims arising out of non-payment of wages at equal rates to men and women workers for the same work or work of a similar nature; and may, by the same or subsequent notification, define the local limits within which each such authority shall exercise its jurisdiction.

(2) Every complaint or claim referred to in sub-section (1) shall be made in such manner as may be prescribed.

(3) If any question arises as to whether two or more works are of the same nature or of a similar nature, it shall be decided by the authority appointed under sub-section (1).

(4) Where a complaint or claim is made to the authority appointed under sub-section (1) it may, after giving the applicant and the employer an opportunity of being heard, and after such inquiry as it may consider necessary, direct:

(*i*) in the case of a claim arising out of non-payment of wages at equal rates to men and women workers for the same work or work of a similar nature, that payment be made to the worker of the amount by which the wages payable to him exceed the amount actually paid;

(*ii*) in the case of complaint, that adequate steps be taken by the employer so as to ensure that there is no contravention of any provision of this Act.

(5) Every authority appointed under sub-section (1) shall have all the powers of a Civil Court under the Code of Civil Procedure, 1908

(5 of 1908), for the purpose of taking evidence and of enforcing the attendance of witnesses and compelling the production of documents, and every such authority shall be deemed to be a Civil Court for all the purposes of section 195 and Chapter XXVI of the **Code of Criminal Procedure, 1973** (2 of 1974).

(6) Any employer or worker aggrieved by any order may be an authority appointed under sub-section (1), on a complaint or claim may, within thirty days from the date of the order, prefer an appeal to such authority as the appropriate Government may, by notification, specify in this behalf, and that authority may, after hearing the appeal, confirm, modify or reverse the order appealed against and no further appeal shall lie against the order made by such authority.

(7) The authority referred to in sub-section (6) may, if it is satisfied that the appellant was prevented by sufficient cause from preferring the appeal within the period specified in sub-section (6), allow the appeal to be preferred within a further period of thirty days but not thereafter.

(8) The provisions of sub-section (1) of section 33C of the **Industrial Disputes Act, 1947** (14 of 1947), shall apply for the recovery of monies due from an employer arising out of the decision of an authority appointed under this section.

8. ***Duty of employers to maintain registers:*** On and from the commencement of this Act, every employer shall maintain such registers and other documents in relation to the workers employed by him as may be prescribed.

9. ***Inspectors:*** (1) The appropriate Government may, by notification, appoint such persons as it may think fit to be Inspectors for the purpose of making an investigation as to whether the provisions of this Act, or the rules made there under, are being complied with by employers, and may define the local limits within which an Inspector may make such investigation.

(2) Every Inspector shall be deemed to be a public servant within the meaning of section 21 of the Indian Penal Code (45 of 1860).

(3) An Inspector may, at any place within the local limits of his jurisdiction, - (*a*) enter, at any reasonable time, with such assistance as he thinks fit, any building, factory, premises or vessel;

(*b*) require any employer to produce any register, muster-roll or other documents relating to the employment of workers, and examine such documents;

(*c*) take on the spot or otherwise, the evidence of any person for the purpose of ascertaining whether the provisions of this Act are being, or have been, complied with;

(*d*) examine the employer, his agent or servant or any other person found in charge of the establishment or any premises connected therewith or any person whom the Inspector has reasonable cause to believe to be, or to have been a worker in the establishment;

(e) make copies, or take extracts from, any register or other document maintained in relation to the establishment under this Act.

(4) Any person required by an Inspector to produce any register or other document or to give any information shall comply with such requisition.

10. *Penalties:* (1) If after the commencement of this Act, any employer, being required by or under the Act, so to do - (a) omits or fails to maintain any register or other document in relation to workers employed by him, or

(b) omits or fails to produce any register, muster-roll or other document relating to the employment of workers, or

(c) omits or refuses to give any evidence or prevents his agent, servant, or any other person in charge of the establishment, or any worker, from giving evidence, or

(d) omits or refuses to give any information, he shall be punishable with simple imprisonment for a term which may extend to one month or with fine which may extend to ten thousand rupees or with both.

(2) If, after the commencement of this Act, any employer - (a) makes any recruitment in contravention of the provisions of this Act, or

(b) makes any payment of remuneration at unequal rates to men and women workers, for the same work or work of a similar nature, or

(c) makes any discrimination between men and women workers in contravention of the provisions of this Act, or

(d) omits or fails to carry out any direction made by the appropriate Government under sub-section (5) of section 6, he shall be punishable with fine which shall not be less than ten thousand rupees but which may extend to twenty thousand rupees or with imprisonment for a term which shall be not less than three months but which may extend to one year or with both for the first offence, and with imprisonment which may extend to two years for the second and subsequent offences.

(3) If any person being required so to do, omits or refuses to produce to an Inspector any register or other document or to give any information, he shall be punishable with fine which may extend to five hundred rupees.

11. *Offences by companies:* (1) Where an offence under this Act has been committed by a company, every person who at the time the offence was committed, was in charge of, and was responsible to, the company for the conduct of the business of the company, as well as the company, shall be deemed, to be guilty of the offence and shall be liable to be proceeded against and punished accordingly:

Provided that nothing contained in this sub-section shall render any such person liable to any punishment, if he proves that the offence was committed without his knowledge or that he had exercised all due diligence to prevent the commission of such offence.

(2) Notwithstanding anything contained in sub-section (1), where any offence under this Act been committed by a company and it is proved that the offence has been committed with the consent or connivance of or is attributable to any neglect on the part of any director, manager, secretary or other officer of the company, such director, manager, secretary or other officer shall be deemed to be guilty of that offence and shall be liable to be proceeded against and punished accordingly.

Explanation: For the purposes of this section, - (a) "company" means any body corporate and includes a firm or other association of individuals; and

(*b*) "director", in relation to a firm, means a partner in the firm.

12. ***Cognizance and trial of offence*:** (1) No court inferior to that of a metropolitan magistrate or judicial Magistrate of the first class shall try any offence punishable under this Act.

(2) No court shall take cognizance of an offence punishable under this Act except upon - (a) its own knowledge or upon a complaint made by the appropriate Government or an officer authorised by it in this behalf, or

(*b*) a complaint made by the person aggrieved by the offence or by any recognised welfare institution or organization.

Explanation: For the purposes of this sub-section "recognised welfare institution or organisation" means a social welfare institution or organisation recognised in this behalf by the Central or State Government.

13. ***Power to make rules*:** (1) The Central Government may, by notification, make rules for carrying out the provisions of this Act.

(2) In particular, and without prejudice to the generality of the foregoing power, such rules may provide for all or any of the following matters, namely:- (a) the manner in which complaint or claim referred to in sub-section (1) of section 7 shall be made;

(*b*) registers and other documents which an employer is required under section 8 to maintain in relation to the workers employed by him;

(*c*) any other matter which is required to be, or may be, prescribed.

(3) Every rule made by the Central Government under this Act shall be laid, as soon as may be after it is made, before each House of Parliament, while it is in session, for a total period of thirty days which may be comprised in one session or in two or more successive sessions, and if, before the expiry of the session immediately following the session

or the successive sessions aforesaid, both Houses agree in making any modification in the rule or both Houses agree that the rule should not be made, the rule shall thereafter have effect only in such modified form or be of no effect, as the case may be; so, however, that any such modification or annulment shall be without prejudice to the validity of anything previously done under that rule.

14. ***Power of central government to give orders*****:** The Central Government may give directions to a State Government as to the carrying into execution of this Act in the State.

15. ***Act not to apply in certain special cases*****:** Nothing in this Act shall apply - (*a*) to cases affecting the terms and conditions of a woman's employment in complying with the requirements of any law giving special treatment to women, or

(*b*) to any special treatment accorded to women in connection with - (i) the birth or expected birth of a child, or

(*ii*) the terms and conditions relating to retirement, marriage or death or to any provision made in connection with the retirement, marriage or death.

16. ***Power to make declaration*****:** Where the appropriate Government is, on a consideration of all the circumstances of the case, satisfied that the differences in regard to the remuneration, or a particular species of remuneration, of men and women workers in any establishment or employment is based on a factor other than sex, it may, by notification, make a declaration to that effect, and any act of the employer attributable to such a difference shall not be deemed to be contravention of any provision of this Act.

17. ***Power to remove difficulties*****:** If any difficulty arises in giving effect to the provisions of this Act the Central Government may, by notification, make any order, not inconsistent with the provisions of this Act, which appears to it to be necessary for the purpose of removing the difficulty:

Provided that every such order shall, as soon as may be after it is made, be laid before each House of Parliament.

18. ***Repeal and saving*****:** (1) The Equal Remuneration Ordinance, 1975 (12 of 1975), is hereby repealed.

(2) Notwithstanding such repeal, anything done or any action taken under the Ordinance so repealed (including any notification, nomination, appointment, order or direction made there under) shall be deemed to have been done or taken under the corresponding provisions of this Act as if this Act were in force when such thing was done or action was taken.

The Payment of Bonus Act, 1965

Preamble

An Act to provide for the payment of Bonus to persons employed in certain establishments and for matters connected therewith. Be it enacted by the Parliament in the sixteenth year of the Republic of India as follows :

1. ***Short title, extent and application*:** (1) This Act may be called the Payment of Bonus Act,1965

    (2) It extends to the whole of India [Note: The words "except the State of Jammu and Kashmir" omitted by Act 51 of 1970, Sec. 2 and Schedule (w.e.f. 1st September,1971).

    (3) Save as otherwise provided in this Act, it shall apply to -

    (*a*) Every factory; and

    (*b*) Every other establishment in which twenty or more persons are employed on any day during an accounting year :

[(Note: Ins. by Act 23 of 1976, Sec. 3 (w.e.f. 25th September, 1975) Provided that the appropriate Government may, after giving not less than two months' notice of its intention so to do, by notification in the official Gazette, apply the provisions of this Act with effect from such accounting year as may be specified in the notification, to any establishment or class establishments [including an establishment being a factory within the meaning of sub-clause (ii) of Cl. (m) of Sec. 2 of the Factories Act, 1948 (63 of 1948)] employing such number of persons less than twenty as may be specified in the notification ; so however, that number of persons so specified shall in no case be less than ten.]

(4) Save as otherwise provided in this Act, the provisions of this Act shall in relation to a factory or other establishment to which this Act applies, have effect in respect of the accounting year commencing on any day in the year 1964 and in respect of every subsequent accounting year :

[(Note: Added by Act 51 of 1970, Sec. 2 and Schedule (w.e.f. 1st September, 1971) Provided that in relation to the State of Jammu and Kashmir, the reference to the accounting year commencing on any day in the year 1964 and every subsequent accounting year shall be construed as reference to the accounting year commencing on any day in the year 1968 and every subsequent accounting year.]

[(Note: Ins. by Act 23 of 1976, Sec. 3 (w.e.f. 25th September, 1975) Provided further that when the provisions of this Act have been made applicable to any establishment or class of establishments by the issue of a notification under the proviso to sub-section (3), the reference to the accounting year commencing on any day in the year 1964 and every subsequent accounting year or, as the case may be, the reference to the accounting year commencing on any day in the year 1968 and every subsequent accounting year shall in relation to such establishment or class of establishments, be construed as a reference to the accounting year specified in such notification and every subsequent accounting year.]

(5) An establishment to which this Act applies [Note: The words, brackets, letter and figure "under Cl. (b) of sub-section (3)" omitted by Act 23 of 1976, Sec.8 (w.e.f. 25th September, 1975)] shall continue to be governed by this Act notwithstanding that the number of persons employed therein falls below twenty [(Note: Ins. by Act 23 of 1976, Sec- 3, (w.e.f. 25th September, 1975) or, as the case may be, the number specified in the notification issued under the proviso to sub-section (3)].

2. ***Act 21 of 1965 to have modified effect for a particular period:*** The Payment of Bonus Act, 1965 (hereinafter referred to as the principal Act) shall:

(*a*) In relation to a factory or other establishment to which the principal Act applies immediately before the commencement of this Act, and

(*b*) In relation to a banking company and the Industrial Reconstruction Corporation of India to which the principal Act applies on and from such commencement by virtue of this Act.

Have effect in respect of the accounting year commencing on any day in the year 1976 [and in respect of the accounting year commencing on any day in the year 1977], as if the amendments specified in Sections 3 to 19 has been made in that Act.

Explanation: In this section, the expressions "banking company" and "accounting year" shall have the meanings respectively assigned to them in clauses (8) and (1) of Section 2 of the principal Act".

3. ***Definitions:*** In this Act, unless the context otherwise requires:

(1) "Accounting year" means:

(*i*) In relation to a corporation, the year ending on the day on which the books and accounts of the corporation are to be closed and balanced:

(*ii*) In relation to a company, the period in respect of which any profit and loss account of the company laid before it in annual general meeting is made up, whether that period is a year or not;

(*iii*) In any other case:

(*a*) The year commencing on the 1st day of April ; or

(*b*) If the accounts of an establishment maintained by the employer thereof are closed and balanced on any day other than the 31st day of March, then, at the option of the employer, the year ending on the day on which its accounts are so closed and balanced :

Provided that an option once exercised by the employer under para. (b) of this sub-clause shall not again be exercised except with the previous permission in writing of the prescribed authority and upon such conditions as that authority may think fit :

(2) "Agricultural income" shall have the same meaning as in the Income-tax Act ;

(3) "Agricultural income-tax law" means any law for the time being in force relating to the levy of tax on agricultural income ;

(4) "Allocable surplus" means:

(*a*) In relation to an employer, being a company [(Note: Ins. by Act 66 of 1980 (w.e.f. 21st August,1980) (other than a banking company)] which has not made the arrangements prescribed under the Income-tax Act for the declaration and payment within Indian of the dividends payable out of its profits in accordance with the provisions of Sec.194 of that Act, sixty-seven per cent of the available surplus in an accounting year ;

(5) In any other case, sixty per cent of such available surplus ; (Note: Certain words omitted by Act 23 of 1976, Sec. 4 (w.e.f. 25th September, 1975)

(6) "Available surplus" means the available surplus computed under Sec.5;

(7) "Award" means an interim or a final determination of any industrial dispute or of any question relating thereto any Labour Court. Industrial Tribunal or National Tribunal constituted under the Industrial Disputes Act, 1947 (14 of 1947), or by any other authority constituted under any corresponding law relating to investigation and settlement of industrial disputes in force in a State and includes an arbitration award made under Sec. 10-A of that Act or under that law;

(8) "Banking company" means a banking company as defined in Sec. 5 of the Banking Companies Act, 1949 (10 of 1949), and includes the State Bank of India, any subsidiary bank as defined in the State Bank of India (Subsidiary Bank) Act, 1959 (38 of 1959), [(Note: Ins. by Act 23 of 1976 Sec. 4 (w.e.f. 25th September, 1975) any corresponding new bank specified in the First Schedule to the Banking Companies (Acquisition and Transfer of Undertakings) Act, 1970, (5 of 1970), [Note: Ins. by Act 66 of 1980, (w.e.f. 21st August, 1980) any corresponding new bank constituted under Sec. 3 of Banking Companies (Acquisition and Transfer of Undertakings) Act, 1980] any co-operative bank as defined in Cl. (bii) of Sec. 2 of the Reserve Bank of India Act, 1934 (2 of 1934),] and any other banking institution which may be notified in this behalf by the Central Government.

(9) "Company" means any company as defined in Sec. 3 of the Companies Act, 1956 (1 of 1956), and includes a foreign company within the meaning of Sec. 591 of that Act;

(10) "Co-operative society" means a society registered or deemed to be registered under the Co-operative Societies Act, 1912 (2 of 1912), or any other law for the time being in force in any State relating to co-operative societies;

(11) "Corporation" means any body corporate established by or under any Central, Provincial or State Act but does not include a company or a co-operative society:

(12) "Direct tax" means:

(*a*) Any tax chargeable under:

(*i*) The Income-tax Act;

(*ii*) The Super Profits Tax Act, 1963 (14 of 1963);

(*iii*) The Companies (Profits) Surtax Act, 1964 (7 of 1964);

(*iv*) The agricultural income-tax law; and

(*b*) Any other tax which, having regard to its nature or incidence, may be declared by the Central Government, by notification in the official Gazette to be a direct tax for the purposes of this Act;

(13) "Employee" means any person (other than an apprentice) employed on a salary or wage not exceeding [(Note: Subs. by Act No. 67 of 1985, Sec. 2, for the words "one thousand and six hundred rupees" (w.e.f. 7th November, (1985)) two thousand and five hundred rupees] per mensem in any industry to do any skilled or unskilled manual, supervisory, managerial, administrative, technical or clerical work for hire or reward, whether the terms of employment be express or implied;

(14) "Employer" includes:

(*i*) In relation to an establishment which is factory, the owner or occupier of the factory, including the agent of such owner or occupier, the legal representative of a deceased owner or occupier and where a person has been named as a manager of the factory under Cl. (f) of sub-section (1) of Sec. 7 of the Factories Act, 1948, the person named; and

(*ii*) In relation to any other establishment, the person who, or the authority which, has the ultimate control over the affairs of the establishment and where the said affairs are entrusted to a manager, managing director or managing agent, such manager, managing director or managing agent;

(15) "Establishment in private section" means any establishment other than an establishment in public sector;

(16) "Establishment in public sector" means an establishment owned, controlled or managed by:

(*a*) A Government company as defined in Sec. 617 of the Companies Act, 1956 (1 of 1956);

(*b*) A corporation in which not less than forty per cent of its capital is held (whether singly or taken together) by:

(i) The Government; or

(ii) The Reserve Bank of India; or

(iii) A corporation owned by the Government or the Reserve Bank of India;

(17) "Factory" shall have the same meaning as in Cl. (m) of Sec. 2 of the Factories Act, 1948 (63 of 1948);

(18) "Gross profits" means the gross profits calculated under Sec. 4;

(19) "Income-tax Act" means the Income-tax Act, 1961 (43 of 1961);

(20) "Prescribed" means prescribed by rules made under this Act;

(21) "Salary or wage" means all remuneration (other than remuneration in respect of overtime work) capable of being expressed in terms of money, which would, if the terms of employment, express or implied, were fulfilled, be payable to an employment or of work done in such employment and includes dearness allowance (that is to say, all cash payments, by whatever name called, paid to an employee on account of a rise in the cost of living, but does not include:

(i) Any other allowance which the employee is for the time being entitled to;

(ii) The value of any house accommodation or of such of light, water, medical attendance or other amenity or of any service of any confessional supply of food grains or other articles;

(iii) Any traveling concession;

(iv) Any bonus (including incentive, production and attendance bonus);

(v) Any contribution paid or payable by the employer to any pension fund or provident fund or for the benefit of the employees under any law for the time being in force;

(vi) Any retrenchment compensation or any gratuity or other retirement benefit payable to the employees or any ex gratia payment made to him;

(vii) Any commission payable to the employee.

(viii) Any commission payable to the employee.

Explanation: Where an employee is given in lieu of the whole or part of the salary or wage payable to him, free food allowance or free food by his employer, such food allowance or the value of such food shall, for the purpose of this clause, be deemed to form part of the salary or wage of such employees.

(22) Words and expressions used but not defined in this Act and defined in the Industrial Disputes Act, 1947 (14 of 1947), shall have the meanings respectively assigned to them in that Act.

4. ***Establishments to include departments, undertakings and branches*:** Where an establishment consists of different departments or undertakings or has branches, whether situated in the same place or in different places, all such departments or undertakings or branches shall be treated as parts of the same establishment for the purpose of computation of bonus under this Act:

Provided that where for any accounting year a separate balance-sheet and profit and loss account are prepared and maintained in respect of any such department or undertaking or branch, then, such department or undertaking or breach shall be treated as separate establishment for the purpose of computation of bonus under this Act for that year, unless such department or undertaking or branch was immediately before the commencement of that accounting year treated as part of the establishment for the purpose of computation of bonus.

5. ***Computation of gross profits*:** The gross profits derived by an employer from an establishment in respect of any accounting year shall:

(*a*) In the case of a banking company, be calculated in the manner specified in the First Schedule ;

(*b*) In any other case, be calculated in the manner specified in the Second Schedule.

6. ***Computation of available surplus*:** The available surplus in respect of any accounting year shall be the gross profits for that year after deducting therefrom the sums referred to in Sec. 6.

[(Note: Added by Act 8 of 1969, Sec. 2) Provided that the available surplus in respect of the accounting year commencing on any day in the year 1968 and in respect of every subsequent accounting year shall be the aggregate of:

(*a*) The gross profits for that accounting year after deducting therefrom the sums referred to in Section 6; and

(*b*) An amount equal to the difference between:

(*i*) The direct tax, calculated in accordance with the provisions of Section 7, in respect of an amount equal to the gross profits of the employer for the immediately preceding accounting year; and

(*ii*) The direct tax, calculated in accordance with the provisions of Section 7, in respect of an amount equal to the gross profits of the employer for such preceding accounting year after deducting therefrom the amount of bonus which the employer has paid or is liable to pay to his employees in accordance with the provisions of this Act for that year.

7. ***Sums deductible from gross profits*****:** The following sums shall be deducted from the gross profits as prior charges, namely:

(*a*) Any amount by way of depreciation admissible in accordance with the provisions of sub-section (1) of Section 32 of the Income-tax Act, or in accordance with the provisions of the agricultural Income-tax law, as the case may be:

Provided that where an employer has been paying bonus of his employees under a settlement or an award or agreement made before the 29th May, 1965, and subsisting on that date after deducting from the gross profits notional normal depreciation, then the amount of depreciation to be deducted under this clause shall, at the option of such employer (such option to be exercised once and within one year from that date) continue to be such notional normal depreciation;

(*b*) Any amount by way of [(Note: Subs. by Act 66 of 1980) development rebate or investment allowance or development allowance] which the employer is entitled to deduction from his income under the Income-tax Act;

(*c*) Subject to the provisions of Section 7, any direct tax which the employer is liable to pay for the accounting year in respect of his income, profits and gains during the year;

(*d*) Such further sums as are specified in respect of the employer in the [(Note: Ibid) Third Schedule].

8. ***Calculation of direct tax payable by the employer*****:** [(Note: Subs. by Act 68 of 1969) Any direct tax payable by the employer] for any accounting year shall, subject to the following provisions, be calculated at the rates applicable to the income of the employer for that year, namely:

(*a*) In calculating such tax no account shall be taken of:

(*i*) Any loss incurred by the employer in respect of any previous accounting year and carried forward under any law for time being in force relating to direct taxes;

(*ii*) Any arrears of depreciation which the employer is entitled to add to the amount of the allowance for depreciation for any following accounting year or years under sub-section (2) of Section 32 of the Income-tax Act;

(*iii*) Any exemption conferred on the employer under Section 84 of the Income-tax Act or of any deduction The Orient Tavern which he is entitled under sub-section (1) of Section 101 of that Act, as in force immediately before the commencement of the Finance Act, 1965 (10 of 1965);

(*b*) Where the employer is a religious or a charitable institution to which the provisions of Section 32 do not apply and the whole or any part of its income is exempt from tax under the Income-tax Act, then, with respect The Orient Tavern the income so exempted, such institution shall be treated as if it were a company in which the public are substantially interested within the meaning of that Act;

(*c*) Where the employer is an individual or a Hindu undivided family, the tax payable by such employer under the Income-tax Act shall be calculated on the basis that the income derived by him from the establishment is his only income;

(*d*) Where the income of any employer includes any profits and gains derived from the export of any goods or merchandise out of India any rebate on such income is allowed under any law for the time being in force relating to direct taxes, then, no account shall be taken of such rebate;

(*e*) No account shall be taken of any rebate [(Note: Subs. by Act 66 of 1980) other than development rebate or investment allowance or development allowance)] or credit or relief or deduction (not hereinafter mentioned in this section) in the payment of any direct tax allowed under nay law for the time being in force relating to direct taxes or under the relevant annual Finance Act, for the development of any industry.

9. ***Eligibility for bonus:*** Every employee shall be entitled to be paid by his employer in an accounting year, bonus, in accordance with the provisions of this Act, provided he has worked in the establishment for not less than thirty working days in that year.

10. ***Disqualification for bonus:*** Notwithstanding anything contained in this Act, an employee shall be disqualified from receiving bonus under this Act, if he is dismissed from service for:

(*a*) Fraud; or

(*b*) Riotous or violent behaviour while on the premises of the establishment; or

(*c*) Theft, misappropriation or sabotage of any property of the establishment.

11. ***Payment of minimum bonus:*** Subject to the other provisions of this Act, every employer shall be bound to pay to every employee in respect of the accounting year commencing on any day in the year 1979 and in respect of every subsequent accounting year, a minimum bonus which shall be 8.33 per cent of the salary or wage earned by the employee during the accounting year or one hundred rupees, whichever is higher, whether or not the employer has any allocable surplus in the accounting year:

Provided that there an employee has not employed fifteen years of age at the beginning of the accounting year, the provision of this section shall have effect in relation to such employee as if for the words “one hundred rupees”, the words “sixty rupees” were substituted.

12. ***Payment of maximum bonus:*** (1) Where in respect of any accounting year referred to in Sec.10, the allocable surplus exceeds the amount of minimum bonus payable to the employees under that section, the employer shall, in lieu of such minimum bonus, be bound to pay to every employee in respect of that accounting year bonus which shall be an amount in proportion to the salary or wage earned by the employee during the accounting year subject to a maximum of twenty per cent of such salary or wage.

(*2*) In computing the allocable surplus under this section, the amount set on or the amount set-off under the provisions of Sec.15 shall be taken into account in accordance with the provisions of that section.

13. ***Calculation of bonus with respect to certain employees:*** Where the salary or wage of an employee exceeds one thousand and six hundred rupees per mensem, the bonus payable to such employee under Sec.10, or as the case may be, under Sec.11, shall be calculated as if his salary or wage were one thousand and six hundred rupees per mensem.

14. ***Proportionate reduction in bonus in certain cases:*** Where an employee has not worked for all the working days in an accounting year, the minimum bonus of one hundred rupees or, as the case may be, of sixty rupees, if such bonus is higher than 8.33 per cent of his salary or wage for the days he has worked in that accounting year, shall be proportionately reduced.

15. ***Computation of number of working days:*** For the purposes of Sec. 13, an employee shall be deemed to have worked in an establishment in any accounting year also on the days on which:

(*a*) He has been laid off under an agreement or as permitted by standing orders under the Industrial Employment (Standing Orders) Act, 1946 (20 of 1946), or under the Industrial Disputes Act, 1947 (14 of 1947) or under any other law applicable to the establishment;

(*b*) He has been on leave with salary or wage;

(*c*) He has been absent due to temporary disablement caused by accident arising out of and in the course of his employment; and

(*d*) The employee has been on maternity leave with salary or wage, during the accounting year.

16. ***Set-on and set-off of allocable surplus:*** (1) Where for any accounting year, the allocable surplus exceeds the amount of maximum bonus payable to the employees in the establishment under Sec.11, the, the excess shall, subject to a limit of twenty per cent of the total salary or wage of the employees employed in the establishment in that accounting year, be carried forward for being set-on in the succeeding accounting year and so on up to and inclusive of the fourth accounting year to be utilized for the purpose of payment of bonus in the manner illustrated in the Fourth Schedule.

(2) Where for any accounting year, there is no available surplus or the allocable surplus in respect of that year falls short of the amount of minimum bonus payable to the employees in the establishment under Section 10, and there is no amount or sufficient amount carried

forward and set on under sub-section (1) which could be utilized for the purpose of payment of the minimum bonus, then, such minimum amount or the deficiency, as the case may be, shall be carried forward for being set-off in the succeeding accounting year and so on up to and inclusive of the fourth accounting year in the manner illustrated in the Fourth Schedule.

(3) The principle of set-on and set-off as illustrated in the Fourth Schedule shall apply to all other cases not covered by sub-section (1) or sub-section (2) for the purpose of payment of bonus under this Act.

(4) Where in any accounting year any amount has been carried forward and set-on or set-off under this section, then, in calculating bonus for the succeeding accounting year, the amount of set-on or set-off carried forward from the earliest accounting year shall first be taken into account.

17. ***Special provisions with respect to certain establishments:*** (1) Where an establishment is newly set up, whether before or after the commencement of this Act, the employees of such establishment shall be entitled to be paid bonus under this Act in accordance with the provisions of sub-section (1-A), (1-B) and (1-C).

(1-A) In the first five accounting years following the accounting year in which the employee sells the goods produced or manufactured by him or renders services, as the case may be, from such establishment, bonus shall be payable only in respect of the accounting year in which the employer derives profit from such establishment and such bonus shall be calculated in accordance with the provisions of this Act in relation to that year, but without applying the provisions of Sec. 15.

(1-B) For the sixth and seventh accounting years following the accounting year in which the employer sells the goods produced or manufactured by him or renders services, as the case may be, from such establishment, the provisions of Sec. 15 shall apply subject to the following modifications namely:

(*i*) For the sixth accounting year:

Set on or set-off, as the case may be, shall be made in the manner illustrated in the [(Note: Subs. by Act 66 of 1980, (w.e.f. 25th September,1975) Fourth Schedule] taking into account the excess or deficiency, if any, as the case may be, of the allocable surplus set-on or set-off in respect of the fifth and sixth accounting year;

(*ii*) For the seventh accounting year:

Set-on or set-off, as the case may be, shall be made in the manner illustrated the [(Note: Subs. by Act 66 of 1980, (w.e.f. 25th September,1975) Fourth Schedule] taking into account the excess of deficiency, if any, as the case may be, of the allocable surplus set-on or set-off in respect of the fifth, sixth and seventh accounting years.

(1-C) From the eighth accounting year following the accounting year in which the employer sells the goods produced or manufactured by him or renders services, as the case may be, from such establishment, the provisions of Sec. 15 shall apply in relation to such establishment as they apply in relation to any other establishment.

Explanation I: For the purpose of sub-section (1), an establishment shall not be deemed to be newly set up merely by reason of a change in its location, management, name or ownership.

Explanation II: For the purpose of sub-section (1-A), an employer shall not be deemed to have derived profit in any accounting year unless -

(*a*) He has made provision for that year's depreciation, to which he is entitled under the Income-tax Act or, as the case may be, under the agricultural income-tax law ; and

(*b*) The arrears of such depreciation and losses incurred by him in respect of the establishment for the previous accounting years have been fully set-off against his profits.

Explanation III: For the purposes of sub-sections (1-A), (1-B) and (1-C) sale of the goods produced or manufactured during the course of the trail running of any factory or of the prospecting stage or an oil-field shall not be taken into consideration and where any question arises with regard to such production or manufacture, the decision of the appropriate Government, made after giving the parties reasonable opportunity of representing the case, shall be final and shall not be called in question by any court or other authority.

(2) The provisions of [(Note: Subs. by Act 23 of 1976, (w.e.f. 25th September, 1975) sub-sections (1), (1-A), (1-B) and (1-C) shall, so far as may be, apply to new departments or undertakings or branches set up by existing establishments :

Provided that if an employer in relation to an existing establishment consisting of different departments or undertakings or branches (whether or not in the same industry) set up at different periods has, before the 29th May, 1965, been paying bonus to the employees of all such departments or undertakings or branches irrespective of the date on which such departments or undertakings or branches were set up, on the basis of the consolidated profits computed in respect of all such departments or undertakings or branches, then, such employer shall be liable to pay bonus in accordance with the provisions of this Act to the employees of all such departments or undertakings or branches (whether set up before or after that date) on the basis of the consolidated profits computed as aforesaid.

18. ***Adjustment of customary or interim bonus against bonus payable under the Act:*** Where in any accounting year

(*a*) An employer has paid any puja bonus or other customary bonus to an employees ; or

(*b*) An employer has paid a part of the bonus payable under this Act to an employee before the date on which such bonus becomes payable;

Then, the employer shall be entitled to deduct the amount of bonus so paid from the amount of bonus payable by him to the employee under this Act in respect of that accounting year and the employee shall be entitled to receive only the balance.

19. ***Deduction of certain amounts from bonus payable under the Act:*** Where in any accounting year, an employee is found guilty of misconduct causing financial loss to the employer, then, it shall, be lawful for the employer to deduct the amount of loss from the amount of bonus payable by him to the employee under this Act in respect of that accounting year only and the employee shall be entitled to receive the balance, if any.

20. ***Time-limit for payment of bonus:*** [(Note: Subs. by Act 23 of 1976, (w.e.f. 25th September, 1975) All amounts] payable to an employee by way of bonus under this Act shall be paid in cash by hi employer.

(*a*) Where there is a dispute regarding payment of bonus pending before any authority under Sec. 22, within a month from the date on which the award becomes enforceable or the settlement comes into operation, in respect of such dispute;

(*b*) In any other case, within a period of eight months from the close of the accounting year:

Provided that the appropriate Government or such authority as the appropriate Government may specify in this behalf may, upon an application made to it by the employer and for sufficient reasons, by order, extend the said period of eight months to such further period or periods as it thinks fit; so, however, that the total period so extended shall not in any case exceed two years.

(Note: Sub-sections (2) to (7) inserted by Act 68 of 1972, Sec. 4 omitted by Act 23 of 1976, Sec. 13 (w.e.f. 25th September, 1975).

(Note: Sub-section (8) inserted by Act 39 of 1973, Sec. 4, omitted by Act 55 of 1973, Sec. 2 (w.e.f. 1st September, 1973).

21. ***Application of Act to establishments in public section in certain cases:*** [(Note: Renumbered by Act 66 of 1980)1] If in any accounting year an establishment in public section sells any goods produced or manufactured by it or renders any services, in competition with an establishment in private sector, and the income from such sale or services or both is not less than twenty per cent of the gross income of the establishment in public sector for that year, then, the provisions of this Act shall apply in relation to such establishment in public sector as they apply in relation to a like establishment in private sector.

[(Note: Ins. by Sec. 11, ibid) (2) Save as otherwise provided in sub-section (1), nothing in this Act shall apply to employees employed by any establishment in public sector.]

22. ***Recovery of bonus due from an employer:*** Where any money is due to an employee by way of bonus from his employer under a settlement or an award or agreement, the employee himself, or any other person authorised by him in writing in this behalf, or in the case of the death of the employee, his assignee or heirs may, without prejudice to any other mode of recovery made an application to the appropriate Government for the recovery, of the money due to him, and if the appropriate Government or such authority as the appropriate Government may specify in this behalf is satisfied that any money is so due, it shall issue a certificate for that amount to the Collector who shall proceed to recover the same in the same manner as an arrear of land revenue:

Provided that every such application shall be made within one year from the date on which the money became due to the employee from the employer:

Provided further that any such application may be entertained after the expiry of the said period of one year, if the appropriate Government is satisfied that the applicant had sufficient cause for not making the application within the said period.

Explanation: In this section and in [(Note: Subs. by Act 66 of 1980, (w.e.f. 21st August, 1980) Secs. 22,23,24 and 25], "employee" includes a person who is entitled to the payment of bonus under this Act but who is no longer in employment.

23. ***Reference of dispute under this Act:*** Where any dispute arises between an employer and his employees with respect to the bonus payable under this Act or with respect to the application of this Act to an establishment in public sector, then, such dispute shall be deemed to be an industrial dispute within the meaning of the Industrial Dispute Act, 1947 (14 of 1947), or of any corresponding law relating to investigation and settlement of industrial disputes in force in a State and the provisions of that Act or, as the case may be, such law, save as otherwise expressly provided, apply accordingly.

24. ***Presumption about accuracy of balance-sheet and profit and loss account of corporations and companies:*** (1) Where, during the course of proceedings before any arbitrator or tribunal under the Industrial Disputes Act, 1947 (14 of 1947), or under any corresponding law relating to investigation and settlement of industrial disputes in force in a State (hereinafter in this section [(Note: Subs. by Act 23 of 1976, Sec. 16 for land in Secs. 24 and 25, (w.e.f. 25th September, 1975) and in [(Note: Subs. by Act 66 of 1980, (w.e.f. 21st August, 1980) [Secs. 24 and 25]] referred to as the "said authority") to which any dispute of he nature specified in Sec. 22 has been referred, the balance-sheet and the profit and loss account of an employer, being a corporation or a company (other than a banking company), duly audited by the Comptroller and Auditor-General of India or by auditors duly qualified to act as auditors of companies under sub-section (1) of Sec.226 of the Companies Act,, 1956 (1 of 1956), are produced before it, then the said authority may presume the statements and the particulars contained in such balance-sheet and profit and loss account to be accurate and it shall not be necessary for the corporation or the company to prove the accuracy of such statements and particulars by the filing of an affidavit or by any other mode:

Provided that where the said authority is satisfied that the statements and particulars contained in the balance-sheet or the profit and loss account of the corporation or the company are not accurate, it may take such steps as it thinks necessary to find out the accuracy of such statements and particulars.

(2) When an application is made to the said authority by any trade union being a party to the dispute or where there is not trade union, by the employees being a party to the dispute, requiring any clarification relating to any item in the balance-sheet or the profit and loss account, it may, after satisfying itself that such clarification is necessary, by order, direct the corporation or, as the case may be, the company, to furnish to the trade union or the employees such clarification within such time as may be specified in the direction and the corporation or, as the case may be, the company shall comply with such direction.

25. ***Audited accounts of banking companies not to be questioned:*** (1) Where any dispute of the nature specified in Sec.22 between an employer, being a banking company, and its employees has been referred to the said authority under that section and during the course of proceedings the accounts of the banking company duly audited are produced before it, the said authority shall not permit any trade union or employees to question the correctness of such accounts, but the trade union or the employees may be permitted to obtain from the banking company such information as is necessary for verifying the amount of bounds due under this Act.

(2) Nothing contained in sub-section (1) shall enable the trade union or the employees to obtain any information which the banking company is not compelled to furnish under the provisions of Sec. 34-A of the Banking Regulation Act, 1949 (10 of 1949).

26. ***Audit of accounts of employers, not being corporations or companies:*** (1) Where any dispute of the nature specified in Section 22 between an employer, not being a corporation or a company, and his employees has been referred to the said authority under that section and the accounts of such employer audited by any auditor duly qualified to act as auditor of Companies under sub-section (1) of Section 226 of the Companies Act, 1956 (1 of 1956), are produced before the said authority, the provisions of Section 23, shall, so far as may be, apply to the accounts so audited.

(2) When the said authority finds that the accounts of such employer have not been audited by any such auditor and it is of opinion that an

audit of the accounts of such employer is necessary for deciding the question referred to it, then it may, by order, direct the employer to get his accounts audited within such time as may be specified in the direction or within such further time as it thinks fit and thereupon the employer shall comply with such direction.

(3) Where an employer fails to get the accounts audited under sub-section (2) the said authority may, without prejudice to the provisions of Sec.28 get the accounts audited by such auditor or auditors as it thinks fit.

(4) When, the accounts are audited under sub-section (2) or sub-section (3) the provisions of Sec.23 shall, so far as may be, apply to the accounts so audited.

(5) The expenses of, and incidental to, any audit under sub-section (3) (including the remuneration of the auditor or auditors) shall be determined by the said authority (which determination shall be final) and paid by the employer and in default of such payment shall be recoverable from the employer in the manner provided in Sec.21

27. ***Maintenance of register, records, etc:*** Every employer shall prepare and maintain such registers, records and other documents in such form and in such manner as may be prescribed.

28. ***Inspectors:*** (1) The appropriate Government may, by notification in the official Gazette, appoint such persons as it thinks fit to be Inspectors for the purpose of this Act and may define the limits within which they shall exercise jurisdiction.

(2) Require an employer to furnish such information as he may consider necessary;

(*a*) At any reasonable time and with such assistance, if any, as he thinks fit, enter any establishment or any premises connected therewith and require any one found in charge thereof to produce before him for examination any accounts, books, registers and other documents relating to the employment of persons or the payment of salary or wage or bonus in the establishment;

(*b*) Examine with respect to any matter relevant to any of the purposes aforesaid, the employer, his agent or servant or any other person found in charge of establishment or any premises connected therewith or any person whom the Inspector has reasonable cause to believe to be or to have been an employee in the establishment;

(*c*) Make copies of, or take extracts from, any book, register or other document maintained in relation to the establishment;

(*d*) Exercise such other powers as may be prescribed.

(3) Every Inspector shall be deemed to be a public servant within the meaning of the Indian Penal Code (45 of 1860).

(4) An person required to produce any accounts, book, register or other document or to give information by an Inspector under sub-section (1) shall be legally bound to do so.

[(Note: Subs. by Act 66 of 1980 (w.e.f. 21st August, 1980) (5) Nothing contained in this section shall enable an Inspector to require a banking company to furnish or disclose any statement or information or to produce, or give inspection of, any of its books of account or other documents, which a banking company cannot be compelled to furnish, disclose, produce or give inspection of, under the provisions of Sec. 34-A of the Banking Regulation Act, 1949(10 of 1949)].

29. *Penalty*: If any person:

(*a*) Contravenes any of the provisions of this Act or any rule made thereunder; or

(*b*) To whom a direction is given or a requisition is made under this Act fails to comply with the direction or requisition.

He shall be punishable with imprisonment for a term which may extend to six months, or with fine which may extend to one thousand rupees, or with both.

30. *Offences by companies:* (1) If the person committing an offence under this Act is a company, every person who, at the time the offence was committed, was in charge of, and was responsible to, the company for the conduct of business of the company, as well as the company, shall be deemed to be guilty of the offence and shall be liable to be proceeded against and punished accordingly:

Provided that nothing contained in sub-section (1), where an offence under this Act has been committed by a company and it is proved that the offence has been committed with the consent or connivance of, or is attributable to any neglect on the part of, any director, manager, secretary or other officer of the company, such director, manager, secretary or other officer shall also be proceeded against and punished accordingly.

Explanation: For the purposes of this section -

(*a*) "Company" means any body corporate and includes a firm or other association of individuals ; and

(*b*) "Director", in relation to a firm, means a partner in the firm.

31. *Cognizance of offences:* (1) No court shall take cognizance of any offence punishable under this Act, save on complaint made by or under the authority of the appropriate Government, [(Note: Ins. by ibid, See.16) or an officer of that Government (not below the rank of a Regional Labour Commissioner in the case of an officer of the Central Government and not below the rank of a labour commissioner the case of an officer of the State Government) specially authority in this behalf by that Government.]

(2) No Court inferior to that of a presidency magistrate or a magistrate of the first class shall try any offence publishable under this Act.

32. ***Protection of action taken under the Act:*** No suit, prosecution or other legal proceeding shall lie against the Government or any officer of the Government for anything which is in good faith done or intended to be done in pursuance of this Act or any rule made thereunder.

32A. ***Special provision with respect to payment of bonus linked with production or productivity:*** Notwithstanding anything contained in this Act:

(*i*) Where an agreement or a settlement has been entered into by the employees with their employer before the commencement of the Payment of Bonus (Amendment) Act, 1976 (23 of 1976), or

(*ii*) Where the employees enter into any agreement with their employer after such commencement,

For payment of an annual bonus linked with production or productivity in lieu of bonus based on profits payable under this Act, then, such employees shall be entitled to receive bonus due to them under such agreement or settlement, as the case may be :

[(Note: Ins. by Act 66 of 1980, (w.e.f. 21st August, 1980)) Provided that any such agreement or settlement whereby the employees relinquish their right to receive the minimum bonus under Sec.10 shall be null and void in so far as it purports to deprive them of such right:]

[(Note: Subs. by ibid) Provided further that] such employees shall not be entitled to be paid such bonus in excess of twenty per cent, of the salary or wage earned by them during the relevant accounting year.]

33. ***Act not to apply to certain classes of employees:*** Nothing in this Act shall apply to:

(*i*) Employees employed by any insurer carrying on general insurance business and the employees employed by the Life Insurance Corporation of India;

(*ii*) Seaman as defined in Cl. (42) of Sec.3 of the Merchant Shipping Act, 1958 (44 of 1958);

(*iii*) Employees registered or listed under any scheme made under the Dock Workers (Regulation of Employment) Act, 1948 (9 of 1948), and employed by registered or listed employers;

(*iv*) Employees employed by an establishment engaged in any industry carried on by or under the authority of any department of the Central Government or a State Government or a local authority;

(*v*) Employees employed by;

  (*a*) The Indian Red Cross Society or any other institution of a like nature (including its branches);

  (*b*) Universities and other educational institutions;

  (*c*) Institutions (including hospitals, chambers of commerce and society welfare institutions) established not for purposes of profit;

(*i*) Employees employed through contractors on building operations;

(*ii*) (Note: Clause (vii) omitted by Act 66 of 1980, (w.e.f. 21st August, 1980) (*iii*) Employees employed by the Reserve Bank of India;

(*iv*) Employees employed by;

(*a*) The Industrial Finance Corporation of India;

(*b*) By Financial Corporation established under Sec.3, or any Joint Financial Corporation established under Sec. 3-A of the State Financial Corporations Act, 1951 (63 of 1951);

(*c*) The Deposit Insurance Corporation;

(*d*) [(Note: Subs. by Act 61 of 1981) the National Bank for Agriculture and Rural Development;]

(*e*) the Unit Trust of India;

(*f*) the Industrial Development Bank of India;

(Note: Omitted by Act 66 of 1980, (w.e.f. 21st August, 1980))

(*g*) Any other financial institution [(Note: Ins. by ibid) Other than a banking company], being an establishment in public sector, which the Central Government may, by notification in the official Gazette, specify having regard to;

(*i*) Its capital structure;

(*i*) Its objectives and the nature of its activities;

(*ii*) The nature and extent of financial assistance or any concession given to it by the Government; and

(*iii*) Any other relevant factor;

(*i*) (Note: Clause (x) omitted by Act 23 of 1976, Sec. 20, (w.e.f. 25th September, 1975)

(*ii*) Employees employed by inland water transport establishments operating on routes passing through any other country.

34. ***Employees and employers not to be precluded from entering into agreements for grant of bonus under a different formula:*** Nothing contained in this Act shall be construed to preclude employees employed in any establishment or class of establishments from entering into agreements with their employer for granting them an account of bonus under a formula which is different for that under this Act:

Provided that no such agreement shall have effect unless it is entered into with the previous approval of the appropriate Government:

Provided further that any such agreement whereby the employees relinquish their right to receive the minimum bonus under sub-section (2-A) of Section 10 shall be null and void in so far as it purports to deprive them of such right:

Provided also that such employees shall not be entitled to be paid bonus in excess of:

(*a*) 8.33 per cent of the salary or wage earned by them during accounting year if the employer has no allocable surplus in the accounting year or the amount of such allocable surplus is only so much that, but for the provisions of sub-section (2-A)of Section 10, it would entitle the employees only to receive an amount of bonus which is less than the aforesaid percentage, or

(*b*) Twenty per cent, of the salary or wage earned by them during the accounting year.

34-A. ***Effect of laws and agreements inconsistent with the Act:*** Subject to the provisions of Sections 31-A and 34, the provisions of this Act shall have effect notwithstanding anything inconsistent therewith contained in any other law for the time being in force or in the terms of any award, agreement, settlement or contract of service.

35. ***Saving:*** Nothing contained in this Act shall be deemed to affect the provisions of the Coal Mines Provident Fund and Bonus Schemes Act, 1948 (46 of 1948), or of any scheme made there under.

36. ***Power of exemption:*** If the appropriate Government, having regard to the financial position and other relevant circumstances of any establishment or class of establishments, is of opinion that it will not be in public interest to apply all or any of the provisions of this Act thereto, it may, by notification in the official Gazette, exempt for such period as may be specified therein and subject to such conditions as it may think fit to impose, such establishment or class of establishments from all or any of the provisions of this Act.

37. ***Power of make rules:*** (1) The Central Government may make rules for the purpose of carrying into effect the provision of this Act.

(2) In particular, and without prejudice to the generality of the foregoing power, such rules may provide for;

(*a*) The authority for granting permission under the proviso to sub-clause (iii) of Cl. (I) of Sec.2;

(*b*) The preparation of registers, records and other document and the form and manner in which such registers, records and documents may be maintained under Sec. 26;

(*c*) The powers which may be exercised by an inspector under Cl. (e) of sub-section (2) of Sec. 27;

(*d*) Any other matter which is to be, or may be prescribed.

(3) Every rule made under this section shall be laid as soon as may be after it is made, before each House of Parliament while it is in session for a total period of thirty days, which may be comprised in one session [(Note: Subs. by Act 23 of 1976, (w.e.f. 25th September, 1975) or in two or more successive session], and if before the expiry of the session [(Note: Subs. by Sec. 21, ibid, (w.e.f. 25th September, 1975) immediately following the session or the successive sessions aforesaid], both Houses agree in making any modification in the rule or both Houses agree that the rule should not be made, the rule shall thereafter have effect only in such modified form or be of no effect as the case may be; so however, that any such modification or

annulment shall be without prejudice to the validity of anything previously done under that rule.

38. ***Application of certain laws not barred*:** Save as otherwise expressly provided, the provisions of this Act shall be in addition to and not in derogation of the industrial Disputes Act, 1947 (14 of 1947) or any corresponding law relating The Orient Tavern investigation and settlement of industrial disputes in force in a State.

39. ***Repeal and saving:*** (1) The Payment of Bonus Ordinance, 1965 (3 of 1965) is hereby repealed.

(2) Notwithstanding such repeal, anything done or any action taken under the said Ordinance shall be deemed to have been done or taken under this Act as if this Act commenced on the 29th May, 1965.

THE FIRST SCHEDULE

[See Sec. 4 (a)]

Composition of Gross Profits

Accounting Year Ending....

Item No.	Particulars sub-items	Amount of main items	Amount of	Remarks
1.	Net Profit as shown in the profit and loss Account after making usual and necessary provisions			
2.	Add back provision for: Bonus to employees Depreciation Development Rebate Reserve (If, and to the extent, charged to Profit and Loss Account) Any other reserves. (If, and to the extent, charged to Profit and Loss Account) Total of item No. Rs.			
3.	Add back also: (a) Bonus paid to employees in respect of previous accounting years. (If, and to the extent, charged to Profit and Loss Account) (b) The amount debited in respect of gratuity paid or payable to employees in excess of the aggregate of - The amount, if any, paid to, or provided for payment to, an approved gratuity fund ; and The amount actually paid to employees on their retirement or on termination of their employment for any reason. (c) Donations in excess of the amount admissible for income-tax. (d) Capital expenditure (other than capital expenditure on scientific research which is allowed to as a deduction under any law for the time being in force relating to direct taxes) and capital losses (other than losses on sale of capital assets on which depreciation has been allowed for income-tax). (If, and to the extent, charged to Profit and Loss Account)			

Item No.	Particulars sub-items	Amount of main items	Amount of	Remarks
	(e) Any amount certified by the Reserve Bank of India in terms of sub-section (2) of Sec. 34-A the Regulation Act, 1949 (10 of 1949)			
	(f) Losses of, or expenditure relating to any business situated outside India.			
Total of Item No. 3 Rs.				
4.	Add also income, profits or gains (if any) credited directly to published or disclosed reserves, other than -			
	(i) Capital receipts and capital profits (including profits on the sale of capital assets on which depreciation has not been allowed for income-tax);			
	(ii) Profits of and receipts relating to, any business situated outside India ;			
	(iii) Income of foreign banking companies from investments outside India.			
Net total Item No. 4 Rs.				
5.	Total of Item Nos. 1,2,3 and 4. Rs.			
6.	Deduct: (If, and to the extent, credited to Profit and Loss Account)			
	(a) Capital receipts and capital profits (other than profits on the sale of assets) on which depreciation has been allowed for income-tax.			
	(b) Profits of, and receipts relating to any business situated outside India.			
	(c) Income of foreign banking companies from investments outside India.			
	(d) Expenditure or losses (if any) debited directly to published or disclosed reserves, other than - Capital expenditure and capital losses (other than losses on sale of capital assets on which depreciation has not been allowed for income-tax); Loses of any business situated outside India.			
	(e) In the case of foreign banking companies proportionate administrative (overhead) expenses of Head Office allocable to Indian business.(If, and to the extent, credited to Profit and Loss Account)			
	(f) Refund of any excess direct tax paid for previous accounting years, relating to bonus, depreciation, or development rebate, if written back.(If, and to the extent, credited to Profit and Loss Account)			
	(g) Cash subsidy, if any, given by the Government or by any body corporate established by any law for the time being in force of by any other agency through budgetary grants, whether given directly or through any agency for specified purposes and the proceeds of which are reserved for such purposes. (If, and to the extent, credited to Profit and Loss Account)			
Total of Item No. 6 Rs.				
7.	Gross Profits for purposes of bonus (Item No. 5 minus Item No. 6) Rs.			

Explanation: In sub-item (b) of item 3, "approved gratuity fund" has the same meaning assigned to it in Cl. (5) of Sec. 2 of the Income-tax Act.]

The Second Schedule

[(Note: Subs. by ibid, Sec. 19)

See Sec. 4 (B)]

Computation of Gross Profits

Accounting Year ending ....

Item No.	Particulars sub-items	Amount of main items	Amount of	Remarks
1.	Net Profit as per Profits and Loss Account.			
2.	Add back provision for Bonus to employees. Depreciation. Direct taxes, including the provision (if any) for previous accounting years. (If, and to the extent, charged to Profit and Loss Account.) [(Note: Subs. by Act 66 of 1980, Sec.19) Development rebate/Investment allowance/Development allowance reserve.] (If, and to the extent, charged to Profit and Loss Account.) Any other reserves Total of Item No. 2 Rs.			
3.	Add back also: (If, and to the extent, charged to Profit and Loss Account.) (a) Bonus paid to employees in respect of previous accounting years. [(aa) (Note: Ins. by Act 23 of 1976, Sec. 26 (w.e.f. (25th September, 1975)). The amount debited in respect of gratuity paid or payable to employees in excess of the aggregate of - The amount, if any, paid to, or provided for payment to, an approved gratuity fund ; and The amount actually paid to employees on their retirement or on termination of their employment for any reason.] (b) Donations in excess of the amount admissible for income-tax. (c) Any annuity due, or commuted value of any annuity paid, under the provisions of Sec. 280-D of the Income-tax Act during the accounting year. (d) Capital expenditure (other than capital expenditure on scientific research which is allowed as deduction under any law for the time being in force relating to direct taxes) and capital losses (other than losses on sale) of Capital assets on which depreciation has been allowed for income-tax or agricultural income-tax).			

Item No.	Particulars sub-items	Amount of main items	Amount of	Remarks
	(e) Losses of, or expenditure relating to, any business situated outside India.			
Total of Item No. 3				
4.	Add also Income, profits or gains (if any) credited directly to reserves, other than - Capital receipts and capital profits including profits on the sale of capital assets on which depreciation has not been allowed for income-tax or agricultural income-tax ; Profits of, and receipts relating to, any business situated outside India ; Income of foreign concerns from investments outside India.			
Net total of Item No. 4				
5.	Total of Item Nos. 1,2,3 and 4.			
6.	Deduct : (a) Capital receipts and capital profits (other than profits on the sale of assets on which depreciation has been allowed for income-tax or agricultural income-tax).			
	(b) Profits of, and receipts relating to, any business situated outside India.			
	(c) Income of foreign concerns from investments outside India.			
	(d) Expenditure or losses (if any) debited directly to reserves, other than-Capital expenditure and capital losses (other than losses on sale of capital assets on which depreciation has not been allowed for income-tax or agricultural income-tax); Losses of any business situated outside India.			
	(e) In the case of foreign concerns proportionate administrative (over head) expenses of Head Office allocable to Indian business.(In the proportion of Indian Gross Profit (Item No. 7) to Total World Gross Profit (as per Consolidated Profit and Loss Account, adjusted as in Item No.2 above only).			
	(f) Refund of any direct tax paid for previous accounting years and excess provision, if any, of previous accounting years relating to bonus, depreciation, taxation or development rebate or development allowance, if written back. (Ins. by Sec. 26. (w.e.f. 25th September, 1975)			
	(g) [(Note: Subs. by Act 23 of 1976) Cash subsidy, if any, given by the Government or by body corporate established by any law for the time being in force or by any other agency for specified purposes and the proceeds of which are reserved for such purposes.]			
Total of Item No. 6 Rs.				
7.	Gross Profits for purposes of bonus (item No. 5 minus Item No. 6)			
Rs.				

[(Ins. by Sec 26. (w.e.f. 25th September, 1975) **Explanation:** In sub-item (aa) of Item 3, "approved gratuity fund" has the same meaning assigned to it in Cl. (5) of Sec. 2 of the Income-tax Act.]

The Third Schedule

[See Sec. 6 (D)]

Item No.	Category of employer	Further sums to be deducted
1.	[(Note: Subs. by ibid, Sec. 20) Company, other than a banking company]	The dividends payable on its preference share capital for the accounting year calculated at the actual rate at which such dividends are payable; 8.5 per cent of its paid-up equity share capital as at the commencement of the accounting year; 6 per cent of its reserves shown in its balance-sheet as at the commencement of the accounting year, including any profit carried forward from the previous accounting year : Provided that where the employer is a foreign company within the meaning of Sec. 591 of the Companies Act, 1956 (1 of 1956) the total amount to be deducted under this Item shall be 8.5 per cent on the aggregate of the value of the net fixed assets and the current assets of the company in India after deducting the amount of its current liabilities (other than any amount shown as payable by the company to its Head Office whether towards any advance made by the Head Office or otherwise or any interest paid by the Company to its Head Office) in India.
2.	[(Note: Subs. by ibid, Sec. 20) Company, other than a banking company]	The Dividends payable on its preference share capital for the accounting year calculated at the rate at which such dividends are payable; 7.5 per cent of its paid-up equity share of capital as at the commencement of the accounting year; 5 per cent of its reserves shown in its balance-sheet as at the commencement of the accounting year, including any profits carried forward from the previous accounting year ; Any sum which, in respect of the accounting year, is transferred by it- To a reserve fund under sub-section (1) of Sec. 17 of the banking Regulation Act, 1949 (10 of 1949); or To any reserves in India in pursuance of any direction or advice given by the Reserve Bank of India,

Item No.	Category of employer	Further sums to be deducted
		Whichever is higher: Provided that where the banking company is foreign company within the meaning of Sec. 591 of the Companies Act, 1956 (1 of 1956), the amount to be deducted under this item shall be the aggregate of: The dividends payable to its preference shareholders for the accounting year at the rate at which such dividends are payable on such amount as bears the same proportion to its total preference share capital as its total working funds in India bear to its total world working funds; 7.5 per cent, of such amount as bears the same proportion to its total paid-up equity share capital as its total working funds in India bear to its total working funds; 5 per cent of such amount as bears the same proportion to its total disclosed reserves as its total working funds in India bear to its total working funds; any sum which, in respect of the accounting year, is deposited by it with the Reserve Bank of India under sub-clause (ii) of Cl. (b) of sub-section (2) of Sec. 11 of the Banking Regulation Act, 1949 (10 of 1949), not exceeding the amount required under the aforesaid provision to be so deposited.]
3.	Corporation	8.5 per cent of its paid-up capital as at the commencement of the accounting year; 6 per cent of its reserves, if any, shown in its balance-sheet as at commencement of the accounting year including any profits carried forward from the previous accounting year.
4.	Co-operative society	8.5 per cent, of the capital invested by such society in its establishment from its books of accounts at the commencement of the accounting year; Such sum as has been carried forward in respect of the accounting year to reserve fund under any law relating to cooperative societies for the time being in force.
5.	Any other employer not failing under any of the aforesaid categories.	8.5 per cent, of the capital invested by him in his establishment as evidenced from his books of accounts at the commencement of the accounting year; Provided that where such employer is a person to whom Chapter XXII-A of the Income-tax Act applies

Item No.	Category of employer	Further sums to be deducted
		the annuity deposit payable by him under the provisions of that chapter during the accounting year shall also be deducted :Provided further that where such employer is a firm, an amount equal to 25 per cent, of the gross profits derived by it from the establishment in respect of the accounting year after deducting depreciation in accordance with the provisions of Cl. (a) of Sec.6 by way of remuneration to all the partners taking part in the conduct of business of establishment shall also be deducted, where oral or written, provides for the payment of remuneration to any such partner, and -The total remuneration payable to all such partners is less than the said 25 per cent, the amount payable, subject to a maximum of fortyeight thousand rupees to each such partner; or The total remuneration payable to all such partners is higher than the said 25 per cent. Such percentage, or a sum calculated at the rate of forty-eight thousand rupees to each such partner, which ever is less. Shall be deducted under this proviso: Provided also that where such employer is an individual or a Hindu undivided family,- An amount equal to 25 per cent of the gross profits derived by such employer from the establishment in respect of the accounting year after deducting depreciation in accordance with the provisions of Cl. (a) of Sec. 6, or Fortheight thousand rupees whichever is less, by way of remuneration to such employer, shall al so be deducted.
6.	Any employer failing under Item No. 1 or Item No. 3 or Item No. 4 or Item No. 5 and being a licensee within the meaning or the Electricity (Supply) Act, 1948 (54 of (1948).	In additional the sums deductible under any of the aforesaid Items, such sums as are required to be appropriated by the licensee in respect of the accounting year to a reserve under the Sixth Schedule to that Act shall also be deducted.

Explanation: The expression "reserves" occurring in column (3) against Item Nos. [(Note: Omitted by Act 23 of 1976, and by Act 43 of 1977, Sec. 19 (w.e.f. 3rd July 1977) 1 (iii), 2 (ii), and 3 (ii)] shall not include any amount set apart for the purpose of;

(*i*) Payment of any direct tax which, according to the balance-sheet, would be payable;

(*ii*) Meeting any depreciation admissible in accordance with the provisions of Cl. (a) of Sec. 6;

(*iii*) Payment of dividends which have been declared but shall include-

(a) Any amount, over and above the amount referred to in Cl. of payment of any direct tax; and

(*b*) Any amount set apart for meeting any depreciation in excess of the amount admissible in accordance with the provisions of Cl. (a) of [Sec. 6].

THE FOURTH SCHEDULE

(See Secs. 15 and 16)

In this Schedule, the total amount of bonus equal to 8.33 per cent of the annual salary or wage payable to all the employees is assumed to be are entitled to be paid (twenty per cent of the annual salary or wage of all the employees) would be Rs. 2,50,000.

Year	Amount equal to sixty per cent or sixty-seven per cent, as the case may be, or available surplus allocable as bonus	Amount payable as bonus	Set on or the year forward	set off carried	Total set on or set off carried forward
Rs. of year					
1.	1,04,167	1,04,167**	Nil	Nil	
2.	6,35,000	2,50,000*	Set on 2,50,000*	Set on 2,50,000	(2)
3.	2,20,000	2,50,000* (inclusive of 30,000 from year-2)	Nil	Set on 2,20,000	(2)
4.	3,75,000	2,50,000*	Set on 1,25,000	Set on 2,20,000 1,25,000	(2) (4)
5.	1,40,000	2,50,000* (inclusive of 1,10,000 from year-2)	Nil	Set on 1,10,000 1,25,000	(2) (4)
6.	3,10,000	2,50,000*	Nil 60,000	Set on + 1,25,000 63,300	(2) (4) (6)
7.	1,00,000	2,50,000* (inclusive of 1,25,000 from year-4 and 25,000 from year-6)	Nil	Set on 35,000	(6)
8.	Nil (due to loss)	1,04,167** (inclusive of 35,000 from year-6	Set off 69,167	Set off 69,167	(8)

Cont...

9.	10,000	1,04,167**	Set off 94,167	Set off 69,167 94,167	(8) (9)
10.	2,15,000	1,04,167** (after setting off 69,167 from year-8 and 41,666 from year-9)	Nil	Set off	(9)

Notes: *Maximum
** Minimum
The balance of Rs.1,10,000 set on from Year-2 lapses.]

4.2 Institutions Related to Reward Systems

In India, institutional set up for regulating compensation system is two fold viz. wage board for regulating compensation in industries belonging to private sector including newspaper establishments and working journalists while pay commissions tend to regulate the compensation of public servants.

A brief description of wage boards and pay commissions are given below:

Wage Boards:

In the 1950s and 1960s, when the organized labour sector was at a nascent stage of its development without adequate unionization or with trade unions without adequate bargaining power, government in appreciation of the problems which arise in the arena of wage fixation due to absence of such bargaining power, constituted various wage boards. The first wage board was set up in 1957 by the government for cotton textile industry and 30 wage boards have been so far set up by the government. Since then a large number of industries has been brought under the scope of wage boards. Wage boards seek to:

- To improve conditions for better industrial relations in the country;
- To standardize wage structure uniformly across a given industry; and
- To pave the way for wage settlements in consonance of social and economic policies of the government.

The wage boards are tripartite in character in which representatives of workers, employers and independent members participate and finalize the recommendations. Usually a member of the parliament is nominated as member to represent the interests of the public. The chairman of the board is appointed by the appropriate government in consultation with the Chief Justice of the concerned High Court or Supreme Court of India. In determining wage structures for a particular industry or class of industries, a wage board considers the needs and imperatives of that industry, prevalent system of payment including piece rate systems, categories of employees, ability of industry to pay and other matters of public interest.

Wage board passes its award based on the majority opinion and is signed by the members and the chairman of the board from the date as may be specified in its written award. The award of wage board remains valid for a period of three years from its date of passing award and may be extended by mutual agreement between the parties.

Fifth wage board has been set up in April 2000 for working journalists and other newspaper employees under the Working Journalists and other Newspaper Employees (Conditions of Service) and Miscellaneous Provisions Act, 1955. Except for the wage boards for journalists and non-journalists newspaper and news-agency employees, which are statutory wage board, all other wage boards are non-statutory in nature. Therefore, recommendations made by these wage boards are not enforceable under the law. However, the importance of the non-statutory wage boards has consequently declined over a period of time and no non-statutory wage board has been set up after 1966, except for sugar industry, where last such wage board was constituted in 1985. The trade unions, having grown in strength in these industries, are themselves able to negotiate their wages with the management. This trend is likely to continue in future.

Pay Commissions

Pay commission is an administrative system/mechanism that the Government of India set up in 1956 to determine the salaries of government employees. Compensation level, structure and system is based upon the recommendations of pay commission being set up by the central government, although some of the state governments set up their own pay commissions. Most of the states in India implement the recommendation of the central pay commissions. Government of India has set up so far six pay commissions. The first pay commission reported in 1947, second in 1959, third in 1973, fourth in 1984, fifth in 1996 and sixth is expected to submit report shortly. Pay commissions also cover compensation of employees working in the public sectors such as nationalized banks and industrial establishments.

The pay commission set up from time-to-time seeks to study current compensation of the employees and collects data from the market through external surveys. Generally, these surveys use questionnaire method and an expert person/agency is appointed to collect and process the data and submit report to the pay commission. For example, Indian Institute of Management has been entrusted with certain survey responsibility by the sixth pay commission. The pay commission also initiates intense discussions and dialogues with all concerned, that is, employers, employee's representatives, trade unions, and public with purpose of getting a wider and deeper insight into the issues. While conducting external surveys, cost of living is also considered based on consumer price index and to provide for appropriate neutralization for meeting the rise in cost of living. Upon preparation of recommendations, it is presented to the government which can accept the recommendations fully or partially or may even reject the recommendations of pay commission. Once, the recommendations of the pay commission are accepted by the government, it is implemented.

We shall briefly describe the purposes and recommendations of the six pay commissions as follows:

1. **First Pay Commission:** The first pay commission was established in the early stages of independent India and it was felt that compensation of government employees cannot be set solely based on the classical economic reasoning of demand and supply. India being a welfare state and government being responsible for faithful implementation of constitutional provisions, therefore it was felt it in the interest of fairness, justice and adequacy, the government employees should be paid a 'living wages' to ensure a minimum standard of quality of life. The idea was based on government acting as a 'model employer'. However, the Fair Wages Committee, 1948 also submitted its report on wage policy to be adopted and their report differentiated between living wage, fair wage and minimum wage. Thus, it is clear that pay commission's living wage was actually a minimum wage.

   Further, pay commission also recommended for payment of dearness allowance to government employees to prevent any economic hardships being caused to them on account of rise in cost of living.

2. **Second Pay Commission :** The second pay commission took the concept of living wage (model employer premise) further as a matter of social policy. It argued that living wage is essential for attracting competent employees and maintaining efficiency. Minimum wages should be considered in view of economic concerns only but to satisfy the principles of social justice also. It reached the conclusion that government should compensate above minimum wages and provide fair wages to the public servants.

3. **Third Pay Commission :** The third pay commission gave the criteria of a sound pay system as follows:

   - *Inclusiveness*: The pay structure adopted for the civil service should be broadly implemented by autonomous, quasi-governmental organizations also. The large scale appointment of temporary employees should be discouraged and brought down to minimum.
   - *Comprehensibility*: The pay structures should provide compensation to all employees and at all levels in a comprehensive manner. Equal payment should be made for equal work.
   - *Adequacy*: The pay level and structure should be internally and externally equitable so that government employees are not put any disadvantageous position with respect to other employees.

The pay commissions did not consider that government should become a model employer by paying high compensation to public servants, rather it should compensate employees based on the recommendations of the pay commissions. Further, pay commission observed that dearness allowance should be treated as part and parcel of compensation structure of employees given increases in cost of living.

4. **Fourth Pay Commission :** The fourth pay commission focused on the criteria for fixing pay levels and structures for government employees. It concluded that market comparison cannot be relied upon for determining pay system for employees in public service as compared to employees working private sector. This is because the motto of public sector is service whereas that of private sector business is profit. Also, while observing ability to pay, it concluded that it is feasible for private sector organization and it is extremely difficult to assess the government's ability to pay. Therefore, it recommended that government should pay 'fair wages' to the public servants. The fairness concept is based on two premises viz. fairness to the employees as well as to people they serve.

   Further, pay commission concurred that dearness allowance should be treated as part and parcel of compensation structure of employees and recommended that full neutralization of rise in cost of living should be paid @ 80% to employees drawing basic pay up to Rs. 3,500 per month, 75% to employees drawing basic pay between Rs. 3500 and Rs. 6000 per month and 65% to for employees with basic pay above Rs. 6000 per month.

5. **Fifth Pay Commission :** The pay commission recommended for pay revision based on work organization and manpower planning. It also recommended that 40% increase in pay with 30% reduction in manpower over a three year period. It emphasized new means of recruitment including contract employment and bringing about innovation in training, performance appraisal, career progression, transfer policies and greater accountability of government employees.

6. **Sixth Pay Commission :** The sixth central pay commission submitted its report under the chair of Justice B.N. Srikrishna in March 2008 which has been accepted by Government of India on 14-08-2008. The commission has increased the pay of the central government employees on an average of 40% and abolished the position of Grade D in the services. It has recommended for a minimum pay of Rs. 6,660 per month and maximum of Rs. 80,000 per month. For secretary level positions, consolidated/fixed pay has been provided. With this, the pay differential between junior employees and senior officers has increased from 1:10 to 1:12. The commission has justified huge increases in compensation of the employees on the ground that it intends to encourage performance of the employees. The sixth pay

commission's financial burden is likely to be to the tune of Rs. 12,561 crores and will benefit 45 lakh central government employees. A perusal of the financial burden contributed by previous five commissions indicates that sixth pay commissions recommendations entail maximum increase in financial liability of the government as follows:

Pay Commission	Formed on Burden	Report Submitted	Financial (Rupees in Crores)
FIRST	May 1946	May 1947	Unavailable
SECOND	August 1957	August 1959	39.62
THIRD	April 1970	March 1973	144.60
FOURTH	June 1983	May 1987	1282
FIFTH	April 1994	January 1997	17,000
SIXTH	July 2006	March 2008	20,000 (expected)

According to the reports of the sixth pay commission, house rent allowance for A-1 category of cities continue remain unchanged at 30% while for A, B-1 and B-2 categories of cities, the house rent allowance has been increased to 20%. For C category and other cities, house rent allowance stands at 10%. For retired employees, pension has been increased by 50% and the stipulation of minimum service period of 33 years has been dispensed with. These recommendations has been implemented with effect from 01.01.2006. The implementation entails a one time arrear payment of Rs. 18,060 crores on the government. Additionally, the commission has recommended that for select posts requiring higher qualification and skill levels, appointment must be made on contract basis. Appointees showing good performance should be granted 3.5% increment instead of 2.5%. However, one of the key features of the sixth pay commission pertains to introduction of performance related incentive scheme (PRIS) in the government. Under this scheme government employee shall be eligible for pecuniary remuneration over and above their pay based on performance. It follows that 'pay-for-performance' model has now been found critical for improving individual performance of government employees. Employees of public sector undertakings are asking for a 100% hike in compensation in place of 40% hike recommended by sixth pay commission.

CHAPTER REVIEW

➢ Payment of Wages Act, 1936

- All employees drawing wages of upto Rs. 10,000/- per month.
- For establishment with personnel > 1000; by 10th day and for < 1000; by 7th day of subsequent month.
- All payments in currency notes or coin or both or bank transfer (with employee's consent).
- Deduction as permitted by law and total deductions should not exceed 50% of wages and amount of fine shall not exceed 3% of wages.

- Deduction for absence for whole or any part of the day or absence of 10 or more personnel in collectivity.

➢ Minimum Wages Act, 1948

- The appropriate government to fix minimum rates of wages for employees employed under part-I or part-II of schedule.
- Wage can be fixed or revised based upon scheduled employments, classes of work, adults, apprentices, children and adolescents and localities.
- Minimum wages could be for time, piece or both.
- Fixing or revising minimum wages is done through by appointing committee and by issuing notification.
- Employer to pay to every employee minimum rates of wages.

➢ Equal Remuneration Act, 1976

- No employer shall reduce the rate of remuneration based on gender of the employee.
- No discrimination on promotion, training or transfer except where employment of women is restricted.

➢ Payment of Bonus Act, 1965

- All employees drawing wages upto Rs. 10,000/- per month and having worked in an establishment for at least 30 days.
- Salary or wages includes basic pay, dearness allowance but no other allowances e.g. overtime, house rent, incentives or commission.
- Computation of gross profit, as per first schedule for banking company and second schedule for others.
- Minimum bonus is 8.33% and maximum bonus is 20% of the salary.
- Wages up to Rs 3,500 per month, bonus payable on actual wages and above 3500 but below 10,000, bonus payable on a notional wages of Rs. 3,500 per month.
- Set off and set on: schedule IV.
- Disqualified for bonus for Fraud, Riotous or violent behaviours, Theft, misappropriation or sabotage and Misconduct of causing financial loss.
- Payment by 30th September of following year.

➢ Wage Boards

- Statutory and non-statutory in nature.
- Set up to protect workers from exploitation of capitalists.
- Tripartite in character comprising of representatives of workers, employers and independent members.

- The chairman of the board is appointed by the appropriate government in consultation with the Chief Justice of the concerned High Court or Supreme Court of India.
- The award of wage board remains valid for a period of three years, extendable by mutual agreement between the parties.
- Fifth wage board has been set up in April 2000 for working journalists and other newspaper employees under the Working Journalists and other Newspaper Employees.
- Importance of the non-statutory wage boards has declined.

➢ Pay Commissions

- *First pay commission*: model employer, demand and supply inappropriate, and payment of dearness allowance.
- *Second pay commission*: furthered model employer premise as a matter of social policy and living wage is essential for attracting competent employees and maintaining efficiency.
- *Third pay commission*: appointment of temporary employees, Equal payment should be made for equal work, externally competitive compensation to prevent misbalance with other employees and dearness allowance should be treated as part and parcel of compensation structure.
- *Fourth pay commission*: market comparison cannot be relied upon for determining pay system; motto of public sector is service rather than profits, and DA for basic pay upto Rs. 3,500 per month, 75% to employees drawing basic pay between Rs. 3500 and Rs. 6000 per month and 65% to for employees with basic pay above Rs. 6000 per month.
- *Fifth pay commission*: 40% increase in pay with 30% reduction in manpower over a three year period, increasing contract employment and bringing about greater accountability of government employees.
- *Sixth pay commission*: 40% average increase in pay. Group 'D' category of employees abolished and compensation of secretary level personnel has been recommended for substantial rise. The pay differential between junior employees and senior officer stands increased to 1:12.

A. Conceptual Review Questions

1. Discuss the role of wage boards in determination of compensation.
2. Explain the recommendations of various pay commissions in India.
3. Draw out the salient features of the following wage laws:
   (*a*) The payment of wages act, 1936
   (*b*) The minimum wages act, 1948
   (*c*) The equal remuneration act, 1976
   (*d*) The payment of bonus act, 1965

B. Analytical Questions

1. Why reward and compensation needs to be statutorily regulated and monitored?
2. Are the wage laws relevant in present era of globalization, liberalization and privatization? If no, then what changes are necessary?
3. "Pay commissions have paved the way for increasing burden on state exchequer rather than improving performance of government servants". Critically evaluate the statement.

CASE INCIDENT

Chamiyya Printing is a small printing house specializing in dye printing on fabrics. It employs around 170 employees mostly on casual basis. In an inspection conducted by state labour department, it was observed that around 103 employees were paid less than the prescribed minimum wages. The minimum wages inspector issued show cause notice to the employer and initiated legal action against the employer. However, even after elapse of two years no legal action has been taken against the defaulting employer. The company continues to be paying less than minimum wages to the employees by greasing the palms of the inspectors and other officials.

Mazdoor Kranti, a trade union, has recently taken up the cause of minimum wages of the employees of the company. The secretary Mr. Nilesh Jain has alleged that that it is not an isolated case as there are many more of such defaulting employers who are thriving under corrupt management-inspector nexus. The laws exist on the books only and there is no real will on the part of the inspectors to implement minimum wages act in latter and spirit. He has approached the state labour commissioner to ensure that minimum wages are paid and strict legal action is taken against the defaulting employers. However, even that has not yielded relieve to the aggrieved employees as only 32 cases has been disposed off. The state labour commissioner puts on the blame on lack of adequate manpower and other legal procedural wrangling.

Finally, enough is enough. Mr. Jain has approached the state minister for labour through his connection in the ruling party and has been assured that government is envisaging settling the minimum wage related cases at the earliest by organizing special lok adalats. Months have passed but nothing so far has materialized. In the meantime Mr. Jain is getting threats from local goons to stop pursuing the cases or face dire consequences. He is perplexed and fears for the safety of his family members.

QUESTIONS

1. Why labour department is not taking legal action against chamiyya printing?

2. Why did the efforts of Mr. Nilesh Jain fail to produce desired results?
3. What should Mr. Jain do now? Please advise him as a professional expert.

EXPERIENTIAL EXCERCISES

1. Working individually or in groups, interview five employees each of fifteen private and fifteen government sector on their perception of fairness and adequacy of reward and compensation systems in operation in their respective organizations in your locality. Prepare a brief report on pay satisfaction, job satisfaction, performance linkages to rewards and improvement in productivity and organization performance.
2. Organize a debate in the class by dividing students into two groups *viz.* Group A and Group B with the following group activities:
   (*a*) Group A: Students of this group will represent employees of public sector enterprises. They should prepare relevant details and supporting data.
   (*b*) Group B: Students of this group will represent employees of private sector enterprises. They should prepare relevant details and supporting data.

Group A and Group B shall debate on tenacity of performance based pay.

❑❑❑

Practice-Based Templates

The appendices comprises of performance appraisal forms, performance management audit form, a typical compensation structure and compensation survey questionnaire. The underpinning idea is to familiarize students with real-world organizational systems and practices pertaining to performance and reward management. It is expected that students will find it interesting and useful while undertaking summer internships.

Performance Appraisal Forms

Employee Performance Evaluation and Development Form

PURPOSE

To provide evaluation and developmental tool for the employee's current performance in order to:

- Improve or maintain performance on their present job
- Identify specific area of improvement
- Identify training needs

Name : ____________________

Ticket No. : ____________________ Category : ____________________

Department : ____________________

Review Period : ____________________

Evaluated by : ____________________ Date : ____________________

Signature of the employee : ____________________ Date : ____________________

Performance Evaluation

Parameters	Comments, if any	Mid Term Rating	Annual Rating

Overall Rating :

Performance Rating Scale – Performance that

9	Consistently exceeds standards by a significant degree while overcoming exceptional challenges or applying unique solutions.
7-8	Consistently exceeds standards with contribution above what is normally expected.
4-5-6	Consistently meets and sometimes exceeds standards, making valued contributions to the success of the business at the level that is expected.
2-3	Marginally meets but occasionally is below acceptable standards, contributing at a level requiring more supervision and guidance than should be required.
1	Consistently does not meet standards over the rating period.

Ongoing Performance Review/Feedback

Summary of achievements, performance.

•

•

•

Feedback and areas of improvements.

•

•

•

Date of Meeting : ______________

Summary of achievements, performance.

•

•

•

Feedback and areas of improvements.

•

•

•

Date of Meeting : ______________

Summary of achievements, performance.

•

•

•

Feedback and areas of improvements.

•

•

•

Date of Meeting : ______________

Employee Development and Career Planning Form

Name : ____________________ Current Position : ____________________

Service : ____________________ Time in Current Job : ____________________

Total Business Exp: ____________________

Employee's Interests and Aspirations

Indicate employee's current career interests and identify reason(s) for each:

a. Short Term (1-3 years) : ____________________

____

b. Mid Term (3-6 years): ____________________

____

c. Long Term (6-12 years) : ____________________

____

Development Needs

(Include feedback from Performance Evaluation, SOL, People Development, Key Business Challenges, Interests / Aspirations)

Skills Need To Be Developed:

- ____________________
- ____________________
- ____________________

Training Required:

- ____________________
- ____________________
- ____________________

Developmental Plans

Action Plans	When	Who	Status

Career Planning and Employee Development is a joint responsibility of the Employee and the Manager.

Employee	Date	Plan Start and End Date	
Manager	Date	Next Level Manager	Date

Individual Performance Review
Individual Contributor

Employee's Name:	
Department:	
Position Title:	
Time in Position:	
Location:	

Key Business Unit/Function Objectives for the Year ....

(List three to five key objectives for your business area)

Personal Objectives for the Year ....

(Based on business objectives given above, list up to 3 to 6 personal objectives and the key actions you will complete to accomplish each objective)

Example: Objective 1	- Key Action 1 - Key Action 2 - Key Action 3, etc.

OBJECTIVE #1	KEY ACTIONS *(to accomplish objective)*

Results *(to be completed by employee at year-end)*
Rating *(to be completed by manager at year-end)*
Objective Rating #1 E M+ M M- U

OBJECTIVE #2	KEY ACTIONS *(to accomplish objective)*

Results *(to be completed by employee at year-end)*
Rating *(to be completed by manager at year-end)*
Objective Rating #2 E M+ M M- U

OBJECTIVE #3	KEY ACTIONS *(to accomplish objective)*

Results *(to be completed by employee at year-end)*
Rating *(to be completed by manager at year-end)*
Objective Rating #3 E M+ M M- U

OBJECTIVE #4	**KEY ACTIONS** *(to accomplish objective)*

Results *(to be completed by employee at year-end)*					
Rating *(to be completed by manager at year-end)*					
Objective Rating #4	**E**	**M+**	**M**	**M-**	**U**

OBJECTIVE #5	**KEY ACTIONS** *(to accomplish objective)*

Results *(to be completed by employee at year-end)*					
Rating *(to be completed by manager at year-end)*					
Objective Rating #5	**E**	**M+**	**M**	**M-**	**U**

OBJECTIVE #6	**KEY ACTIONS** *(to accomplish objective)*

Results *(to be completed by employee at year-end)*					
Rating *(to be completed by manager at year-end)*					
Objective Rating #5	**E**	**M+**	**M**	**M-**	**U**

Building Organization Capability Competencies

(Rating of employees competencies – to be completed by employee and manager at year-end)

Rating Key:	E M+ M M- U	
Develops & Motivates Self : Draws on expertise of others and leverages abilities of others to help achieve goals and strategies. Seeks ways to develop and motivate self. Develops self through goal setting, self monitoring performance and seeking feedback.	E M+ M M- U	E M+ M M- U
Holds Self Accountable: Establishes high performance standards for self. Sets and meets goals and expectations. Drives for clear direction with linkages to company and unit strategies and plans. Ensures that well-defined goals and performance standards are set and understood. Seeks timely, complete and actionable feedback, whether positive or corrective. Establishes and adheres to aggressive project plans. Clarifies responsibilities and deadlines. Acts on formal and informal feedback to improve performance. Provides constructive informal feedback and suggestions to others. Coaches/mentors other employees when it can help them improve their performance.	E M+ M M- U	E M+ M M- U
Leads, Manages & Coaches Based on Situation : Sets goals for self and participates actively in determining team/ unit goals that support function/business plan. Effectively coaches the performance of peers and up to immediate manager.	E M+ M M- U	E M+ M M- U
Culturally Aware: Being able to understand and respect the customs, language, norms and accepted business approaches of one's own and other cultures. Must be able to modify one's own behavior in order to show respect and operate effectively in varying cultures. Must be able to adapt to different cultural perspectives of customers, potential customers, partners, etc.; including different negotiating styles, business etiquette and personal conduct required to successfully conduct business.	E M+ M M- U	E M+ M M- U
Participates in Change: Challenges the status quo and champions new and innovative ideas that create value for the company. Acts as a catalyst of change while motivating others to support the change.		

Contd...,

Rating Key:	E M+ M M- U	
Readily adapts to changing circumstances. Has a change mindset. Understands that change is required if Goodyear is to remain competitive. Actively and visibly supports the need for change. Willingly changes direction or behavior in response to changing priorities.	E M+ M M- U	E M+ M M- U
Excellent Communicator : Expresses ideas and exchanges information clearly and persuasively. Delivers information effectively using appropriate and multiple channels. Communicates openly and honestly to all levelsof the organization; shares relevant information with others. Actively listens and seeks to understand others' points of view. Maintains an approachable manner that instills trust and confidence. Explains technical, professional and complex information at a level appropriate to the audience. Presents information (verbally or in writing) in an organized, clear, and meaningful way. Effectively communicates facts, ideas, opinions, or concerns.	E M+ M M- U	E M+ M M- U
Excellent Team Member : Contributes to an environment which encourages others to contribute, achieve and develop themselves and become active members of a team. Acts in a way that supports and encourages situations for people to belong. Contributes to an environment in which others desire to work – a place that fosters a high energy level, enthusiasm, commitment and trust. Seeks to clarify their role and understand their contribution to the unit's success. Works well others and exhibit the interpersonal skills and motivation to succeed as a team. Willingly share recognition and reward with the team. Treats others with respect and openness. Shows genuine interest in others and sensitivity to their needs. Supports performance efforts of others.	E M+ M M- U	E M+ M M- U

Employee Self-Assessment of Overall Performance

(Summarize your overall performance against objectives and listed competencies for performance period. Describe key contributions and accomplishments, along with any other achievements.)

Manager's Evaluation of Employee's Overall Performance

(Summarize assessment of employee's overall performance against objectives and listed competencies for ______________ (year) performance. Review employee's self-assessment and include any pertinent responses).

Development Action Plan

(Agreement on future actions that will be taken to help improve performance to objectives and/or listed competencies, or to develop the employee in one of the High Performance Individual Profile competencies.)

Circle Overall Objective and Competency Ratings:
(to be completed by manager at year-end)

Overall Objective Rating:	E	M+	M	M-	U
Overall Competency Rating:	E	M+	M	M-	U

Based on performance to objectives and competencies, this employee has been rated: (circle one)

(to be completed by manager at year-end)

E M+ M M- U

Employee Signature____________________________________Date _______

Manager Signature____________________________________Date _______

Reviewer Signature____________________________________Date _______

Comments from Optional Mid-Year Assessment

Performance Review Form

Performance Plan (From: .... To ....)

Name	Dept.	Location	Empl. Code
Designation	DOJ	Qualification	Certifications

Major Responsibilities and Expectations from the Role

Key Result Areas (Financial Parameters–KRAs which are objective, databased and clearly measurable)	Weightage (in %) (1)	Achievement (in %) (2)	Final Achievement Score (1 x 2)/ 100

Learning & Growth (Self and Team Development, New Skills and Competencies,			
Stakeholders – both Internal and External customers			
Business Processes – Improvements in Operational Efficiencies			
Total	100%		

- Developmental Comments: Training Needs, Job Rotation, Understudy Programmes, Change of Assignment, etc.
- Ability to take on Higher Responsibility.

Please use this page to state the appraisee's potential to take on higher responsibility. While doing so, please mention specifically the higher responsibility (role / title), timeframe for taking up the same and development inputs required, if any.

New Role / Higher Responsibility

Position/Title	Brief Description of the Role	Time Frame	Development Inputs Required, if any

Competencies	Tick Relevant	P = Proficient S = Strength D = Developmental Need	Comments
Builds Relationship & Partnership	☐		
Communication Skills	☐		
Interpersonal Effectiveness	☐		
Visionary Leadership	☐		
Change Leadership	☐		
Coaching	☐		
Empowerment	☐		
Team Development	☐		
Accountability	☐		
Integrity	☐		
Maturity	☐		
Result Orientation	☐		
Decision Making	☐		
Functional Expertise	☐		
Managing the Job	☐		
Strategic Thinking & Execution	☐		

Performance Feedback	Training Needs	
Appraiser's comments on the dialogue held with appraisee	• • •	• • •

Overall Rating (Based on KRAs Achievement Score)	
Appraiser Rating	Reviewer Rating

Appraisee's Name	Appraiser's Name	Reviewer's Name
Date	Date	Date

Competency	Associate Self-Rating	Manager's Rating
Develops & Motivates Self : Draws on expertise of others and leverages abilities of others to help achieve goals and strategies. Seeks ways to develop and motivate self. Develops self through goal setting, self monitoring performance and seeking feedback.	E M+ M M- U	E M+ M M- U
Holds Self Accountable : Establishes high performance standards for self. Sets and meets goals and expectations. Drives for clear direction with linkages to company and unit strategies and plans. Ensures that well-defined goals and performance standards are set and understood. Seeks timely, complete and actionable feedback, whether positive or corrective. Establishes and adheres to aggressive project plans. Clarifies responsibilities and deadlines. Acts on responsibilities feedback to improve performance. Provides constructive performance. and suggestions to others. Coaches/mentors other employees when it can help them improve their performance.	E M+ M M- U	E M+ M M- U
Leads, Manages & Coaches Based on Situation : Sets goals for self and participates actively in determining team/unit goals that support function/business plan. Effectively coaches the performance of peers and up to immediate manager.	E M+ M M- U	E M+ M M- U
Culturally Aware : Being able to understand and respect the customs, language, norms and accepted business approaches of one's own and other cultures. Must be able to modify one's own behaviour in order to show respect and operate effectively in varying cultures. Must be able to adapt to different cultural	E M+ M M- U	E M+ M M- U

Contd...,

Competency	Associate Self-Rating	Manager's Rating
perspectives of customers, potential customers, partners, etc.;including different negotiating styles, business etiquette and personal conduct required to successfully conduct business.		
Participates in Change : Challenges the status quo and champions new and innovative ideas that create value for the company. Acts as a catalyst of change while motivating others to support the change. Readily adapts to changing circumstances. Has a change mindset. Understands that change is required if Goodyear is to remain competitive. Actively and visibly supports the need for change. Willingly changes direction or behavior in response to changing priorities.	E M+ M M- U	E M+ M M- U
Excellent Communicator : Expresses ideas and exchanges information clearly and persuasively. Delivers information effectively using appropriate and multiple channels. Communicates openly and honestly to all levels of the organization; shares relevant information with others. Actively listens and seeks to understand others' points of view. Maintains an approachable manner that instills trust and confidence. Explains technical, professional and complex information at a level appropriate to the audience. Presents information (verbally or in writing) in an organized, clear, and meaningful way. Effectively communicates facts, ideas, opinions, or concerns.	E M+ M M- U	E M+ M M- U
Excellent Team Member : Contributes to an environment which encourages others to contribute, achieve and develop themselves and become active members of a team. Acts in a way that supports and encourages situations for people to belong. Contributes to an environment in which others desire to work – a place that fosters a high energy level, enthusiasm, commitment and trust. Seeks to clarify their role and understand their contribution to the unit's success. Works well others and exhibit the interpersonal skills and motivation to succeed as a team. Willingly share recognition and reward with the team. Treats others with respect and openness. Shows genuine interest in others and sensitivity to their needs. Supports performance efforts of others.	E M+ M M- U	E M+ M M- U

PERFORMANCE MANAGEMENT AUDIT FORM

Instruction for Auditors: Performance management audit involves examination, evaluation, analysis and suggestions pertaining to the organization's performance management philosophy, policy, process, format and implementation bottlenecks. During the audit of performance management system, if you come across deficiencies or gaps, then please note down the extent of gap with suggested improvement strategy. In third column, please write 'S' for satisfactory and 'NS' for Not Satisfactory.

SL. No.	Audit Criteria	Rating	Gap Identified	Improvement Strategy
1.	**Performance Management Philosophy** *Does performance management serve the following objectives?* • Strategic and business plans of the organization • Participative and empowering work culture • Open and interactive communication • Leadership commitment • Concern for internal and external customers • Realistic performance expectations • Ethical behaviour and action • Written down policy and procedures			
2.	**Performance Management Policies and Procedures** *Does it cover the following aspects?* • Objectives of performance management and appraisal • Key performance indicators • Position descriptions • Formats of performance planning, personal development plans, and appraisal • Guidelines for managers and employees for ethical conduct • Appreciation, rewards and recognition for excellent performance • Appeal procedures			
3.	**Performance Management Process** *Does performance management process serve the following objectives?* • Performance expectations are based on job description and/or competency mapping			

SL. No.	Audit Criteria	Rating	Gap Identified	Improvement Strategy
	• Performance expectations are jointly decided by manager and employee • Performance plans are made in advance • Established performance standards • Performance plans are documented and signed by manager and employee • Training and development intervention for improving competencies/performance • Supporting, coaching and mentoring employees to achieve performance plans • Defined appraisal periods • Objective rating instruments • Multiple feedback on employee performance • Feedback provided to employee • Effective reward systems • Decisions on rewards based on performance • Reassignment of individuals • Beneficial to both employee and organization • Satisfaction of employees with the process			
4.	**Performance Appraisal Formats** *Is performance appraisal format:* • Relevant to performance management process • Strategically agile • Comprehensive yet precise • Easy to use • Objective and development oriented • Manager and employee trained on performance appraisal techniques			
5.	**Performance Management Implementation** *Are issues and concerns in implementation of performance management properly addressed?* • Acceptance of performance management system by managers and employees • Appraisal workshops and training conducted • Leadership commitment and resource allocation • Normalization of all ratings made by a committee • Analysis of overall trends and issues • Report on results • Learning, mentoring, counseling and coaching for performance improvement • Review for system effectiveness **Oover All Observations and Comments**			

A Typical Compensation Structure

S. No.	Component	Rate Per Month
1.	*Basic Pay*	50% of total pay
2.	*House Rent Allowance*	50% of Basic Pay for employees residing in Metro Cities and 40% of Basic for employees residing in Non-Metro cities.
3.	*Transport Allowance*	15% of Basic Pay.
4.	*Special Allowance*	25% of Basic Pay.
5.	*Education Allowance*	10% of Basic Pay
6.	*Other Allowance*	10% of Basic Pay
7.	*Medical Reimbursement*	Rs. 1250
8.	*Leave Travel Assistance*	10% of Basic Pay.
9.	*Company PF*	Rs. 780
10.	*Bonus*	Rs. 292 (Payable annually)
	Total	
11.	*Performance Pay* performance assessment.	Rs. 100,000/- per annum based on

For example, a candidate Mr. O.P. Singh has been selected on a compensation of Rs. 50,000/- per month, then his compensation break-up shall be as follows:

S. No.	Component	Amount Per Month	Calculation Tip
1.	Basic Pay	Rs. 23,840/-	Rs. 50,000 – (Rs. 1250 + Rs. 780 + Rs. 292) = Rs. 47678 divided by 2
2.	House Rent Allowance	Rs. 9,536/-	40% of Rs. 23, 840/-
3.	Transport Allowance	Rs. 3,576/-	15% of Rs. 23, 840/-
4.	Special Allowance	Rs. 3,576/-	15% of Rs. 23, 840/-
5.	Education Allowance	Rs. 2,384/-	10% of Rs. 23, 840/-
6.	Other Allowance	Rs. 2,384/-	10% of Rs. 23, 840/
7.	Medical Reimbursement	Rs. 1250	Fixed
8.	Leave Travel Assistance	Rs. 2,384/-	10% of Rs. 23, 840/
9.	Company PF	Rs. 780	Fixed
10.	Bonus	Rs. 292	Fixed
	Total	**Rs. 50,002**	
11.	Performance Pay	Rs. 100,000/- per annum based on performance assessment.	

Compensation Survey Questionnaire

Instruction for Data Collector: Response to questions must be obtained from atleast 30 companies and each question must be answered properly.

Personal Information

Name | Title

Phone | Address

E-mail

Company Information

Type of Business | Annual turnover

Location | Number of employees

Compensation Policy and Practices Information

Are your employees represented by a Union?

If yes, how many employees are represented by a union?

Does your company utilize a traditional pay structure?

If yes, please answer the following questions:

How is progression in the job grade determined?

How often is the pay structure reviewed?

When was the last time it was adjusted?

Does your company give a general increase?

If yes, what percentage?

Does your company give Dearness Allowance?

If yes, what percentage?

Does your company utilize a broad band system?

If yes, what is the band width?

Does your company have an incentive system?

If yes, please answer the following questions:

What type of incentive system?

What was the average incentive paid last year?

What is this year's projected average incentive?

Does your company have a formal employee performance management and appraisal process?

If yes, please answer the following questions:

How often are employees appraised?

How has performance appraisal outcomes being linked to reward processes?

What was the average performance pay for last year?

What is this year's projected average increase?

Benefit Information

Please mark the benefit plan offered to your employees:

Employee Perception

Are employees satisfied with current overall pay systems?

If yes, how and why?

If no, how and why?

Do employees prefer monetary or non-monetary rewards?

If yes, why?

If no, why?

A Prudent Advice

You as a management graduate working in a business enterprise shall not only be responsible for your own performance but that of your subordinates and the enterprise itself. Today, with dramatic and drastic changes in business landscape, you need to be a good LEADER FIRST and then a good Manager. This is primarily because you shall be responsible for not only creating and sharing vision but more importantly executing strategy. Execution is not only the biggest issue facing business enterprises today, but it is a mechanism for change and transition from better to the best.

Bossidy and *Charan* (2002) enlists the following seven essential leadership behaviour that form the core of strategy execution:

- Know your people and your business;
- Insist on realism;
- Set clear goals and priorities;
- Follow through;
- Reward the doers;
- Expand people's capabilities; and
- Know yourself.

Therefore, grasp the constructs of performance and reward management as provided in this book extremely well so that you as a new age HR professional assume central role for continuous performance improvement of the employees and the business enterprise in order to take your organization to the pinnacle of excellence, both profitably, ethically and responsibly.

❑❑❑

References and Select Bibliography

The following publications present key concepts which facilitated in formulating the ideas presented in **Performance and Reward Management**. The list is by no means intended to be complete but provided here as a complementary addendum to the end notes and other references throughout.

Armstrong, Michael, *Performance Management: Key Strategies & Practical Guidelines*, second edition, 2000, Kogan page, London.

Armstrong, Michael and Baron, Angela, *Managing Performance: Performance Management In Action*, Chartered Institute of Personnel and Development, 2004, London.

Armstrong, M. and Murlis, H., *Reward Management*, 1991, Kogan Page Ltd., London.

Adams, J. (1963) 'Toward an Understanding of Inequity', *Journal of Social Psychology*, Vol. 67, 1963, Pp. 422-436.

Amos, T.L., Ristow, A. and Ristow, L., *Human Resource Management*, 2004, 2nd edition, Juta and Co. Ltd., Lansdowne.

Brumbrach, P., *Performance Management*, 1988, The Cornwell Press, London.

Brown, R.D., *Performance Appraisal as a Tool for Staff Development*, 1988, Jossey-Bass, San Francisco.

Bacal, R., *Performance Management*, 1999, McGraw-Hill, New York.

Beach, Dale S., *Personnel Management*, 1985, Macmillan Publishing, New York.

Barney, J., "Firm Resources and Sustained Competitive Advantage", *Journal of Management*, Vol. 17, No. 1, 1991, Pp. 99-120.

Barney, J.B., "Organizational Culture: Can It Be Source of Competitive Advantage?", *Academy of Management Review*, Vol. 11, No. 3, 1996, Pp. 656-665.

Boyett, J.B., and Boyett, J.T., *The Gainsharing Design Manual,* 2004, ASJA Press, Lincoln, Nebraska.

Berger, Lance A., "Creating a Talent Management System for Organizational Excellence: Connecting the Pots", In Lance A. Berger and Dorothy R. Berger, *The Talent Management Handbook: Creating Organizational Excellence by Identifying, Developing and Promoting Your Best People*, McGraw-Hill Professional, New York.

Branham, Leigh, *The 7 Hidden Reasons Employee Leave: How To Recognize the Subtle Signs and Act Before It's Too Late*, 2005, AMACOM.

Baron, R.A., *Behaviour in Organizations*, 1983, Allyn & Bacon, Inc., New York.

Cameron, K. and Whitten, D., *Organizational Effectiveness: A Comparison of Multiple Models*, 1981, Academic Press, London.

Carter, Louis, Giber, David, Goldsmith, Marshall, and Bennis, Warren (eds.), *Best Practices in Leadership Development Handbook*, 2000, Jossey-Bass, San Francisco.

Carrell, M.R. and Kuzmits, F.E., *Personnel: Management of Human Resources*, 1952, Charles E. Merril Publishing, London.

Dessler, Gary, *Human Resource Management*, Prentice Hall of India Pvt. Ltd., New Delhi, 7th edition, 2002.

De Cieri, H. L., Kramer, R., Noe, R. A., Hollenbeck, J. R., Gerhart, B., Wright, P. M., *Human Resource Management in Australia: Strategy-people-performance,* 2nd edition, McGraw-Hill Australia Pvt Ltd., Macquarie Park NSW.

De Waal, A., "The Power of World-class Performance Management: Use It!", *Measuring Business Excellence*, Vol. 6, No. 3, 2002, Pp. 9-19.

Delpo, Amy, *The Performance Appraisal Handbook: Legal and Practical Rules for Managers*, 2007, Nolo Publishers.

Source : Dr. Jain, Mahaveer, "Definition of Leadership", Developing Behavioural Skills on Leadership for Trade Union Leaders, Readings, January 12-17, 2009, V.V. Giri National Labour Institue, Noida, Pp. 8.

Source : Dr. Jain, Mahaveer, "Feedback: An Art of self and Organizational Excellence", Developing Behavioral Skills on Leadership for Trade Union Leaders, Readings, January 12-17, 2009, V.V. Giri National Labour Institute, Noida, Pp. 96-97.

Fletcher, C., "Performance Appraisal and Management: The Developing Research Agenda", *Journal of Occupational and Organizational Psychology*, 2001, Vol. 73, No. 4, Pp. 473-487.

Fombrun, C., Tichy, N.M. and Devanna, M.A., *Strategic Human Resource Management*, 1984, John Wiley and Sons, Inc., New York.

Follet, M.P., "The Essentials of Leadership", *Proceedings of the Rowntree Lecture Conferences*, 1933, University of London Press, London.

Gerhart, B. and Rynes, S.L., *Compensation: Theory, Evidence, and Strategic Implications*, 2003, SAGE Publications, Inc., London.

Grönhaug, K. and Nordhaug, O., "Strategy and Competence in Firms", *European Management Journal*, Vol. 10, No. 4, Dec. 1992, Pp. 438-444.

Guinn, Kathleen A., "Performance Management for Evolving Self-directed Work Teams", *American Compensation Association (ACA) Journal*, Winter 1995, Vol. 4, No. 4, Scottsdale, AZ, Pp. 74–81.

Gupta, B.L. and M.T., Joseph, "Audit the Performance Appraisal System of Education Institutions", *Business Manager*, Vo. 11, No. 6, December 2008, Pp. 11-17.

Gilley, Jerry W., *The Manager as Coach*, 2007, Greenwood Publishing.

Gomez, Louis R. and Mejia, David Balkin, *Managing Human Resources*, 1999, 2nd edition, Prentice Hall College Division, New Jersey.

Gomez–Mejia, Luis R., Balkin, David B., and Cardy, Robert L., *Managing Human Resources*, 2002, 3rd edition, Prentice Hall of India Pvt. Ltd., New Delhi.

Harris, H., *Getting Employees to Fall in Love with Your Organization*, 1996, AMACOM, New York.

Holton, E.F. III, Bates, R.A., and Ruona, W.E.A., "The Development of a Generalized Learning Transfer System Inventory", *Human Resource Development Quarterly*, Vol. 11, No. 4, 2000, Pp. 344-346.

Hackman, R., Oldham, G., "Motivation Through the Design of Work: Test of a Theory", *Organizational Behaviour and Human Performance*, Vol. 16, 1976, Pp. 250-279.

Hendry, C. and Pettigrew, A., "Patterns of Strategic Change in the Development of Human Resource Management", *British Journal of Management*, Vol. 3, No. 2, 1992, Pp.137-156.

Hofstede, G., Neuijen, B., Ohayv, and D.D., Sanders, G., "Measuring Organizational Cultures: A Qualitative and Quantitative Study across Twenty Cases", *Administrative Science Quarterly*, Vol. 35, 1990, Pp. 286-316,

Hale, Richard and Whitlam, Dr. Peter, *Powering Up Performance Management*, 200, Gower Publishing Ltd., Hampshire.

Heneman, H. G. III, and Schwab, D. P., "Work and Rewards Theory", In D. Yoder and H. G. Heneman, Jr. (eds.), *ASPA Handbook of Personnel and Industrial Relations*, 1979, 6(1)-6(22) Bureau of National Affairs, Washington, D.C.

Source: "HR News", Business Manager, Vol. 11, No. 6, December 2008, PP. 20-28.

Kaplan, R.S. and Norton, D.P., "The Balanced Scorecard–Measures that Drive Performance", *Harvard Business Review,* Vol. 70, No. 1, 1992, Pp. 71-79.

Kaplan, R. and Norton, D., *The Strategy-focused Organization*, 2001, Harvard Business School Press.

Kotter, J.P. and Heskett, J.L., *Corporate Culture and Performance*, 1992, Free Press, New York.

Kaplan, A., *Leadership and Management*, 1998, Olive Publications, Durban.

Kakar, Sudhir, "Authority Pattern and Subordinate Behaviour in Indian Organizations", *Administrative Science Quarterly*, Vol. 16, No. 3, 1971, Pp. 298-314.

Kakar, Sudhir, *The Inner Experience: A Psychoanalytic Study of Childhood and Society in India*, 1978, Oxford University Press, New Delhi.

Kothari, R., *Politics in India*, 1970, Orient Longman, New Delhi.

Kreitner, R., and Kinicki, A., *Organizational Behaviour*, 1992, 2nd edition, Richard D. Irwin Inc.

Kessler, I., 'Payment Systems' In M. Poole and M. Warner (eds.), *The IEBM Handbook of Human Resource Management*, 1998, International Thomson Business Press, London.

Lawler, E.E., *Treat Employees Right*, 2003, Jossey-Bass Inc., San Francisco.

Lansbury, R., "Performance Management: A Process Approach", in Readings in *Human Resource Management ed. R.J. Stone*, 1988, John Wiley & Sons Australia Ltd., New York.

Lave, J., *Learning, Apprenticeship, Social Practice*, Vol. 3, 1991, Nordisk Pedagogik.

Locke, E., "Toward a theory of task motivation and incentives", Organizational *Behaviour and Human Performance*, Vol. 31, 1968, Pp. 157-189.

Lebas, M. and Euske, K., "A Conceptual and Operational Delineation of Performance" In A. Neely (Ed.), *Business Performance Measurement: Theory and Practice*, 2002Cambridge University Press, Cambridge, UK.

Liedtka, Jeanne M., Haskeins, Mark E., Rosenblum, John W, "The Generative Cycle: Linking Knowledge and Relationships", *Sloan Management Review*, Fall 1997, Volume 39, No. 1.

Lawler II, E.E., Performance Management: The Next Generation, *Compensation and Benefits Review*, May-June 1994, Pp. 16-19.

Lawler, E.E., *Treat People Right*, 2003, Jossey-Bass Inc., San Francisco.

La Motta, T., *Recognition: The Quality Way*, 1995, Quality Resources, New York.

Martocchio, J.J., *Strategic Compensation*, 1998, Prentice-Hall Inc., New Jersey.

Milliman, J.F., Zawacki, R.F., Norman, C., Powell, L. and Kirksey, J., "Companies Evaluate Employees from All Perspectives", *Personnel Journal*, Vol. 73, No. 11, 1994, Pp. 99-103.

Mondy, R.W., Noe, R.M., and Premeaux, S.R., *Human Resource Management*, 8th edition, Upper Saddle River, Prentice Hall, 2002, New Jersey.

Mohrman, A.M., Resnick-West, S.M. and Lawler III, E.E., *Designing Performance Appraisal Systems: Aligning Appraisals and Organizational Realities*, 1989, Jossey-Bass, San Francisco.

McAfee, R.B. and Champagne's, P.J., "Performance Management: A Strategy for Improving Performance and Productivity", *Journal of Managerial Psychology*, Vol. 8, No. 5, 1993, Pp. 24-32.

Murthy, K.R. and Clevland, J.N., *Understanding Performance Appraisal*, 1995, Sage Publications, California.

Monnot, M.J., Colarelli, S. and Hemingway, M., "Strategic Human Resource Management" in Greenhaus, J.H. and Callanan, G. (eds.), *The Encyclopedia of Career Development*, Sage Pub., Thousand Oaks.

Miles, R.E. and Snow, C.C., *Organizational Strategy, Structure and Process*, 1978, McGraw-Hill Book Company, New York.

Mendonca, M and Kanungo, R.N., "Impact of Culture on Performance Management in Developing Countries", *International Journal of Manpower*, Vol. 17, No. 4, 1996, Pp. 65-75.

Mohrman, S.A. and Mohrman Jr., A.M., "Organizational Change and Learning" In J.R. Galbraith and E.E. Lawler II et al., *Organizing for the Future: The New Logic for Managing Complex Organizations*, Jossey-Bass, San Francisco CA, Pp. 87-108.

McCormick, I. and Tifflin, J., *Industrial Psychology*, 1979, Allen and Unwin, New York.

McAfee, B., Quarstein, V. and Ardalan, A., "The Effect of Discretion, Outcome Feedback and Process Feedback on Employee Job Satisfaction", *Industrial Management and Data Systems*, Vol. 95, No. 5, 1995, Pp. 7-12.

McLarney, Carolan, "Mary Follet on Leadership", *GITAM Journal of Management*, Vol. 7, No. 1, Januaryy-March 2009, Pp. 12-23.

Mantravadi, P. and Reddy, A.V., "Types of Merger and Impact on Operating Performance: Indian Experience", *GITAM Journal of Management*, Vol. 7, No. 1, January-March 2009, Pp. 88-112.

Meyer, T., *Creating Competitiveness through Competencies: Currency for the 21st Century*, 1996, Knowledge Resources (Pvt) Ltd., Randburg.

Moore, D.R., Cheng, M. and Dainty, A.R.J., "Competence, Competency and Competencies: Performance Assessment in Organizations", *Work Study*, Vol. 51, No. 6, 2002, Pp. 314-319.

Mondy, R.W., Noe, R.M., and Premeaux, S.R., *Human Resource Management*, 2002, 8th edition, Prentice Hall, New Jersey.

Nelson, B., *1001 Ways to Recognize Employees*, 1994, Workman Publishing, New York.

Nelson, B., "Motivating Employees with Informal Awards", 1995, *Management Accounting*, Vol. 77, No. 5, Pp. 30-35.

Neale, F., *The Handbook of Performance Management*, 1991, Institute of Personnel Management, London.

Noe, R.A., Hollenbeck, J.R., Gerhart, B. and Wright, P.M., *Human Resource Management: Gaining Competitive Advantage*, 2000, 3rd edition, Irwin McGraw-Hill, Boston.

O'Neal, S., "The Reward and Recognition Phenomena", *Compensation and Benefits Review*, Vol. 24, No. 6, 1992, Pp. 48-52.

O'Neal, S. and Palladino, M., "Revamp Ineffective Performance Management", *Personnel Journal*, Vol. 71, No. 2, 1992, Pp. 93-102.

Odiorne, G.S., *Management by Objectives*, 1965, Pitman Publishing Company, New York.

Ovando, M.N., "Constructive Feedback: A Key to Successful Teaching and Learning", *International Journal of Educational Management*, Vol. 8, No. 6, 1994, Pp. 19-22.

Price, Alan, *Human Resource Management in a Business Context*, International Thomson Business Press, 2nd edition, 2003.

Pillai, P.A., "Integrated Performance Management to Create a Performing Culture in an Organization", In Dipti Sethi (ed.), *Performance Management and Culture: Implications and Insights*, 2007, ICFAI University Press, Hyderabad.

Pritchard, R.D., Holling, H., Lammers, F. and Clark, B.D., *Improving Organizational Performance with the Productivity Measurement and Enhancement System: An International Collaboration*, 2002, Nova, New York.

Poister, T.H., *Measuring Performance in Public and Non-Profit Organizations*, 2003, Jossey-Bass, San Francisco.

Roberts, G.E., "Employee Performance Appraisal System Participation: A Technique that Works", *Public Personnel Management*, Vol. 32, No. 1, 2003, Pp. 89-98.

Rudman, Richard, *Performance Planning and Review*, 2003, 2nd edition, Allen & Unwin, Australia.

Ravichandran, K. and Ravithilagan, D.J.E., "Transformation of the Performance Appraisal System: The Changing Scenario", In Dipti Sethi (ed.), *Performance Management and Culture: Implications and Insights*, 2007, ICFAI University Press, Hyderabad.

Rao, Dr. T.V., *Appraising and Developing Managerial Performance*, 1992, Academy of HRD, Ahmedabad.

Source : Recognition and Rewards: The Changing Face", Cover Feature, *Business Manager*, Vol. 11, No. 6, December 2008, PP. 20-26.

Ross, T.L. and Ross, R.A., "Gain Sharing: Sharing Improved Performance" In M. Rock and L. Berger (eds.), *The Compensation Handbook*, McGraw-Hill, New York, Pp. 176-189.

Robbins, S.P., DeCenzo, D.A., Stuart-Kotze, R. and Stewart, E.B., *Fundamentals of Management*, 2005, 4th edition, Pearson Education, Canada.

Sheal, P.R., *The Staff Development Handbook: An Action Kit to Improve Performance*, 1999, Kogan Page, London.

Schneier, C.E., Beatty, R.W., and Baird, L.S., *The Performance Management Sourcebook*, 1987, HRD Press, Massachusetts.

Singh, R.P., "Human Side of Performance Management", Business Manager, Vol. 11, No. 2, August 2008, Pp. 10-14.

Schiehll, E. and Morissette, "Motivational, Measurement, and Rewards from a Performance Evaluation Perspective", *RAC*, Vol. 4, No. 3, September-December 2000, Pp. 7-24.

Sharpley, "Perception, Motivation and Performance", *DSA Business Psychology*, 2002, available online at www.dsa-int.com

Swapnika, C. and Kodwani, A., "High Performance Work Systems and Organizational Culture", In Dipti Sethi (ed.), *Performance Management and Culture: Implications and Insights*, 2007, ICFAI University Press, Hyderabad.

Scott, W.R., *Organizations: Rational, Natural and Open Systems*, 1992, 3rd edition, Prentice Hall, Englewood Cliffs, New Jersey.

Schein, E.H., *Organizational Culture and Leadership*, 1992, 2nd edition, Jossey-Bass, San Francisco.

Spangenberg, H., *Assessing Managerial Competence*, 1990, Juta & Co Ltd., Cape Town.

Stolovitch, Harold D. and Keeps, Erica J., *Training Ain't Performance*, 2004, ASTD.

Storey, John, "Human Resource Policies for Knowledge Work" In Ray, T., Quintas and Little, S. (eds.), *Managing Knowledge: An Essential Reader*, 2005, Sage Publications, London.

Schermerhorn, Hunt, and Osborn, *Human Resource Management*, Houghton Mifflin Company, Boston, 2004.

Storey, John, and Sisson, Keith, *Managing Human Resources & Industrial Relations*, Open University Press, 1993.

Stroh, L.K., Northcraft, G.B., Neale, M.A., Kern, M., and Langlands, C., *Organizational Behaviour: A Management Challenge*, 2001, 3rd edition, Lawrence Erlbaum.

Source : Subramanian, Iyer, "Performance Evaluation", Business Manager, Vol. 11, No. 9, March 2009, Pp. 24-28.

Tilburg, E.V., "Performance Reward Contingencies: The Role and Relationship in the Job Performance – Job Satisfaction Question", *The Journal of the AATEA*, Summer, 1988.

Vroom, V., *Work and Motivation*, 1964, Wiley, New York.

Vallance, S., "Performance Appraisal in Singapore, Thailand and the Philippines: A Culture Perspective", *Australian Journal of Public Administration*, Vol. 58, No. 3, 1999, Pp. 78-95.

Wilson, T.B., *Innovative Reward Systems for the Changing Workplace*, 1994, R.R. Donnelley & Sons Organization, USA.

Waal, A.A. de, *Power of Performance Management: How Leading Companies Create Sustained Value*, 2001, John Wiley & Sons, New York.

Zawacki, Robert A. and Couger, J. Daniel, "Evaluating Performance Appraisal Systems for I.S. Personnel" *ACM Digital Library* (New York, 0-89791-262-4/88/0400-0144, 1998), Pp. 144–147.

❑❑❑

Index

❑❑❑